D1117852

TRUE
CANADIAN
HEROES
AT SEA

Arthur Bishop

Foreword by
Vice-Admiral D.N. Mainguy, CMM
Former Vice-Chief of the Defence Staff

Library and Archives Canada Cataloguing in Publication

Bishop, William Arthur, 1923–
    True Canadian heroes at sea / Arthur Bishop.

Includes bibliographical references and index.
ISBN 1-55267-870-9

1. Canada—History, Naval. 2. Heroes—Canada—Biography. 3. Veterans—Canada—Biography. 4. Sailors—Canada—Biography. I. Title.

FC231.B57 2005   359'.0092'271   C2005-903450-5

This collection produced for Prospero Books.

Key Porter Books Limited
Six Adelaide Street East, Tenth Floor
Toronto, Ontario
Canada M5C 1H6

www.keyporter.com

Text design: Peter Maher
Electronic formatting: Jean Lightfoot Peters

Printed and bound in Canada

06 07 08 09 10 5 4 3 2 1

Contents

Foreword

True Canadian Heroes at Sea is the third volume in Arthur Bishop's series on Canada's Military Heritage, which includes *True Canadian Heroes in the Air* and *True Canadian Heroes on the Battlefield*.

This book tells the tales of courageous incidents at sea involving Canadians, from the Indian Mutiny to the Korean War. The tales are well told and make good reading. Thanks to the courage and dedication of those who fought in the wars of the 20th century, I never had to take part in a war.

Some of the names of those whose deeds are described in this book are resonant of the role models of my youth, as well as others I served with. As a boy, I met Rowland Bourke, who worked in the Esquimalt Dockyard and had spectacles like Coke-bottle bottoms. He used to say he got the Victoria Cross because he couldn't see to get out of the way. I knew Louis Audette because he had the patience to listen to a very unsure teenager, when I was wrestling with whether my future should be in the Navy.

I served with many others in this book. Herbie Rayner was my captain at Royal Roads; I was Ralph Hennessy's navigator in the *Algonquin*; Max Bernays was the coxswain of the *Fraser* when I was the anti-submarine officer. I commanded HMCS *Protecteur* under Andy Collier when he was Commander of the Canadian Fleet, and I served many of the others in various capacities.

Arthur Bishop has done a service to the heritage of this country in producing *Courage at Sea*. He has stuck to the discipline of writing about courageous incidents, and in this way has produced a sharply focused, most readable book—a good companion to more formal histories. I hope those whose deeds are recorded here will continue to serve as role models for the youth of Canada.

D.N. Mainguy
Vice-Admiral (Ret.)
29 July 1994

Acknowledgements

I begin by thanking my very good friend *Willis McLeese* for his generous help. Willis has come to my aid several times in the past, and his support again in this instance is much appreciated. I should also like to mention that Willis was one very solid sailor-warrior himself.

My heartfelt thanks to three people who helped in the research for this volume: *Carl Christie*, senior research director of the Directorate of History, who came to my assistance in more ways than one; *Anne Melvin*, the librarian of the Royal Canadian Military Institute, was, throughout, her usual helpful self; and *John Grodzinski*, researcher and author, who supplied me with much information and many ideas.

Frank Dunbar was of much assistance in countless ways, as well as making helpful suggestions. *Dick Donaldson* of the Naval Officers Association, editor of *The Starshell*, provided me with a valuable list of published sources.

Charles V. Rolfe of the Hampton Gray VC Chapter of the Canadian Naval Air Group supplied me with details on the action that won Gray his Victoria Cross.

I should especially like to thank *Peter Berry*, an ex-permanent RCN officer, for his advice and help, and also for introducing me to *Admiral Dan Mainguy*, who kindly consented to write the foreword to this volume.

As usual, this book would have been much more difficult to write without the help of my editor, *Don Loney*. At the same time, I would also like to thank *David McCabe* for a masterful job of close-editing; and *Glenn Wright*, foremost authority on naval affairs, for his expertise in vetting my manuscript.

Marilyn Gurney, Director, Maritime Command Museum in Halifax, for providing the picture of the Sailor's Memorial. *Dalton Waller*, whose advice and counsel was of great help.

My wife *Cilla* was once again a tower of strength in putting up with my foibles and other shortcomings during this volume's preparation.

Finally, I should like to offer thanks to my *Selection Committee*, who will remain anonymous. Their job is one of the most difficult tasks in preparing a book of this nature, and our points of view and selections were often at loggerheads. But on one point we were always in complete agreement. Our selections were, in all cases, made as representative—rather than total, or final—of all those who have served Canada at sea.

Introduction—Setting Sail

At precisely 12:45 p.m. on the 105th anniversary of the Battle of Trafalgar, the Canadian Navy set sail on a course that no armada, for its size, ever matched in performance. Although the Naval Service Act had been given royal assent five months earlier, on October 21, 1910, the service actually took on tangible form when an aged cruiser, *Niobe*, purchased from the British government, docked at Halifax for use as a training ship. A year later, King George V made official the designation Royal Canadian Navy. Those bureaucratic proceedings aside, however, the real genesis of Canada's naval tradition had, in effect, been launched a century earlier.

During the War of 1812 a British frigate intercepted a slave ship bound from the west coast of Africa to the United States. Bringing its captive cargo to Halifax, the slaves were set free. The Nova Scotia government allowed them to settle and helped them find employment. Transplanted into a Maritime province, most of these new "immigrants" naturally gravitated towards the marine trade. The son of one of them went so far as to join the Royal Navy—and became the first of four Canadian sailors to win the Victoria Cross.

Ironically and regrettably, outside the Navy service itself, these recipients of our highest award for valour are virtually unknown, and they have received little or no public recognition. Lamentably, the same is true to an even greater extent of the bravery of countless other Canadian seamen. Our "silent service" has for too long remained silent about the deeds and achievements of those who served us at sea, and who helped to build the RCN to a greatness that ranks it among the leading navies of the world.

It's time to redress this grievous omission by piping them aboard our Military Heritage retrospective, and acknowledging them with the esteem—and the place in our history—that they so richly merit. Full speed ahead!

*"Courage is the best gift of all: courage
stands before everything."*
PLAUTUS

"Courage mounteth with occasion."
WILLIAM SHAKESPEARE

The Indian Mutiny
1855–1859

Resentment over the British East India Company imposing its will on the Hindu way of life had been rising steadily for nearly half a century. By 1855 it boiled over into rebellion, and one of its earliest results was the fall of Delhi to the insurgent forces. It was September 1857 before the British recaptured the city. The climax to the mutiny came with the fall of Lucknow that November. In effect, the rebellion had ended, though it was another two years before the unrest was finally quelled.

Lucknow
November 16, 1857

HALL William Edward

"First Canadian to Be Awarded Naval Victoria Cross—Won in a Land Action"

In May 1857, the British warship HMS *Shannon* and another vessel were diverted from Hong Kong, where they had been escorting troops in anticipation of a Chinese insurrection, to Calcutta, where they arrived in August to play out their role in the Indian Mutiny. Aboard *Shannon* was William Hall, son of a freed slave from Halifax, who was the ship's "Captain of the Foretop." Hall had already been decorated for bravery in the Crimean War with two British medals, bearing the Sebastopol and Inkerman clasps, and a Turkish medal. But his finest hour was yet to come.

The two ships steamed up the Ganges River to Allahabad, carrying two naval brigades. They were equipped with six 8-inch guns, two field guns and two 24-pound howitzers, and their assignment was to support a regiment of Seaforth Highlanders and Indian Sikh warriors in lifting the siege of Lucknow. A British garrison 300 miles north of Delhi at the foot of the Himalayas, Lucknow was surrounded by 50,000 Sepoy rebels who had already captured Delhi and Cawporne, killing all white soldiers, as well as every white woman and child.

By mid-afternoon of November 16, the 5,000-man relief force had broken through the outer walls of the city. Now they faced the seven-foot-thick walled Shah Nujiff mosque, inside of which 30,000 Sepoys had garrisoned themselves. The naval detachment brought up their guns to within 200 yards of the wall and began pounding shells against it—but to no avail. Worse still, rifle fire from the mutineers inflicted appalling casualties. The two 24-pound howitzer naval guns were now moved within 20 feet of the wall, but the crew of one gun was mowed down. Of the other crew, only Hall and a wounded gunner were left alive.

William Hall, Naval Brigade, Royal Navy

Undeterred, Hall continued to work his howitzer in the face of a relentless return rifle fusillade. Fire. Sponge out. Reload. Fire. And repeat the procedure—all the while, musket shells whizzing about him. Finally, one of his own shells breached the wall, the British troops poured through and the Sepoy mutineers fled in disarray. The mutiny was over. For his action, Hall was awarded the Victoria Cross.

William Hall was born in 1827 in Horton's Bluff, N.S., where he attended school before joining the Royal Navy. During the Crimean War he served aboard HMS *Rodney* as an able seaman. Hall remained with the Royal Navy until 1876, retiring to Nova Scotia with the rank of Petty Officer.

In Halifax on October 1, 1901, Hall was given a place of honour in a parade of British war veterans during a visit by the Duke of York. His impressive array of decorations, including an Indian Mutiny service medal, attracted the attention of the future King George V, who shook hands with him and chatted about his career in the service.

Hall died in Hantsport in the Annapolis Valley on August 25, 1904, and was buried there in an unmarked grave. In 1947, however, the Hantsport Branch of the Royal Canadian Legion, British Service League, erected a cairn in his honour, and in Halifax the coloured branch of the Legion was named after him.

VC BCRMs TM IMM P/O Born April 18, 1827 Died August 25, 1904
RefScs: C&TOTCN 117 CVC 18–19 TGM Nov. 10, 1989 TOTNA 47–49 VM 11

The Royal Canadian Navy in World War I 1914–1918

When war began, the Royal Canadian Navy had 350 men and two British cast-off cruisers, *Rainbow* and *Niobe*, both of which had seen better days. By the time the conflict ended in 1918, this embryonic force had grown to 9,600 men, some 100 vessels and a fledgling Naval Service, the nucleus of a future fleet. But during the war, the RCN never did come to grips with the enemy; they had to be content at first with assuming such responsibilities as assessing and directing shipping in Canadian ports.

With the United States' entry into the war in April 1917, the Germans extended operations of their U-boats—*Unterseebooten*—to include merchant shipping in North American waters. Against this threat, the RCN organized the East Coast Patrols, in the Gulf of St. Lawrence and along the shores of Nova Scotia and Newfoundland.

The Canadian Navy boasted only two submarines, and these were acquired in the manner of a distress sale. Fashioned and outfitted for the Chilean Navy by a Seattle shipbuilding firm, they'd been rejected as substandard and put on the block. But in July 1914, war was imminent. Canada's west coast was threatened by the powerful presence of the Imperial German Naval Fleet in the Pacific, and with the antiquated *Niobe* as its only naval defence, the British Columbia government persuaded Ottawa to buy the subs—just over a million dollars for both.

The submarines proved to be a sound investment for two very good reasons: first, they inspired public confidence that measures were being taken to protect the province; and second, though the vessels would never go into battle (they did carry out patrol duties), they provided a valuable training platform for the growing service.

At the beginning of 1917, Canadian Vickers in Montreal, through an arrangement with Bethlehem Steel Corporation's shipyards in Massachusetts, had begun building submarines for the Royal Navy. British crews arrived at the Maisonneuve ship-yards to take possession, sailing them down the St. Lawrence and across the Atlantic. Vickers had turned out so many sub-marines in just six months that the RN ran out of crews to man them—RCN to the rescue. There were now men available from Esquimalt, B.C., with sufficient training (on the "CC boats," as they were called) to cover the shortfall. When they reached England, many of the men were accepted—not without some opposition—into the RN Submarine Service.

They set a proud standard for a small country. Altogether, during the course of the conflict, the Canadian Navy recruited 3,000 seamen for service with the Royal Navy, and an unrecorded number of Canadians enlisted directly, one of whom was awarded the Victoria Cross for bravery in action.

Following the war, two modernized subs were acquired by the RCN via the RN—free of charge. These replaced the worn-out CC boats. But, in 1921, when the Navy was once again a target for government cutbacks, the submarines, among other vessels, got the axe. Canada would not add another submarine to her fleet until 1961.

Off the North American Pacific Coast
August, 1914

GERMAN Tony
HOSE Walter
KINGSMILL Charles
SPEE von Graf

"Canada's First Futile Flirtation with the War at Sea"

By the time the Great War broke out on August 4, 1914, Walter Hose had done his best to bring *Rainbow* up to operational standards. A cast-off ancient Royal Navy light cruiser, she had been commissioned into the Royal Canadian Navy as a training ship two years earlier. On the day before the war, she was at sea patrolling the Straits of Juan de Fuca with only half her proper complement, a third of which were volunteer reservists with no seagoing experience. Her wireless range was limited to 200 miles. Armed with two 6-inch guns and four 12-pounders, the modern high-explosive (HE) shells, to replace the outdated gunpowder ammunition aboard, was in storage at a shore-based magazine awaiting delivery because the railway company lacked experience handling explosives. On August 4 Hose received a signal that a quantity of the HE shells had finally arrived in Vancouver Then a second signal arrived, from Canadian Naval Service Headquarters this time: *Nurnberg* and *Liepzig* reported off Magdalen Bay [Mexico] steering north. Do your utmost to protect *Algerine* and *Shearwater* steering north of San Diego. Remember Nelson and the British Navy. All Canada is watching.

Hose faced a dilemma. Ironically, the two British steam-and-sail sloops had been part of an international squadron, of which the heavily armed German cruiser *Leipzig* was also a part, protecting foreign interests in the Mexican civil war. Her sister ship, *Nurnberg*, was in the vicinity as well. Overnight the situation had changed, putting the two virtually defenceless RN sloops at the mercy of the two first-class "enemy" fighting ships. Should he take the time to sail to Esquimalt in British Columbia and pick up the HE ammunition first or, remembering Nelson, press on and take his chances with his outmoded gunpowder shells and hope for the best? Predictably Hose, a former RN commander who already had several seagoing commands to his credit (see Between Wars: Weathering the Storm), opted to steer south. Coaxing all the 19 knots of which the 20-year old *Rainbow* was capable he pondered the tactics he would need to tackle the fast 25-knot German cruisers with HE explosives fired from their ten 4-inch guns with a range of 10,000 yards compared to his own gunpowder ammunition at 4,000. A frightening prospect—and with all Canada watching!

Hose put into San Francisco to refuel hoping for news of *Shearwater* and *Algerine*. There wasn't any. It didn't help either that the without radios the sloops had no means of communication. However, both German cruisers had been spotted off San Diego heading north—about a day away. Hose steamed out of the bay to patrol the area around the Farallones Islands west of the Golden Gate bridge right in the path of the enemy squadron and also in hope of sighting the two British ships as well. He had calculated their position to be somewhere to the west, possibly steering north.

Meanwhile he girded for the uneven confrontation he must face against a better-armed enemy force at odds of two to one. Weighing his chances he calculated that the only chance he had to hamper the progress of his stronger protagonists was to take advantage of the Pacific fog off the California coast. Using the misty blanket for cover he planned to draw the Germans into a fight at close enough range to inflict sufficient damage and force them to withdraw for repairs, allowing *Algerine* and *Shearwater* enough time to make for the safety of Esquimalt.

To get ready for the inevitable battle Hose took every possible precaution including having *Rainbow*'s crew tear out all the ship's peacetime flammable woodwork and toss it overboard. After waiting anxiously, by August 10 there was still no sign of either the German or the British ships and with his coal running low and in the hope that the sloops would by this time be well out of enemy range Hose decided to withdraw up along the coast.

Unbeknownst to him, however, *Leipzig* had been spotted west off the Farallones. She had learned that *Rainbow* had berthed at San Francisco and was now on her trail. Hose had reckoned, however, that the Germans would be trailing him anyway and he calculated that he had enough of a head start to keep a safe distance between himself and the enemy by continuing north where he estimated his British "charges" would be. But then a moment of panic. At 8:00 on the morning of August 12, a large, three-funnelled ship suddenly loomed ahead, closing fast. Hose signalled "Action stations. Full speed ahead!" *Rainbow*'s unseasoned crew held their collective breath, their nerves on edge, ready for instant battle. Then, a moment later—false alarm! The "enemy" was identified as SS *Prince George*, a British merchant vessel hastily impressed into service as a hospital ship.

Earlier, back at Esquimalt, naval personnel were certain they would never see *Rainbow* again, the dated battle wagon cumtraining ship, cum-dated old battle wagon once more, was unsuited and poorly equipped to take on a pair of the most modern warships afloat, a confrontation that could end only in disaster. Moreover, there were no reinforcements to send for such an ugly eventuality, not even any torpedoes for the two submarines the RCN had acquired from the Americans. It was small consolation at least, knowing that any wounded would be cared for, *Prince George* having been speedily complemented with a medical staff and marked as a hospital ship before sailing south.

Thankfully, *Shearwater*, at any rate, had by this time reached the Juan de Fuca Straits and was out of danger. That left only *Algerine* still needing protection. Following the nerve-racking initial meeting with the hospital ship, Hose wasted no time heading into Esquimalt for a fast refuelling where good news awaited him: the high-explosive shells had finally arrived. But his elation quickly turned to chagrin when he learned the fuses were missing. Regardless he set out again to search for the remaining British sloop, which he found the next afternoon some 60 miles to the south being coaled from a passing collier. *Algerine* signalled: "I am damn glad to see you." Historian Commander Tony German opined that while escorting her safely back to port: "Walter Hose and his whole ship's company no doubt echoed the words."

Now the Germans were reported off San Francisco where *Liepzig* had sailed in to refuel. Her captain was said to have boasted that the German Navy would soon clear the Pacific of the Royal Navy and made a gift of a pair of Japanese bear cubs to the city zoo, an ironic statement and gesture as it turned out. When the news of *Leipzig*'s whereabouts reached Hose at Esquimalt—the missing fuses having been found and awaiting his arrival—after refuelling he wasted no time heading south again, determined to come to grips with the enemy at last.

He was well underway when Canadian Naval Service HQ received belated official permission from the British Admiralty for *Rainbow* to engage *Leipzig* and drive her from the Pacific trade route. But next day, when it was reported that the German cruiser had been joined by her sister ship *Nurnberg*, the Admiralty changed its mind and reversed the order, recalling *Rainbow* to Esquimalt to await the arrival of HMS *Newcastle*, a fast new British cruiser en route from Yokohama. Three days later on September 1, a three-funnelled cruiser, presumably one of the German ships, was reported off Prince Rupert. Together *Rainbow* and *Newcastle* hastened to the area. However, it was all in a lost cause. In fact, neither *Leipzig* nor *Nurnberg* had been closer than 2,500 miles from the British Columbia coast.

By this time the entire Pacific naval war zone had suddenly changed dramatically with Hose's ancient warship caught up in the vortex of a jumbled complex, and her role was now relegated to that of radio liaison. Japan had entered the war on the Allied side. A powerful new armoured cruiser from her navy, *Idzumo*, was on the way to bolster the British and Canadian force.

This turn of events forced German Admiral Graf von Spee to forfeit his plans to destroy British shipping in the Pacific. By an overnight stroke of fate the hunter had been transformed into the hunted. Now, pursued by all RN naval ships in the vicinity, Spee had to concentrate his efforts into getting all his ships safely back home. Typical of his aggressive nature, Hose wanted to join in the chase. Permission denied—on the grounds that if *Rainbow* was lost, the

RCN, its director Sir Charles Kingsmill in particular, and the Canadian government in general, would come in for criticism "on account of her age in being sent to engage modern vessels." Accent: fear of criticism. In any event, in December, Spee's German Far East Fleet was solidly trounced by the Royal Navy during a battle off the Falkland Islands in which all but one of the German ships was sunk, bringing the danger to the west coast to an end.

From then on *Rainbow* was confined to local patrols in which she managed to capture two German schooners and tie up enemy ships in neutral ports. Then when the United States entered the war in 1917 the venerable old seahorse was paid off. In Tony German's prescient words: "If old ships dream in their retirement as old sailors do, she had some memories to warm her rusted heart."

RefScs: TSIAOG 37–39

Coronel, Chile
November 1, 1914

CANN Malcolm
HATHEWAY John
PALMER William
SILVER Arthur

"First Royal Canadian Navy Casualties"

In August 1914, with the Royal Canadian Navy barely four years old and the first class of the Royal Naval College of Canada just graduated, a future Royal Navy flagship, the cruiser HMS *Good Hope*, docked at Halifax to refuel. Because of vacancies in the gun room created by an Admiralty clerical error, the vessel took on four of the freshly appointed Canadian midshipmen—Malcolm Cann, John Hatheway, William Palmer and Arthur Silver.

On November 1, in an unequal encounter with German cruisers *Gneisenau* and *Scharnhorst*, from Graf von Spee's fleet at

Coronel off the west coast of Chile, *Good Hope* was quickly reduced to a flaming hulk. It exploded and went down with all hands aboard. The four Canadian midshipmen became the RCN's first casualties, the first of 225 Canadian sailors to perish with other British ships in World War I.

RefScs: RAR 12 RCNIR 34 TSIAOG 32 VR(1) 24

THE GERMAN SUBMARINE SCENARIO— UNRESTRICTED WARFARE

*F*rom the outbreak of hostilities with Germany in 1914 all Canadian shipping was devoted to the war effort, with the RCN responsible for the safeguard of Canadian merchant, troop and ammunition ships sailing out of Halifax. Passengers wishing to travel to the United Kingdom had to do so on passenger ships sailing from New York, the exception being government officials and other civilians involved in war work who were allowed to travel on troopships. But up until the American entry into the war in 1917, although passenger liners leaving the United States for the United Kingdom ostensibly enjoyed neutral status, there existed a danger emanating from what the Germans called the "hunger blockade" or "starvation blocked" imposed by the Royal Navy.*

Great Britain's first act of war was the prevention of material or contraband reaching Germany until economic strangulation had been achieved. As time went on the blockade soon extended to every conceivable commodity, including food, from reaching Germany, whose sea lanes to the outer world were via the North Sea, the English Channel and the Mediterranean.

In November 1914, the blockade was given added muscle when Britain declared the entire North Sea to be a military area and began laying extensive mine fields in the English Channel and the North Sea in support of Royal Navy patrols. Incoming freighters were compelled to divert to designated English ports and submit to a search and examination of their cargo. Those found shipping contraband goods to Germany were subject to confiscation of ship as well as cargo.

Strictly speaking this defied the Rules of Blockade set out by the Paris Declaration in 1856, which had been signed by all the major powers, including Great Britain. In effect the Royal Navy could only impose its blockade at the edge of German territorial waters, known as the three-mile limit. But under the First Lord of the Admiralty, Winston Churchill, it resolutely refused to conform to the Paris Declaration knowing that such obeisance—placing the British warships so close to the German mainland—would be suicide

There was the hazard of countless shoaling reefs and tiny islands that were sure to impale the vessels in times of fog and poor visibility. They would be easy targets for the long-range coastal batteries as well as airships and airplanes. Worse still they would be sitting ducks for the Unterseebooten, the key weapons the Germans were about to wield in their counter-blockade.

Though the U-boat was to become a major factor in the war against Allied warships and merchantmen it was initially looked upon with scorn and skepticism by the German Admirals as well as the British Admiralty. However, all this changed overnight when, on September 22, 1914, Lieutenant Commander Otto Weddigen sank three 12,000 ton British armoured warships off the Dutch coast, the Hogue, Cressy and Aboukir, with a loss of 1,500 British servicemen's lives. Weddigen returned home the conquering hero and was personally decorated with the Iron Cross First and Second Class by Kaiser Wilhelm II. In October, Weddington struck again, delivering another crushing blow to the Royal Navy when he sunk the cruiser Hawke off Aberdeen with a loss of 500 officers and men.

Now both Britain and German navies were forced to treat the submarine seriously and with due respect. Weddington's dazzling performance gave impetus to a U-boat campaign as the submarines stalked Royal Navy warships openly, in broad daylight, off the English coast in a battle of attrition. Each day *they encountered hundreds of merchant ships plying their trade and the Germans soon realized that Britain's trade routes and supply ships were her greatest strength as her commercial vehicles were allowed to proceed unmolested in spite of their vulnerability to attack. They now became the U-boat fleet's principle target. In retaliation to the hunger blockade imposed by the Royal Navy, on February 4, 1915, Germany declared all waters around the British Isles to be a war zone and warned that ships entering the area would be liable to destruction without warning. Admiral Von Tirpitz, father of the German Navy, was optimistic that this strategy would starve Britain into submission in a very short time. Ergo: each side was now attempting to starve its opponent, one with a blockade of ships above the sea, the other with a blockade of submarines under it.*

The fleet of 28 U-boats was deployed over various locations around the British Isles with three of them designated for the South Western Approaches up the southern Irish coast and the Irish Sea. This was a particularly lucrative area for targets with ships sailing from America and into such ports as Liverpool, Queenstown and Milfordhaven. The best killing areas turned out to be around Fastnet, Galley Head, Kinsale, Queenstown and Waterford, a stretch of water off the coast of Ireland the U-boat commanders referred to as Torpedo Alley.

To counter this submarine menace Winston Churchill had devised the Q ships, merchant vessels—an assortment of tramp-steamers, fishing trawlers and sailing ships—requisitioned from their owners and dispatched to Queenstown (hence the designation Q boat) for conversion. This entailed changing the name, adjusting the colours, adding a dummy funnel, generally disguising the vessel, which had a gun installed, manned by trained Royal Navy gunners.

The objective was to lure a U-boat to the surface to challenge its supposed victim in the belief that it was an unarmed merchant ship. The Q boat gunners would then unleash a salvo aimed at the base of the conning tower. For a time it worked with the Q boats sinking a dozen or more U-boats. However in some cases the submarines managed to fire off a torpedo in time to avoid total destruction while they were under attack. When the Germans discovered the true nature of the Q boats they no longer surfaced but adopted a shoot first and ask questions later policy.

Churchill then adopted a fresh strategy. In February 1915, he issued secret orders to all merchant ships, including the Lusitania, *urging all British vessels to fly flags of other nations to mislead the U-boats; if ordered by a submarine to halt they were to attempt to ram it at full speed.*

Initially the German submariners observed the Cruise Rules, which had been in force for hundreds of years, when attacking enemy merchant shipping. A warship or submarine could not attack or capture a merchant ship without first making provision for the safety of its civilian crew. Churchill's policy ended any such German chivalry at sea. From then on anything was game.

Old Head of Kinsale, Ireland
May 7, 1915

CHURCHILL Winston
HOLT William Robert George
SCHWEIGER Walther
TURNER William

"Strong Swimming School Boy, Hero of U-Boat Sinking—Gave his Life Jacket to Save Another"

When the luxury liner *Lusitania* set sail from New York for Liverpool on May 1, 1915, among her 360 civilian Canadian passengers was the 15-year-old son of Sir Herbert Holt, president of the Royal Bank of Canada. Robert "Bob" Holt was returning to the English public school he was attending for the final term of the year. The day before, *Kapitanleutnant* Walther Schwieger had steered his German submarine *U-20* through the mouth of Emden naval base with orders to proceed to the Irish

Sea "to attack transport ships, merchant ships and warships." Holt, aboard *Lusitania*, and Schweiger, at the controls of *U-20*, were bound on a collision course.

By 10:00 on the sunny morning of May 7, submarine and liner were a mere 100 miles apart off the coast of Ireland, *Lusitania* south of Browhead, *U-20* south of the Coningbed Lightship. At 1:50 p.m, 12 miles from land and proceeding at 18 knots, the captain of the passenger ship, William Turner, took a sighting on the lighthouse tower of Old Head of Kinsale. Meanwhile Schweiger, having spotted a four-funnel vessel two miles away, which he identified as a large passenger steamer, dove his submarine to a periscope depth of 36 feet and set course to intercept. At 2:10 p.m., 2,300 feet from the target, he gave the order to fire. With a "shudder and a hiss" a torpedo streaked through the water, a trail of bubble in its wake.

Passengers aboard *Lusitania* had just finished their lunch. Young Bob Holt had settled into an armchair on the boat deck lounge, where the orchestra was playing "The Blue Danube," to read *An Irishman's Luck*. Given his Celtic heritage, a propitious title for a novel as it turned out. Those on deck were basking in the light breeze, gazing at the emerald green of the Irish shore. Suddenly they noticed a streak of white rippling the mirror-like calm of the sea off the starboard bow, followed by a torpedo explosion under the bridge, sending splinters and wreckage from the upper structure showering down on those below. Almost immediately a second missile exploded in the forward part of the vessel, igniting volatile coal dust, which blew a hole in the bottom of the boat.

As the call came to man the lifeboats Captain Turner frantically tried to head his doomed ship towards land. But it was impossible; the crippled liner was completely out of control and starting to sink. Nor could he stop the engines to allow the lifeboats to be launched safely. On striking the water, several capsized, spilling the occupants into the ocean. Some passengers had been killed or wounded when the torpedo struck, others thrown over the side of the ship into the sea. "I heard a dull crash," Holt recalled. "Immediately *Lusitania* leaned over on her right side, at about a thirty-five degree angle. People at once began to walk to the upper side of the deck, but there was no panic, although there was a lot of confusion."

Having witnessed the risk of being launched in one of the lifeboats, Holt decided instead to take his chances clambering down the starboard side of the ship and jumping into the water. He was about to climb over the side when he noticed that one of several women around him didn't have a life jacket. Holt gave her his own life preserver then climbed down and leaped into the water, swimming away from the sinking ship as hard as possible. Fortunately he was a strong enough swimmer (which he later credited for saving his life) to avoid being pulled under by the suction from the sinking ship, otherwise he would have drowned. The scene about him was chaos. Panic and tumult were everywhere. "It was terrible," Holt remembered. "People were shouting for help and others were going under. I succeeded in getting hold of an oar and, turning around, I saw the *Lusitania* disappear. She did not sink all at once; her bow entered the water first, and she slid gradually forward until she disappeared."

Holt released the oar he'd been hanging onto and resumed swimming when a man wearing a life belt grabbed him around the waist. With no life preserver of his own, Holt angrily pushed him aside. As he swam on he drew alongside the ship's surgeon and two other men. Together they managed to find an air tank from one of the lifeboats floating about. However it didn't have enough ballast to support all four of them so Holt made off towards a collapsible lifeboat in which were seated a man and a woman. Partly submerged, it was still seaworthy, but it couldn't support an extra person either, if it was to remain afloat, so Holt swam off once more. After a short time he reached a collapsed lifeboat that had turned upside-down and was carrying 30 people. He asked if there was room for one more whereupon one man extended an oar to him. Holt eagerly grabbed it and crawled aboard.

All around them people were hanging onto wreckage, deck chairs and any other objects they could find. Unfortunately the upside-down craft couldn't help them; it had reached the limit of its capacity. However, three men in a collapsible lifeboat that was still intact cruised about picking up as many survivors as it could safely hold. It was of some help but it still left hundreds of wretched souls in the frigid water struggling to stay afloat by clinging to whatever flotsam they could find. Holt described the pathetic scene succinctly when he later wrote: "Everyone in the water in one situation or another was desperately looking for help and hoping to be rescued."

The sight of a sailing boat within half a mile raised their spirits, but only temporarily. Because the sea was so calm and there was no wind, it remained dead in the water, unable to come to their rescue. Next, a steamer could be seen on the horizon. But once again their hopes were dashed when, not having seen them, after half an hour, she sailed away in the opposite direction. To add to their despair all the lifeboats had by this time headed for Queenstown. "There were still people like ourselves awaiting rescue, and those clinging to wreckage were in a perilous position," Holt reported.

However, after waiting forlornly for two hours, deliverance arrived at last when they finally sighted a ship sailing in the direction of their upturned lifeboat. The *Katrina*, a Cardiff ship that had come from the Falkland Islands flying the Greek flag, had been alerted to the *Lusitania* disaster by the coast guard and began a search for survivors. As soon as those on the lifeboat sighted it, Holt tied some handkerchiefs to an oar and began waving it to draw attention. It worked. The *Katrina* pulled alongside, lowered a pair of lifeboats and took the grateful survivors aboard the ship, which promptly headed for Queenstown. The captain and the crew were "exceedingly kind," Holt remembered, helping them to dry their clothes and serving hot tea to warm them after hours in the agonizingly cold water. One of those rescued was a stoker from the *Lusitania* who had one of his arms almost completely blown off when the torpedo struck. He had also suffered a severe head wound. Fortuitously an Italian surgeon had also been among those rescued from the upturned lifeboat. Dressing the head wound was no problem but he diagnosed the condition of the stoker's arm, which had been almost completely severed from his body and was dangling from his shoulder, serious enough to require amputation. However, the *Katrina* had neither anaesthetics nor surgery implements aboard, so the doctor had to perform the operation with a penknife and without the benefit of a narcotic to put his patient to sleep.

As the ship proceeded to Queenstown *Katrina* picked up two more survivors, a man and a woman clinging to a pair of wooden crates floating on the surface. The rescue ship reached Queenstown harbour around midnight and the survivors were transferred to HMS *Julia*. Their ordeal was over but not the tragedy that claimed the lives of 1,189 innocent men, women and children, the shock of this inhuman act of terror reverberating around the world.

In Victoria, B.C., martial law had to be imposed as incensed citizens plundered and destroyed German shops and businesses. In Great Britain riots were widespread throughout the major cities. In London the American ambassador declared, "The United States must declare war or forfeit European respect."

The Germans, who hailed the sinking a great success, alleged that *Lusitania* was carrying munitions and Canadian troops, both claims subsequently proven false by courts of inquiry.

In fact the British were not entirely blameless for the disaster, particularly Winston Churchill who, as First Lord of the Admiralty, had advocated the arming of merchant ships and the "right to ram" U-boats, thereby inducing unrestricted open warfare on the high seas. Many years later, alluding to the American outrage it precipitated, fostering the strong anti-German feelings, and the pro-war sentiments it generated, he stated: "In spite of all its horror, we must regard the sinking of the *Lusitania* as an event most important and favourable the Allies...the poor babies who perished in the ocean struck a blow more deadly than could have been achieved by the sacrifice of a hundred thousand fighting men."

RefScs: LAET 5 63 73 148 190–91 PD TLUTM 36–37 88 97 141–143

Ostend, Belgium
April 23 and May 10, 1918

BOURKE Rowland Richard Louis

"RCN Reject Won DSO, VC for Attacks on Enemy-Occupied Channel Port"

When the Royal Canadian Navy and the Canadian Army turned Rowland Bourke down due to defective eyesight, he refused to be discouraged. He sailed for England, where he talked his way into the Royal Naval Volunteer Reserve. On April 25, and again on May 10, 1918, as commander of a naval motor launch (ML), he took part in two attempts to blockade the port of Ostend on the Belgian coast. For these actions he was awarded the Distinguished Service Order and the Victoria Cross consecutively.

Following the second attack, Bourke commandeered his ML 276 into the smoke-filled harbour, behind the crippled British warship *Vindictive*, to look for survivors. There he engaged enemy machine guns on both piers with his Lewis guns. Bourke pulled his own ship alongside *Vindictive* to see if there were any injured aboard. Finding it abandoned he decided to withdraw, but as he did so he heard cries for help from the water. He re-entered the harbour and after a prolonged search found a British naval lieutenant and two badly wounded ratings clinging to an upended skiff. He and his crew hauled them aboard.

Throughout the rescue Bourke and his crew came under heavy enemy fire at close range. Two of his crewmen were killed and several others wounded. His motor launch also suffered heavy damage, taking 55 hits, one by a 6-inch shell. Although the speed of his vessel was sharply reduced, Bourke managed to steer it out of the harbour, where another British warship, *Monitor*, took him in tow. His citation to the VC read: "This episode displayed daring and skill of a very high order...."

Rowland Bourke was born in London, England, in 1885 and emigrated to Canada in 1902. Before the war ended he had been promoted to the rank of lieutenant-commander and, in addition to

Rowland Bourke, wearing the Victoria Cross received for action as commander of motor launch 276. (DND/PA 161003)

the VC and DSO, he had been awarded the French Chevalier of the Legion d'Honneur. In World War II he served in the Royal Canadian Volunteer Reserve as an administrative officer. Following the war he retired to Esquimalt, B.C.

VC DSO Ld'H LTCOMM Born November 28, 1885
RefScs: C&TOTCN 117–18 CVC 102–03 VM 102–3

Between Wars: Weathering the Storm
1918–1939

HOSE Walter
NELLES Percy Walker

"First Chiefs of Naval Staff Kept Royal Canadian Navy Afloat"

By the end of the war in November 1918, the RCN's contribution had been enormously important in that it had protected merchant shipping from any loss by German submarines in Canadian waters. And yet it had not achieved a single victory.

Canadians were far more impressed with the feats of their air aces and with the overwhelming accomplishments of the army. Ironically, as a nation with one of the longest coastlines in the world—35,000 miles—Canada was a long way from being Navy-minded. In any case, with the cessation of hostilities all her armed services were sharply reduced—the Navy almost to the point of extinction.

Four years later, out of economic necessity, all three services were placed under a single command, that of the Chief of the General Staff. Walter Hose, Director of Naval Service, who during the war had commanded the East Coast Patrols—Canada's principal naval contribution—could not abide by the decision to consolidate forces, and he argued vociferously against it. Finally, Hose resigned in frustration as CGS and, in 1928, he became the RCN's first Chief of the Naval Staff.

Hose realized that Canada would never have a proper navy until it gained public support. He deliberately scrapped the RCN *per se* and concentrated his efforts and monies on resurrecting the Royal Canadian Naval Volunteer Reserve, which had glimmered briefly in 1912 and then flickered out due to lack of support from the Ministry of Naval Service. By opening reserve units across the country, Hose managed to "sell" the Navy to the populace, and at the same time build up a pool of naval-trained Canadians in the event of war.

The year 1933, in the depths of the Depression, saw another major round of budget spending cuts. The new CGS, Andrew

Walter Hose, father of the Royal Canadian Navy. (DND/PA 142594)

McNaughton, considered the army to be sufficient defence against invasion (*à la* War of 1812), and he decided to do away with the Navy altogether. He hadn't reckoned with the aggressiveness and resourcefulness of Walter Hose, however, who used every means and channel available to preserve his service.

In the end, Walter Hose won the day, paving the way for his successor, Percy Nelles, who in 1934 became the first Canadian to be appointed Chief of the Naval Staff. Nelles kept the RCN on an even keel to meet the threat of a new world war, successfully juggling politics and inter-service rivalries.

At the outbreak of World War II, Nelles had at his disposal a piddling force of six destroyers, five minesweepers, two training vessels and personnel consisting of 145 officers and 1,674 men. He could be grateful to his predecessor that a navy existed at all, and that he had the rank to command it.

Walter Hose was born the son of a bishop of Singapore. Joining the Royal Navy at an early age, he served in such actions as the capture of Wei-hai-wei in China by the Japanese in 1894; the Turko-Greek War in 1897; and, during the Boxer Rebellion in 1900–1901, he was awarded the China Medal for his actions on the Yangtze River. After attending the British War Staff Course and serving as a member of the Combined Naval and Military Operations Staff, he retired from the RN in 1912.

Married to a Newfoundlander, Hose joined the RCN that same year and was appointed Commander of *Rainbow*. When the East Coast Patrol was formed in 1917, Hose was given command. During his tenure not one ship was lost to the German U-boats.

At the end of World War I in 1918, he served as Senior Naval Officer in Halifax, overseeing the demobilization of the East Coast Patrol that he had commanded so capably. That same year he was appointed Assistant Minister of Naval Service. Then, in 1920 and 1921, he was successively made Assistant Director and Director of Naval Service. In 1924 he acted as Naval Advisor to Prime Minister Mackenzie King at the Imperial Conference in London. Hose retired from the RCN in 1934. He had, in effect, been "Canada's Father of the Navy," as well as its saviour.

RADM CBE CM Died June 1965
RefScs: EDS 6 MMN 24 RCNIR 69 TOTNA 18 32 TSIAOG 27 30 57 59–61

Percy Nelles (l.), Chief of the Naval Staff at the outbreak of World War II, seen here with M.F. Oliver of Chebogue. (DND/PA 126313)

Percy Nelles, a native of Brantford, Ont., joined the Canadian Naval Service (the precursor of the RCN) in 1908 and first served aboard a Canadian fisheries schooner vessel. In 1911, as a midshipman-in-training along with 37 other cadets, he represented the RCN at the coronation of King George V. After graduating as a junior officer, Nelles served with the Royal Navy aboard several ships until 1917, when he was appointed Flag Lieutenant to the Director of Canadian Naval Service, a post he held until 1922. During that period he attended the Admiralty Staff College in England.

Subsequently Nelles was give command of *Saguenay* and later an RN light cruiser, the first time a Canadian had been given such a command. Nelles held the post of CNS until 1944, when he was made Senior Canadian Flag Officer Overseas. During the invasion of Normandy in June that year, Nelles was in the thick of the naval action, first aboard an RCN destroyer, then boarding a motor torpedo boat to get a closer look at the proceedings.

After serving as head of the Canadian Mission Overseas, in 1945 Nelles retired from the RCN with the rank of full Admiral after 37 years in uniform, during which time he had become the youngest Rear Admiral in the British Commonwealth. He died in June 1951, and was given a burial at sea with full honours from aboard HMCS *Sault Ste. Marie*.

ADM CBE CLM (US) Born January 7, 1892 Died June 13, 1951
RefScs: MMN 34 RCNIR 139–40 TSIAOG 59–61 WPA 83

The RCN against Germany
1939–1945

At the outbreak of World War II, the RCN consisted of barely 1,800 permanent force officers and men, and a reserve force of 1,200. But before the war was through, some 1,000,000 Canadian men and women had performed military duty in some capacity—quite remarkable for a country with a population of just over 12,000,000. Of that total, approximately 15 per cent served with the Royal Canadian Navy.

Beginning the war with only six destroyers, five small minesweepers and two training vessels, the Royal Canadian Navy ended the war with 373 fighting ships, most of which were built in Canada.

During 2,060 days of war, 25,343 Allied merchant ships carried 181,643,180 tons of cargo across the North Atlantic under Canadian escort. RCN ships, by themselves or with other Allied vessels, sank a total of 27 German U-boats and captured, incapacitated or sank 42 surface ships of the Kriegsmarine.

In all operations, 24 Canadian warships were lost; 1,797 Canadians lost their lives; 319 were wounded; 95 were taken prisoner. Members of the RCN received 1,677 British and 64 foreign decorations.

Ninety per cent of the Navy was made up of men and women who joined for the duration of the war only. Once it ended, the majority of them returned to civilian life.

Early Stages
September 1939–May 1940

Although the size and shape of the RCN between 1939 and 1945 was moulded by the need for protection of merchant- and troop-carrying shipping against German U-boats, that threat was given scant attention by British and Canadian authorities at the outbreak of hostilities. The main danger was seen to be the German surface fleet—dreadnoughts and fast, well-armed pocket battleships—which, in fact, sank only a fraction of the tonnage sent to the bottom by enemy submarines before they themselves were either scuttled, sunk or bottled up.

The sinking of *Athenia*, a passenger ship with 1,000 civilians aboard, only one day after Britain's declaration of war, changed that thinking overnight, with a helping hand from Winston Churchill. The British First Sea Lord proclaimed the event a signal that Germany had declared unrestricted, all-out U-boat warfare, and he took immediate advantage of the situation by ordering naval escorts for convoys. The RCN immediately climbed aboard.

By mid-September 1939, the Canadian destroyers Saguenay and St. Laurent had already escorted a convoy 350 miles out of Halifax, where it was taken over by RN ships. On October 10, Canadian destroyers repeated the procedure, escorting the First Canadian Division out to sea. But essentially, at this point, the basic role of the RCN was perceived to be the defence of Canada's own shores.

By the end of the year, the Navy had accumulated a strange assortment of 60 vessels that, in addition to destroyers, included armed merchant ships, converted luxury yachts and fishing vessels. But, most importantly, a plan to initiate a shipbuilding program had been laid. This would include the doughty little corvette—with its rolling ability designed after a whaling craft, to tackle the porpoising quality of the submarine. The corvette would become the chief surface nemesis of the U-boat.

Naval status quo came to an abrupt end in April 1940, when the Germans invaded Norway. Six weeks later they had conquered Holland and Belgium and, by May 23, the Panzers had rattled into Boulogne to cut off the British Expeditionary Force. The next day three RCN destroyers from *Halifax*—*Restigouche*, *Skeena* and *Saguenay*—and *Fraser* from Bermuda, set sail for Plymouth to bolster the Royal Navy destroyers. They were soon to be joined by three *others*—*Assiniboine*, *Ottawa* and *St. Laurent*—after the latter three had been refitted.

Aboard were commanders and first officers most of whom would eventually reach admiral or commodore rank, and whose names would become legend in the lore of the Canadian Navy. In the meantime, while they were en route, one of their brother officers, on course at a gunnery school in Portsmouth, had already distinguished himself during the evacuation of Dunkirk.

Dunkirk
May 27–June 4, 1940

TIMBRELL Robert Walter

"First RCN Officer to Be Decorated in World War II"

On May 26, the day the signal was given to begin evacuating the British army from Dunkirk, Bob Timbrell, who was taking a course at HMS *Excellent* gunnery school in Portsmouth, was detailed off to help rescue the troops. To his surprise, the 20-year-old trainee was assigned as captain of HMS *Llanthony*, a yacht belonging to a Maltese millionaire, one of the ragtag fleet of assorted vessels used in the evacuation. It had no armament other than the .45 Colt revolver Timbrell carried with him, and an inexperienced crew of eight.

At Dunkirk, the jetties were reserved for the destroyers and ferries, so Timbrell had to bring his ship into shore as close he dared and take the troops directly off the beach. On his first trip he succeeded in bringing 100 men back to England, and in three more sallies he brought back 300 more. Then, on the fourth trip, *Llanthony*'s luck ran out—a German bomb hit the forecastle, killing five of the crew. The anchors were lost and the fuel lines damaged, bringing the engine to a stop; the stricken vessel drifted onto the beach, where Timbrell disembarked the hundred troops he had taken aboard a short time earlier.

As the tide began to ebb, Timbrell and his crew went over the side to dig sand out from under the rudders and propellers so they wouldn't be damaged in the rising tide. To make embarking easier, Timbrell came up with the innovative idea of creating his own jetty by having the disembarked (and disgruntled) troops drive abandoned trucks in a line as close to the ship as possible before the tide turned. As the water rose, *Llanthony* was anchored with a Bren gun carrier and armed with machine guns and anti-tank guns. At full tide, with the fuel lines repaired, the troops were re-embarked and *Llanthony* set off for England again.

Timbrell had been so successful he was looked upon as an old hand at the art of evacuation and given command of a flotilla of four trawlers, one of which was lost to a mine their first night out.

On the last day of the evacuation, under constant shelling, bombing and mortar fire, Timbrell and his small fleet sailed back to England with their final load of troops. *Llanthony* was little more than a remnant of the impeccable yacht Timbrell had taken command of just over a week earlier. It was filthy inside and out, and both masts had been shot away. There were holes in the superstructure, and the scruffy-looking crew stank to high heaven. But she and they had performed nobly. For his part in the action, Timbrell was awarded the Distinguished Service Cross, the first RCN officer of the war to be decorated.

Robert Timbrell was born in Vancouver, B.C., and enlisted in the Navy in 1937, eventually attaining the rank of Rear Admiral. In 1940 he survived the sinking of the Canadian destroyer *Margaree*. Following World War II, Timbrell held several posts, including that of Deputy Chief of Plans. Before retiring in 1973, he was Commander of Maritime Command.

RADM DSC MID Born February 1, 1920
RefScs: MMN 44 TOTNA 104–08 TSIAOG 77 85 174

Rescue Work
June 1940

*By the time the Canadian destroyers arrived in Great Britain in
June 1940, the Dunkirk evacuation had ended and France was
on the verge of collapse. The RCN destroyers' initial duties were
to assist the RN in saving pockets of retreating British, Dutch,
Belgian, French and Polish troops—along with civilian VIPs—
from capture.*

Saint-Valéry-en-Caux
June 11, 1940

DeWOLF Harry George
LAY Horatio Nelson
PIERS Desmond William

*"First Exchange of Fire between Canadian Navy and German
Army"*

HMCS *Restigouche* had been ordered to proceed to a point
just off the French coast near Dieppe to pick up troops of the
British 51st Highland Division at Saint-Valéry-en-Caux. On
arrival, the crew observed a variety of vessels evacuating French
and English wounded, but no sign of the Highlanders.

The captain, Nelson Lay, ordered his Number One, Desmond
"Debby" Piers, to assign someone to go ashore and investigate.
Typically, Piers elected himself to carry out the task. He found
the division, firmly holding a six-mile line, but the general in
charge declined Piers's invitation to evacuate his men—a bold but
foolhardy decision that cost him the eventual capture of 6,000 of
his troops. Meanwhile, *Restigouche* had been joined by *St.
Laurent* (built for the RN in 1932, then purchased for the RCN in
1937).

By the time Piers returned to his ship, both destroyers had
come under fire from German Panzer tanks on the cliffs. Harry

Desmond "Debby" Piers aboard Restigouche. *(J.D. Mahoney/PA 136286)*

DeWolf, skipper of *St. Laurent*, returned fire with his 4.7-inch guns, and Lay immediately ordered his own gunners to open up. When German fire cleared the top of *Restigouche*'s bridge by no more than three feet, all hands fell flat on their faces—except Lay, who sat calmly in his seat. (Many years later, Lay recalled the affair. "I noticed the...rest were ducking behind the canvas and the dodgers. This struck me as absurd and I started to laugh. Canvas is no protection against a 3-inch shell and, in any case, when you heard the shell it was well past.")

But enough was enough, and the two Canadian destroyers soon beat a hasty retreat in a zigzag course. This marked the first exchange of fire between the RCN and the German *Wehrmacht*.

Harry DeWolf, born in Bedford, N.S., exhibited leadership at an early age. While attending the Royal Naval College, from which he graduated in 1921, he was made Cadet Captain. After serving on many RN ships, he was given command of *St. Laurent* in 1939.

In 1940, while on escort duty, he supervised the rescue of survivors of the sinking *Arandora Star*. There were some 900 in the water, most of them German and Italian aliens from Britain en route to internment in Canada.

DeWolf held various senior positions throughout and after the war. He served as Chief of the Naval Staff from 1956–1960, and attained the rank of Vice-Admiral before retiring in 1961.

VADM CBE DSO DSC MID (4) OLM (US) OLH (Fr)
KHCOL (Nor)
RefScs: MMN 17 RCNIR 42 TNAR 22 202 203 210
TOTNA 99 112 197 TSIAOG 7–8(Frd) 61 81 85

Nelson Lay was born in Skagway, Alaska, and graduated from the Royal Naval College of Canada in 1918. Nearly two weeks after the St. Valery incident, following the French surrender on June 21 at Compiegne, Lay's *Restigouche*, with the help of *Fraser*, the senior Canadian ship, rescued a party of fugitive diplomats (including Georges Vanier, Canadian minister to France, who served as Canada's Governor General, 1959–1967) from a sardine boat at St. Jean de Luz, near the Spanish border.

Later, while marshalling transports and patrolling for U-boats, they evacuated the better part of a Polish division. For this action, Lay and two of the ship's company were awarded the Polish Cross of Valour.

In 1941 he was Director of Operations at Naval Headquarters. In August 1943, HMS *Nabob*, an RN aircraft carrier manned by an RCN crew under Lay's command, was torpedoed at sea. Lay gave the order to abandon ship, and then managed to save 214 men, including 10 who were injured (see page 154).

At war's end, Lay was Director of Plans and Naval Intelligence. He retired as Vice-Chief of the Naval Staff with the rank of Rear Admiral in November 1958.

RADM OBE COV(Pol) Born January 23, 1903
RefScs: ABW 156 MMN 28 RCNIR 42 152 TOTNA 12 97
TSIAOG 78 185

Desmond Piers became a master of U-boat warfare. In the summer of 1942 he led a spectacular battle against 17 U-boats while escorting the ill-fated SC (slow convoy) 107—Halifax to the United Kingdom—through the "Black Pit," the mid-Atlantic stretch over which there was no air support at the time. A native of Halifax, he became an outspoken critic of the poor quality of equipment supplied to the RCN.

Joining the Navy in 1932, he attained the rank of Rear Admiral. He ended his naval career as Chairman of the Defence Liaison Staff in Washington and Canadian representative on the NATO Military Committee. He later became Chairman of the Nova Scotia Division of the Canadian Corps of Commissionaires.

RADM CM DSC KStLJ Born June 12, 1913
RefScs: BW xi 2440 MMN 36 TNAR 245 TOTNA 126–28
TSIAOG 78–79 85

THE WESTERN APPROACHES JUNE–DECEMBER 1940

*W*hen France surrendered in June 1940 and the Germans overran the country, the English Channel became the first line of defence against invasion, and the Canadian ships remained with the Home Fleet.

With western and central Europe and part of Scandinavia under the Nazi yoke, U-boats were free to circumvent the British Isles from newly established submarine bases as far north as Narvik and as far south as Bordeaux. They began employing tactics that their commander, Karl "Daddy" Donitz, had developed in World War II—the Rudeltactik, or wolf-pack attack. Their method was to get well ahead of a convoy by day then run on the surface like torpedo boats at night for assaults on merchant ships, submerging only if they themselves were threatened with attack.

The U-boats were assisted in their efforts by the Luftwaffe. New long-range, 4-engine Focke-Wulf Kondors, flying from Bordeaux, not only bombed and strafed Allied shipping in the Western Approaches to the British Isles and routes to the Mediterranean, but also acted as spotters for the submarines. In their first 60 days (roughly July through September), the aircraft sank 30 ships. By the beginning of September, with World War II now a year old, the toll in shipping losses from U-boats alone amounted to 470 ships. Two million tons were sent to the bottom—what the U-boat commanders called the "Happy Time." An equal amount of tonnage was lost through mines, aircraft attacks and surface ships.

By October, the danger of a German invasion of England had passed, but the southern ports were bombed so incessantly that, by the end of the month, the Channel was closed to shipping. Atlantic convoys were now re-routed north of Ireland to Liverpool and the Firth of Clyde. RCN destroyers joined the RN'S Clyde Escort Group sailing from Liverpool, Greenock, Rosyth and later Londonderry. North American escorts reached only as far east as a point south of Iceland, and they were too few. As an example, one convoy out of Halifax, HX-79 (and it was a fast one, with an especially heavy escort), lost 13 ships out of 40—in one night alone.

November 6, 1940

MAINGUY Edmond Rollo

"First Royal Canadian Navy U-boat Kill"

Some time after midnight, answering a distress call from a merchant ship, Rollo Mainguy, captain of *Ottawa* and senior officer of the escort, together with a British destroyer, found a surfaced submarine blazing away at the merchant vessel. The U-boat submerged; both escorts closed in and set up a coordinated attack. In turns, one destroyer tracked the submarine while the other dropped depth charges. Over the next three hours they relentlessly made nine different assaults, unloading a total of 80 depth charges—12 tons of explosives.

Through the night they'd heard several explosions. Then, as morning dawned, they saw diesel oil oozing to the surface.

Mainguy and his RN counterpart were certain they had a kill, as was the commander in charge of escort vessels in Liverpool. But, convening much later, the Admiralty's U-Boat Assessment Committee saw things differently. Yes, there were explosions and fuel oil leaking to the surface—a common German trick—and no confirmation that the submarine had been destroyed. Likewise, there was no evidence of any wreckage sighted. So the committee granted the destroyers a "probably damaged." (After the war, Italian officials established and confirmed that one of their U-boats—*Faa di Bruno*—had indeed been sunk on the night of November 6, 1940. Its demise, and the fact that it had been the RCN's first submarine victory of the war, had gone unrecognized all that time.)

Rollo Mainguy, a native of Victoria, B.C., joined the Navy in 1915 and attended the Royal Naval College of Canada, graduating as a midshipman. Between wars he served in various capacities, taking command of *Assiniboine* in 1939 before becoming captain of *Ottawa* the following year. He was then appointed Captain (D) Halifax (that is, in charge of destroyer escorts) in 1941, and held the same post in Newfoundland with the establishment of the Newfoundland Escort Group.

He next served as Chief of Naval Personnel, and as the Third Member of the Naval Board in 1942. In 1944 he was back at sea commanding *Uganda*, a ship that took part in the bombardment of Sakashima and the Japanese-held base of Truk. Mainguy became Commanding Officer Pacific Coast in 1946, and the next year Flag Officer Atlantic Coast. Between 1951 and 1956 he served as Chief of the Naval Staff. After retiring with the rank of Vice-Admiral, he became president of the Great Lakes Waterways Development Association.

VADM OBE MID OLM (US) Born May 11, 1901
RefScs: MMN 30 TDBS 185 TNAR 39fp 100 141 150fp 167
TSIAOG 76 82–83 128fp 205

December 1, 1940

McNAUGHT Clifford

"Suffered from Frightful Burns but Kept Gunners Supplied"

At the same instant that *Saguenay* spotted a submarine on the surface astern of its convoy, the destroyer was struck by a torpedo. The attacker was the Italian submarine *Argo*, and the damage it had inflicted was severe. Flames broke out and raced through the ship—21 members of the crew were killed.

Argo surfaced again, circling to get in a second shot. Clifford McNaught, an able seaman aboard *Saguenay*, was suffering from painful burns to his face, and his hands were horribly mangled. He nevertheless dashed forward to assist the short-handed gun crew by passing shells to them.

Saguenay limped home on one engine, thanks to the tenacity and seamanship of the engineering officer and his crew. McNaught was found huddled by the gun sobbing fretfully, a letdown from the heroic deed he had performed in utter agony.

RefScs: TSIAOG 83

Circa mid-December 1940

RAYNER Herbert Sharples

"Battled Enemy Submarines and Elements at the Same Time"

Convoy escorts had to not only face the danger of being torpedoed and fired at by enemy submarines but also battle the elements—fierce winds, rain, snow, storms, heavy waves and bitter cold. This particularly snowy, stormy December night, on a heavy sea in which *St. Laurent* detached herself from her convoy to rescue survivors of a crippled armed merchant cruiser, was typical of such conditions.

Herbie Rayner, captain of *St. Laurent* (nicknamed *"Sally"* after Sally Rand the fan dancer), learned that U-boats were everywhere—they had sunk 10 ships and torpedoed *Forfar*, a merchant cruiser. *Sally*'s crew plucked the survivors out of the icy water and Rayner had begun escorting the cruiser eastward when U-boats struck again. *Forfar* took another torpedo and was sinking. *St. Laurent* rushed back to the rescue, then picked up a solid series of "pings" on the asdic (anti-submarine detection equipment, later known as SONAR), signifying a U-boat. Rayner had to make a fast decision—continue to pick up survivors or go after the sub. He decided on the latter—U-boats had created enough havoc for one night.

He radioed for help, knowing that one ship alone can easily lose a target. Soon a British destroyer joined him, and the two vessels began a coordinated attack. After eight depth charge drops, diesel oil spread on the surface of the sea. The two commanders were sure they had a kill. *Sally* returned to the task of picking up survivors, some in lifeboats, others grimly clinging to rafts and flotsam.

That completed, *St. Laurent* received an emergency signal that a merchant ship 50 miles away had been torpedoed. *Sally* again rushed to the scene to find the stricken vessel slowed to five knots an hour. Towering seas threatened the merchantman. It was a struggle that lasted three days through snow, squalls and high winds before the ships reached the haven of the Clyde and a berth at Greenock.

Herbert Rayner was born in Clinton, Ont., and joined the RCN in 1928. Having served aboard several RN ships, he was assigned to *Skeena* in 1937. In 1940 he took command of *St. Laurent* from Rollo Mainguy. In 1942 he advanced from Staff Officer Operations to Commanding Officer Atlantic Coast. The next year he was given command of *Huron*.

In 1944 he was appointed Director of Plans, and subsequently was made Captain (D) Halifax. Following the war he served in several senior capacities, and in 1960 became Chief of Naval Staff. Rayner retired in 1965 with the rank of Vice-Admiral, and two years later was made Director of the Anglican Diocese of Ottawa.

VADM DSC & Bar Ld'H(Fr) CdGaP(FR) Born January 16, 1901

RefScs: MMN 38 NAR 112 TOTNA 112 TSIAOG 83–85 158

THE NEWFOUNDLAND ESCORT FORCE APRIL–SEPTEMBER 1941

*U*ntil the spring of 1941, convoys had no protection between a point near Newfoundland, the extent to which the Halifax escort travelled, and the area west of Ireland, where the Western Approaches escorts picked them up. This situation was partly alleviated in April when the Royal Navy established a base in Iceland, providing the convoys with twice the coverage they had been receiving.

It was still not enough. It had not solved the problem of horrendous shipping losses—the wolf packs had extended their hunting fields to the "no-man's-land" between Iceland and Newfoundland. Obviously, complete coverage was the only solution.

In May, the British Admiralty asked the RCN to cover the western Atlantic in addition to protecting its own shores. A new command was created, known as the Newfoundland Escort Force (NEF), with its headquarters and naval base at St. John's, on the east coast of the island. At first the group consisted of a nucleus of RN destroyers from World War I, those destroyers that could be spared from the RCN, and Canadian ships recalled from Western Approaches service. But the foundation of the force was the output of corvettes now pouring from Canadian shipyards.

MURRAY Leonard Warren

"Commander of the Newfoundland Force"

*F*rom St. John's, the NEF picked up convoys from Halifax and Sydney coastal escorts, then conveyed them across the

Atlantic to the Mid-Ocean Meeting Point (MOMP) just south of Iceland, where the Western Approaches escorts took over. From there, the RCN ships proceeded north to Hvalfjord, Iceland to refuel and, if necessary, to refit. They then returned to sea to escort westbound convoys to Newfoundland, delivering them to the Canadian shore escorts.

The officer in charge of this operation (official designation: Commodore Commanding Newfoundland Force) was Leonard Warren Murray, who had been Commander of Canadian Ships and Establishment in the United Kingdom.

Leonard Murray, born in Granton, N.S., had been a cadet at the Royal Naval College class of 1912. He first saw service as an RN midshipman aboard HMS *Berwick* during the Mexican Revolution in 1913. In World War I he served on several RN warships, and between wars held various posts with both the RN and the RCN. In 1939 he became Director of Naval Operations and Training. Murray retired from the Navy in 1946 and made his home in England.

CMDRE CB CBE CdeG(Fr) LoM(US) CoL(Nor) Born June 22, 1896. Died November 11, 1971
RefScs: MMN 33 RCNIR 99fp 139 140 TNAR 39p 49 138 166 164 180 200 208 TSIAOG 68 90 fp 128 192 205

Bay of Biscay
June 24, 1941

CREERY Wallace Bouchier
LAY Horatio Nelson

"The Ever-Present Risk of Collision"

To the list of dangers on the sea in wartime, add to surface and undersea attacks, mines and assault from the air the hazard of collision. Convoys, coordinated forays, even rescue work usually called for close-in sailing—dangerous enough. At night, with total blackouts in force, no radar at work in the early days to judge proximity between ships and, for security reasons, lack of wireless or telephone communications, collision became a manifestly greater risk.

The first such calamity to befall the Royal Canadian Navy in World War II took place following the rescue of Allied diplomats, VIPs and Polish troops from the French coast near the Spanish border. The RN cruiser HMS *Calcutta*, leading two Canadian destroyers, *Fraser* and *Restigouche*, headed north towards Bordeaux, where enemy ships were reported. When no targets presented themselves north of the Gironde River estuary, *Calcutta* wasted no time in giving the order to return to England.

Sometime around 10 p.m., with visibility about one and a half miles, *Calcutta* signalled "single line ahead." Wallace Creery, captain of *Fraser*, immediately altered course to comply. Seeing the silhouette of the Canadian destroyer cutting towards him, *Calcutta*'s skipper concluded that *Fraser* was about to cross his bow, leaving little margin for error. He ordered a sharp turn to starboard, which would have put him on a course inside *Fraser*, had the latter not been swerving to port (Creery's ultimate intention was to have pulled in astern of the leader). The ships were now on a collision course at a combined speed of 34 knots.

Both captains simultaneously barked orders for engines astern and wheels reversed, but—too late. The vessels closed the last 200 yards in a mere 11 seconds. *Calcutta*, still swinging to starboard, sliced into *Fraser*'s port beam like a knife through cheese.

Incredibly, *Fraser*'s entire bridge broke off and plunked itself down on top of *Calcutta*'s forecastle, where it settled—creaking and groaning in rhythm with the roll of the ship. A dazed and horrified Creery and his bridge mates stepped down to the safety of the cruiser's bow, shaking their heads in disbelief.

At the time of the collision, *Restigouche*, under the command of Nelson Lay, trailed three miles astern. When she reached the scene she pulled alongside the after-section of the broken destroyer to take on survivors. It took 10 precarious minutes in a rising swell to transfer 60 of the crew to the ship. For the survivors struggling in the water, *Restigouche* lowered lifeboats (more properly designated Sea-Boats) to augment the one already launched by *Calcutta*, dropped Carley floats and draped scramble nets over the sides.

Meanwhile, the bow of *Fraser* had drifted off into the darkness. The cries of those left marooned, clinging to the guardrails, rallied Lay's ship to their rescue. Just as she approached, *Fraser*'s bow turned turtle, throwing the men into the water. In spite of the darkness and a growing swell, 16 officers and 134 crewmen were saved. A scuttling party was dispatched to open the flood valves, and what was left of *Fraser* sank a few minutes after midnight.

Altogether, 66 men were lost to the disaster, a toll that might have been substantially higher had it not been for Nelson Lay, who persisted in staying on the scene. (Dick Malin, one of Lay's asdic operators, recalled that when a signal flashed from *Calcutta* to leave the scene, Lay turned impatiently to the yeoman who had taken it down and said: "I won't read any more messages for at least an hour!")

Wallace Creery was born in Vancouver in 1900 and joined the Royal Canadian Navy in 1914, attending the Royal Naval College of Canada. During World War I he served on several Royal Navy ships, including HMS *Canada* in 1918. Between wars he held a number of RCN assignments, including that of Director of Naval Operations in 1935.

In 1940 he was Captain in Charge, Halifax, and King's Harbour Master. In 1943 he became Chief of Staff to the Commanding Officer, Atlantic Coast Operations, and later Assistant Chief of Naval Staff. Following World War II Creery held several senior posts, including Flag Officer, Pacific Coast in 1950, and eventually Vice-Chief of Naval Staff and Member of the Naval Board in 1953. He retired as Rear Admiral in 1955. Creery died in Ottawa at age 87 in 1987.

RADM CBE Born February 22, 1900 Died February 3, 1987
RefScs: FDS 35–36 MMN 15 TSIAOG 78–79

South of Greenland
September 9–11, 1941

GRUBB Frederick
HIBBARD James Calcutt
PRENTICE James Douglas

"60-hour Sea Battle—One U-boat Sunk, 16 Merchant Ships Lost"

On August 30, 1941, convoy SC-42, made up of more than 60 ships, left Sydney, Nova Scotia, carrying well over half a million tons of supplies—fuel oil, grain, phosphate, lumber, ammunition, stores and a fleet of trucks—bound for the United Kingdom. At the end of the first week of September, at the west coast meeting point, just east of the Straits of Belle Isle between Labrador and Newfoundland, the convoy was taken over by Group 24 of the Newfoundland Escort Force: the destroyer *Skeena*, captained by the escort's senior officer, Jimmy Hibbard, and three corvettes—*Alberni*, *Kenogami* and *Orillia*.

At the same time in St. John's, James "Chummy" Prentice, Senior Officer Canadian Corvettes, cancelled a scheduled training run to set sail aboard *Chambly*, accompanied by *Moose Jaw*, to link up with SC-42 at a point where he was sure it would run afoul of U-boats. However, on the second day out (September 7) he received a signal to hold his position and await another convoy, due to pass the straits on September 11.

Meanwhile, on September 8, SC-42, which had reached a point south-southeast of Kap Farvel (Cape Farewell) in Greenland, altered its course to due north—heavy German signal traffic left no doubt that U-boats were gathering in force. The convoy held this course for 23 hours then, with the ice-sheathed mountains of Greenland in view, Hibbard ordered a change in course to northeast. As night fell, the convoy, which stretched out over a 25-square-mile area of ocean, wheeled to starboard. The night was clear with a full moon lighting the ships from the south—ideal for the wolf packs.

(l. to r.) Sir Humphrey Walwyn, Governor of Newfoundland, Commander James Prentice and Mrs. Prentice at the presentation of the DSO. (DND/PA 134538)

Out of the dark side to the north, at 11:37 p.m., torpedoes struck *Muneric*. Laden with iron ore, it sank like a rock, leaving no survivors. *Kenogami* swept back along the track of the torpedo when, off her starboard wake, another torpedo came churning through the water, narrowly missing the corvette. *Kenogami* sighted a surfaced U-boat, but the crew was virtually incapable of doing anything about it—at this stage in the war Canadian corvettes were not equipped with searchlights or star shells. They vainly fired their 4-inch gun without illumination, and the U-boat soon escaped.

Shortly after midnight clouds blotted out the moonlight, giving the convoy a chance to turn away. Just before the order was given, a surfaced U-boat slipped inside a shipping lane. Hibbard's *Skeena* cut into the convoy and raced up the same lane after it. The German submarine, well ahead, suddenly swung at right angles, crossed the line of ships, turned again and passed *Skeena* in the opposite direction, a line of merchantmen between them. It then submerged out of sight.

The night was not over. U-boats were everywhere inside the convoy. By morning, seven merchant ships had been torpedoed, and yet another was sunk at noon. Hibbard had also lost the services of one of his corvettes. *Orillia* had stayed behind to pick up survivors. She eventually took the damaged tanker *Tahchee* in tow and set course for Iceland.

Meanwhile, help was on the way. An order had gone out from the Admiralty requesting reinforcements. In the early evening, when the U-boats attacked again, sinking two merchantmen, *Skeena* shot off a pair of star shells (Canadian destroyers *did* have them) to survey the situation. No submarines were sighted, but the flares were seen by Chummy Prentice's group, now rapidly approaching.

Bringing *Chambly* within range of the convoy, Prentice's asdic crew positively identified a submarine. Making a quick attack, the ship dropped two depth charges. Then, just as *Chambly* readied for a second attack, *U-501*, commanded by Hugo Forster, bobbed to the surface a few hundred yards off *Moose Jaw*'s port bow.

Skipper Freddie Grubb ordered his gunners to open fire. He was bearing down fast when the submarine's engines stopped—Forster had decided to surrender. *Moose Jaw* pulled alongside to find most of the U-boat's crew standing with their hands in the air. Forster suddenly leaped from his own deck onto the deck of the corvette. Grubb let it be known he didn't want more boarders from an enemy vessel that could be taken in tow—whereupon the U-boat started up again and attempted to cross *Moose Jaw*'s bow. Grubb decided to ram. As the corvette bore down, the Germans ran for their forward gun, but a few rounds from *Moose Jaw*'s 4-incher shot it away.

Now Prentice pulled *Chambly* alongside *U-501* and sent a boarding party over. When the Germans refused an order to return belowdecks—even at gunpoint—the Canadians lowered themselves down the scaffold to find the lighting system broken and the instruments wrecked; then water began to rush through the broken hull. One Canadian was lost and 11 Germans drowned as the U-boat sank.

During this three-day action, and directly afterwards, SC-42 lost five more ships, two of them within two minutes of one another. The furious 60-hour, one-sided battle finally ended just before noon on September 11, when the escort was joined by four RN destroyers, two corvettes and two sloops from the Western Approaches force, and they all drew within range of air cover from Iceland.

The cost had been frightful—16 ships lost. The reasons were obvious. The escort had been outnumbered by the U-boats three to one. *Orillia*'s departure to take a disabled tanker in tow left the escort short-handed. Also, some of the ships' commanders spent time picking up survivors at the expense of the convoy. Though their compassion was understandable, their judgment was questionable: such actions had put the convoy—their number-one priority—at risk.

Jimmy Hibbard had done his best under the most difficult and trying circumstances. He was not only officially commended for his "energy and initiative," but every surviving captain from the SC-42 signed a letter thanking him and his group for a battle bravely fought.

James Hibbard, born in Hemison-Ste. Malachie, P.Q., went on to become RCN Flag Officer, Pacific Coast in 1955. He had joined the Royal Canadian Naval Volunteer Reserve in 1924 as an Ordinary Seaman and served aboard several RN ships before the war. After leaving the Navy with the rank of Rear Admiral, he was made Honourary Citizen of the City of Victoria, B.C., Trustee of the Maritime Museum of British Columbia, and Honourary Governor of the Vancouver Island Branch of the Canadian Corps of Commissionaires.

RADM DSC & Bar, Ld'H(Fr) CdGaP(Fr) CoL(Nor) Born March 26, 1908

RefScs: ABW 50 MMN 14 NAR 67–71 73 75 RCNIR 198
TSIAOG 17–18 103 105 164

James Prentice was born in 1899 in Victoria, B.C., and joined the RN at age 13. In 1938 he retired and was put at the disposal of the RCN should war break out. In 1939 he was offered a commission, and his first command was captain of *Chambly*, a corvette.

It was a type of ship he came to know and respect better than any other commander. He tested its merits and sought ways to improve its performance. His attack on *U-501* was typical of the method he advocated, which ran contrary to accepted RN practice. Prentice's procedure was to reduce speed (the British *increased* speed) and keep it constant, giving the U-boat no warning and thus preventing the submarine from taking evasive action.

Prentice believed in getting as close as possible to the target before dropping depth charges, even though there was risk of the explosion striking the corvette. In fact, in one depth-charge attack made by *Chambly* around the SC-42, electrical fittings aft were blown and personnel in the boiler room were lifted six feet off the deck.

LTCOMM DSO Born 1899
ABW 47 NAR 39p 45 66–76 141 183 200 208 RAR 62
RCNIR 198 TOTNA 149 TSIAOG 90 105 15 128fp 154 174
UBAC 30 177

Postscript: Hugo Forster's action in leaping from *U-501* onto *Chambly*'s deck and surrendering his U-boat was looked upon as an act of cowardice by his own crew. When they were sent to separate prisoner-of-war camps, his men refused to say goodbye to him. At a POW camp in Canada he was tried *in camera* by other U-boat commanders. After a prisoner exchange in 1944, he returned to Germany, where he was court-martialled by the *Kriegsmarine*. It is rumoured that he was executed by firing squad.

RefScs: TOTNA 151–52

130 Miles East of Greenland
September 19, 1941

FOSTER William
GILDING Charles
HATRICK Raymond
STEPHEN George Hay

"First Canadian Corvette to Be Sunk"

Shortly before four o'clock in the morning, the German submarine *U-74*, commanded by Eitel-Frederich Kentrat, waded into the eastbound convoy SC-44. In short order the U-boat sank four merchant ships and fired a torpedo into the bow stern of *Levis*, one of the convoy's five escorts. Though Kentrat had no way of knowing it, *Levis* presented the perfect target for a submarine: her asdic was down, and she was therefore unable to carry out normal U-boat screening exercises.

Charles Gilding, *Levis*'s captain, was in his cabin when he heard the crash. Momentarily stunned, he made his way on deck but, still groggy, was unable to comprehend what had happened. Ray Hatrick, one of the ship's officers, enlightened him that the ship had been torpedoed. Without hesitation, Gilding gave the order to "Abandon ship," and immediately took charge of launching and manning the lifeboats.

Belowdecks, meanwhile, Ray Hatrick directed the rescue of the injured and made sure that the depth charge firing guns were secure on "Safe." At the same time he signalled an alert to the rest of the escort, and the convoy itself, that a U-boat was at large in the vicinity.

The corvette *Mayflower* arrived on the scene to pick up survivors, assisted by *Agassiz*, the third Canadian corvette escort. Altogether 40 were rescued, leaving behind 17 dead; another crewman died in the water. *Mayflower*'s captain, George Stephen, then sent a lifeboat over to *Levis* to assess the damage. Though she had virtually been severed in two, with her bow dangling forward, the report was sufficiently optimistic for Stephen to order a 10-man party aboard to take *Levis* in tow, stern-first.

Incredibly, the stricken corvette stayed afloat for another 12 hours. At six minutes past five o'clock, with *Levis* listing heavily to starboard and her bow beginning to sink, *Mayflower*'s crew cut the tow line. Four minutes later the corvette turned on her side and sank below the surface. When the bitterly cold sea struck the blazing hot boilers of the engine room a series of explosions created a violent crescendo, a discordant dirge to a warship committed to the deep.

RefScs: CCAN 53–59 FDS 86–87 TSIAOG 108

RE-ROUTING
DECEMBER 1941–FEBRUARY 1942

*F*or nearly two years US Navy destroyers had been conducting undeclared warfare against U-boats to protect American merchant shipping. Then, in December 1941, after the Japanese attacked Pearl Harbor, they had to be withdrawn to support their inadequate Pacific Fleet.

Principally, this move affected the Canadian Navy, which, with 13 destroyers and 17 corvettes, formed the main strength of the Western Atlantic force. The Mid-Ocean Meeting Point was now extended to some 700 miles east of Halifax, and the number of escort groups was bolstered from six to seven. The eastern terminus was changed from Hvalfjord, Iceland to Londonderry, a port being developed by the United States Navy on the Foyle River at the northwest tip of Northern Ireland.

It had further been decided that, instead of trying to bypass the U-boats, Canadian convoy escorts should be beefed up and sail directly from St. John's to Londonderry (under the new arrangement, the NEF as a force ceased to exist, and became part of the Mid-Ocean Escort Force). However, that still left a stretch of 800 sea miles (a zone running southeast from the south coast of Greenland) without air cover from either Iceland or the Maritimes, a zone that came to be known ominously as the "Black Pit."

During the last two months of 1941, German submarine activity subsided somewhat when—over the objections of U-boat commander Karl Donitz—Erich Raeder, Chief of the German Naval Staff, ordered the submarines to operate off Gibraltar in response to British naval successes against Axis supply lines in the Mediterranean. For a short time, the North Atlantic escort trips—the fierce winter weather aside—became milk runs.

When Donitz was finally allowed to redirect some of his U-boats back to the Atlantic, he advocated a new danger for Allied shipping—enemy submarines in the seas off the Nova Scotia and New England coasts.

Meanwhile, early in February 1942, convoy SC-67 sailed for the British Isles, its RCN escort the first to make the famous "Newfie-to-Derry" run that would continue for the next four years.

South of Iceland
February 10, 1942

DAY Alexander
DEANS Russell
SHADFORTH Herbert
LAABS Harold
MacMILLAN Reginald
MILLS Wilfred
WHITWORTH John

"Demise of the First Newfie-to-Derry Convoy and Escort Ships"

The initial Newfie-to-Derry run between St John's, Newfoundland and Londonderry, Northern Ireland was a harbinger of what lay in store for subsequent convoys and their escorts. Through the first days of its voyage, SC-67 encountered fog and heavy weather, but no U-boats were sighted. Then, somewhere around 9:30 on the night of February 10, the Canadian senior escort ship, corvette *Spikenard*, commanded by Bert

Shadforth, was following a zigzag pattern ahead of the convoy when two torpedoes exploded below the wheelhouse, between the bridge and forecastle, blowing away a portion of the ship's side and deck. Almost simultaneously, a torpedo smashed into the nearby tanker *Heina*. *Louisburg*, another Canadian corvette escort, stayed to pick up her survivors.

Aboard *Spikenard* fire had broken out, destroying the bridge, the wireless room and one of her lifeboats. Flames then spread to fuel drums aft of the mast—fire raced up the superstructure and down into the belly of the corvette. Men on the mess decks had to fight their way to the forecastle through a curtain of flames. Many of them, groping forward, stumbled into the gaping hole blasted in the deck plates.

Then a second explosion, and *Spikenard* started to sink immediately, her ship's whistle set off by the blast, blowing constantly with an eerie shriek until waves engulfed the stricken vessel. Within three minutes she was gone.

Incredibly, eight of her crew had managed to survive the debacle, and were later found clinging to a merchant naval raft. Telegrapher Wilf Mills was on the forecastle when the explosion occurred and fire erupted around him. Covering his head with his coat for protection against the flames, he made his way to the upper deck where a Carley float was secured. But his hands were so badly burnt he was unable to cut the rope to release it.

Reg MacMillan, a stoker who was resting in his bunk when the torpedo struck, miraculously appeared to sever it. He, Mills and Russell Deans, who had also escaped through the wall of fire, moved off with it, finally finding their way to a raft that had floated free. They were soon joined by John Whitworth, who was burnt almost beyond recognition; Alex Day, acting chief engine room artificer; Harold Laabs, a petty officer who took charge of the survivors; and two others. The eight men picked up two other survivors after the second explosion—both were so badly injured they died shortly after being taken aboard.

Throughout the night other corvettes in the escort had tried to contact *Spikenard*, but failure to reach her was put down to the possibility of equipment failure—an occurrence common enough to be almost taken for granted. In any case, suspicion that she might be in trouble did not allow a thorough search to be made; the safety of the convoy took priority.

By dawn a British escort joined SC-67. The corvette *Gentian* was immediately dispatched to make a thorough search. When *Spikenard*'s survivors were found, they reported that they had seen the shadowy shape of a ship passing them in the dark, blustery night. But they'd had no flares to attract attention to their plight, and their shouts for help had gone unheard.

All things are relative—but death is death no matter its form or extent. The scope of the sacrifice of those who plied the seas in wartime is horrific. Compare, for example, a bomber, whose destruction meant the demise of seven to 10 airmen. In the case of *Spikenard* and *Heina*, some 100 lives were lost in a matter of minutes. *Spikenard* gave up 57 of her crew, including all five of her officers.

Postscript: Aptly enough, a spike serves as a memorial to *Spikenard*. On an earlier occasion, between escort duties and after several rounds of drinks, a contest was held in the Crow's Nest, the seagoing officers' club in St John's, Newfoundland to see who could hammer a six-inch spike into the floor with the least number of blows. *Spikenard*'s skipper, Bert Shadforth, won hands down.

To commemorate the win, a brass ring with the engraved inscription "Spikenard, his Spike" was inserted around the nail, and eventually mounted on a pillar a few feet from where "Shad" had driven it into the floor. A fitting monument to a gallant captain who went down with his ship, and his crew, who made the supreme sacrifice.

RefScs: CCAN 79–83 EDS 101–04

THE MURMANSK RUN
MAY 1942

*I*mmediately after Russia fell under the flaming sword of the German invasion of June 22, 1941, the Soviets put the pressure on Great Britain to supply munitions the Red Army sorely lacked. Britain, with American help, readily agreed. However, the Russians did not have sufficient ships to carry the huge amounts they were to be supplied with so that the British and Americans had to provide the majority of merchant transports and naval escorts. The route chosen was around the North Cape through the Arctic waters to Murmansk and Archangel, a hazardous 1,500–2,000 mile run hindered by icebergs, tempest, fogs and radar interference.

For the first five months all went well with only one ship lost. But from March 1942 on, the convoys had to run the gauntlet of the Luftwaffe flying from airfields in Norway and northern Germany, U-boats redirected from the Atlantic to Norwegian ports (for fear of a British invasion), German battleships and mine-laying.

Off the Norwegian Coast
May 24–30, 1942

EVANS George

"Under-age Merchant-mariner Veteran of Convoys to Russia"

B y the second year of the war, St John's, Newfoundland, had become the focal base of the Battle of the Atlantic, the harbour crowded with ships of the Royal Navy, the Royal Canadian Navy and the merchant marine. Many other vessels wearing war wound damage suffered from mine explosions or German U-boat torpedoing were towed in to be repaired. American and Canadian army camps and the RCN had been established almost from the outbreak of hostilities. The Crow's Nest seagoing officers club was a landmark tradition. The naval transient trade thrived on Newfie hospitality. It was a heady atmosphere, bristling with excitement for a 15-year-old inundated with tales of derring-do from sailors returning from ocean convoys for a brief spell before shipping out again. Small wonder it inspired in Sea Cadet George Evans such a yearning and dreams of glory that he refused to wait until he was 16 and eligible to join the Canadian Navy. Certainly sea-going adventure aplenty awaited him but on a scale beyond anything he could possibly have dreamed of.

When George Evans was turned down by the Navy recruiting office on Water Street in Newfoundland after lying about his age his response was predicable. "O.K! But you won't see me next year. I'm joining the Merchant Navy even if I have to stow away."

It was no idle threat though it didn't quite come to that. Out fishing with his father the following day, they pulled alongside the gangway of the Norwegian freighter SS *Einvik* to sell the chief steward some of the morning's catch. While his father haggled with the mariner, George made himself scarce and found his way to the galley where the chef asked him if he would like to sign on as cabin boy. George jumped at the chance but was told he would have to produce his birth certificate to prove he was 16. That night he doctored the document and next day was hired on. The date was September 1, 1941. "16"-year old George Evans had no inkling of the trials and tribulations that lay in store before he realized his ambition, one that would place him at the very heart of one of the most embattled convoys of the entire Murmansk run operation.

Next day *Einvik* joined an eastbound convoy en route from Sydney, Nova Scotia. On the second day the freighter began losing steam and, unable to keep up, soon found herself on her own. On the fourth night at sea, 450 miles from the south coast of Iceland, the inevitable happened: the Norwegian steamer took a torpedo in the starboard side, forcing the crew to abandon ship and man the two lifeboats.

On the second day adrift, for the first time since the sinking, the crew—eleven to each life craft—fed themselves on rations salvaged from the stricken freighter. The sea was calm but it was cold and, with no wind, the men were glad to take their turns rowing to keep warm. However, George Evans's hands became badly blistered and his feet swelled up. He became so ill the captain took pity on the lad and made room for him in the bottom of the boat to lie down and sleep. After four days afloat the lifeboats reached the Icelandic fishing village of Storhord. By this time Evans was suffering from acute edema as well as bronchitis and was taken to hospital to recuperate.

After a month, all the survivors of the sinking moved to Reykjavik to board a Norwegian troop ship which, after beating off a wolf pack submarine attack, reached Greenock in Scotland. It was only natural that by this time Evans, still only 15 years old, in a strange land and still convalescing, would grow homesick, longing to be back with his family and friends and the comforts of St. John's. When he learned that the British supply ship *Daytonian* was about to leave for Canada to take on fresh cargo and was short a stoker, a job he had long cherished, he immediately signed on. By the time the merchantman reached Sydney, Nova Scotia, he asked to be paid off. His hopes of getting home to St John's were quickly dashed, however. Request denied; no replacement available. Evans soon found himself in a convoy that, after a hectic voyage in which U-boats sank several ships in the group, though *Daytonian* emerged unscathed, finally arrived in Liverpool in mid-December. (Later, Evans remembered ruefully, it seemed as if such incidents were getting to be a habit with him.) Anxious more than ever to get home after that current experience, he applied to the Newfoundland Commissioner in London, who sympathetically made the necessary arrangements and sent him back to Liverpool. Overjoyed at the prospect, Evans got so drunk celebrating his emancipation the night before the sailing that he overslept and the ship left without him. "Maybe," he would remark later, somewhat sardonically, "I was not really ready to go home for a while."

Broke, marooned of his own making and running out of options, he appealed to the Merchant Navy Department, who arranged for him to join the crew of SS *Aurora*, a British coastal delivery ship dropping cargo off at various ports around the

British Isles. After a stint of a little over three months, on March 20—his 16th birthday—Evans was paid off with orders to report to SS *Pieter de Hoogh*, a Dutch cargo ship taken over from the British at Hull in Scotland.

There was an aura of secrecy aboard, everything hush-hush, the entire crew in the dark as to what to expect. But from the supplies that were being loaded aboard, installation of an Oerlikon anti-aircraft cannon and other armament fore and aft manned by army and navy gunners, and the issue of heavy winter gear, including heavy woollens, leathers and floating suits, there was no doubt that something big and important—not to mention dangerous—was afoot. Evans didn't know it but his date with destiny was about to arrive.

The mystery ended when, on March 22, the cargo shop sailed for Reykjavik, Iceland, where it joined nearly 100 ships assembled in the harbour making up the soon to be renowned Convoy PQ 16—bound for the Murmansk run. Evans approached the prospect with some trepidation. On shore leave making the rounds of the pubs in Hull he'd heard hair-raising accounts about the Russian run. Scary stuff. "It frightened me," he confessed. Too late. The die was cast. Like it or not he was in for a penny, in for a pound.

On the morning of March 24, 1942, PQ 16 set sail for the Denmark Strait, 39 merchant ships escorted by a horde of battleships, destroyers, anti-aircraft ships, submarines, supply tankers and trawler rescue vessels. For protection against air attack several of the merchantmen carried Hurricane fighter planes for catapulting off their ships.

Fog blanketed their destination, causing the convoy to split up until next morning when the mist dispersed. The convoy now reassembled, the merchant ships in nine columns interspersed with the cruiser flotilla of supply tankers and rescue craft. The battleship cruisers remained at a strategically effective distance off each beam with destroyers and corvettes fore and aft on both flanks, acting as close escort.

Just after 5:00 a.m., the harbinger of the relentless assault, destined to plague Convoy PQ 16 for the next six days until it reached port, appeared in the form of a German reconnaissance

Focke-Wulf four-engine Kondor orbiting at a safe distance behind the convoy reporting its position and speed. Even though it was well out of range, one of the destroyers fired off a few rounds that, if nothing else, by baring its teeth, demonstrated the convoy's readiness to fight and, at the same time, gave the ships' crews, understandably impatient and edgy awaiting an enemy assault, a much-needed boost to morale.

All was clear sailing until 2:00 p.m. when a British convoy returning from Murmansk and Archangel reported a submarine ahead and to starboard of the northbound fleet. After spotting it, one of the PQ 16 destroyers gave chase but was unable to reach it in time before the U-boat dived out of sight. In frustration the destroyer dropped depth charges but was unable to determine any result.

At 6:30 p.m. the convoy sustained its first air attack. Two German formations of six twin-engine Junkers JU88s and seven Heinkel He111 bombers came diving out of the sun and set fire to a merchant ship. Immediately one of the freighters catapulted a Hurricane fighter into the air. The pilot shot down one of the bombers and damaged another before he was wounded by return fire from one of the air gunners and had to bail out. Fortunately a rescue trawler reached him in time to pull him out of the sea before the icy Arctic waters claimed him. The crew of the burning merchant ship worked relentlessly under machine-gun fire from the enemy planes but after struggling for 48 hours, although they put the fire out, they were unable to repair the vessel to bring it up to convoy speed. One of the destroyers had to take it in tow back to Iceland. An hour later a dozen JU88s returned but were driven off by ack-ack fire, forcing them to drop their bombs harmlessly into the ocean. PQ 16's initiation into the ravages of war in the Norwegian Sea. Not the "Longest Day" but long enough for a baptism into the rigors of the Murmansk run.

That first night in the Norwegian Sea passed peacefully but next morning at 3:05, a menacing 10-hour duel between the escort destroyers and a pack of U-boats got underway when an American cargo ship took two torpedoes fired from a submarine into its port side and immediately sank. Twenty-nine members of the crew managed to escape, though nine of them later perished in the frigid water. Next, a submarine levelled its sights on one of the destroyers, launching a "fish" at the target, but the projectile went wide. The warship retaliated by dropping 10 depth charges without any result either. Realizing the constant peril in which the convoy now found itself with U-boats all around, the destroyers never let their guard down for a minute. That persistent precaution was about to pay off. At 5:07 a.m. one of the destroyers sighted a pair of partially submerged submarines a mile apart five miles away. They had maneuvered themselves into a vantage point between the right flank of the convoy and the Norwegian coast on their own starboard side, creating a potentially perilous situation. The destroyers went right after them but before they could come within range the U-boats dived for the safety of the deep. This somewhat inconclusive contest between surface protector and *Unterseeboot*, the former somewhat handicapped by severe sub-zero conditions hampering the asdic detection device effectiveness, continued throughout the morning and into the afternoon, only a single freighter, an American, suffering minor damage.

A lull followed, albeit it an agitated one stirred by apprehensions of what to expect next. Then at precisely 6:00 the convoy experienced its third air attack when eight Heinkel 111 torpedo bombers and three Junkers 88 dive bombers descended on the flotilla. It was a harrowing experience George Evans would never forget; crews of his ship, cowering in terror, praying and trembling with fear as bombs rained down, narrowly missing the side of the freighter, and machine-gun fire peppering the decks. Ships virtually leaped from the sea from the concussion of explosions. It was a nightmare. Then, mercifully, suddenly it was all over, for the time being anyway. But the morrow promised far worse to come.

That fateful Wednesday, May 27, 1942, got off to a cataclysmic start at 3:20 a.m. when a formation of seven He111s and three JU88s attacked the convoy. Not a single bomb found a target, but the morale on the ship crews from the explosions in the sea all about them was shattering. After nights on alert without proper sleep, their nerves were stretched to the breaking point. Many suffered from shock and moved about as if in a trance. And with Murmansk still three days away their ordeal was far from over.

But for the moment, a brief hiatus from the hazard of enemy harassment was only to be confronted with the vexation of a totally different type of threat. When the convoy reached a point south of Bear Island, the awesome sight of the majestic snow-packed Mount Misery seemed to project the wretchedness bearing its name down its slopes and out to sea on the vast convoy. The frustration of navigating through and around solid pack-ice, while avoiding collisions and slowing progress, set the ships up as sitting ducks for the purgatory that followed.

Beginning shortly after noon and lasting for an uninterrupted eight hours, PQ 16 sustained the longest, most relentless, destructive air attack ever perpetrated against an Allied convoy in that space of time in any theatre of the entire war.

Relying on the element of surprise generously provided by a cloud cover, a wave of Luftwaffe bombers broke through an overcast at 3,000 feet to enjoy the welcome extra advantage of a haze at 1,500 feet, making it difficult for the ships' anti-aircraft gunners to take accurate aim. Two bombs struck the American merchantman SS *Alamar*, setting the vessel on fire and forcing the crew to abandon ship. A destroyer, joined by a British submarine, picked up survivors from the blazing ship. Simultaneously, explosions from two bombs bracketed another American freighter, SS *Mormacsul*, and so badly damaged the ship on either side it quickly filled with water. Fortunately the crew had time to escape, jumping free, and were plucked out of the freezing sea by a destroyer and a rescue trawler. And that was only the warm-up.

The next victim of the German sky raiders was a Russian merchant vessel, *Stari Bolshevik*. A direct bomb hit set the fo'c'sle on fire. The crew of both men and women sailors exhibited some of the motherland's fortitude by refusing to abandon ship. With the assistance of a French corvette, they fought flame and smoke for a solid 38 hours to bring the conflagration under control—all the while keeping their place in the convoy. Meanwhile the crew of the Canadian freighter SS *City of Joliet* had no choice but to abandon their ship when a couple of near misses caused such a bad leak in two of the holds the vessel rapidly filled with water. They too were saved from drowning by a rescue boat that rushed to the scene. The crew of the British cargo vessel SS *Empire Baffin*, which was also damaged by two stray bombs, was more fortunate; they were able to repair their ship and still maintain their position in the line.

By this time as the result of the German bombers' dogged attacks the rescue trawlers became so overloaded with survivors that they presented easy inviting targets for enemy planes—they had to turn the task over to the destroyers. SS *Empire Lawrence*, one of the British freighters with a catapult Hurricane fighter aboard, was sinking so quickly from a bomb explosion that two of the destroyers pressed into rescue service were ordered to stand by. Shortly after the destroyers took up stations on the scene, *Empire Lawrence* took four more bomb hits. By the time the smoke cleared, the ship was on the verge of going right under. However, even though the destroyers came under machine-gun strafing fire from the JU88s they succeeded in saving the survivors.

Bomb damage and crew casualties were not the sole province of the merchant group, however. The warship contingent also came in for its fair share. A stick of four bombs dropped from a Heinkel landed in the water abreast of the Polish destroyer *Garland*. The first one to hit the sea exploded the others, and the shrapnel riddling the ship from end to end caused severe damage. The fore and aft guns as well as the Oerlikon on the starboard side were taken out of action, the gunners killed and wounded. Fire broke out in the fo'c'sle. By the time it was brought under control 25 crewmen had lost their lives and another 43 had been wounded, one of them so critically a medical officer was transferred from another ship to attend him. It quickly became obvious the man was so seriously injured he need hospital attention. *Garland* proceeded immediately to Murmansk in advance of the convoy, full speed ahead—at a swift 24 knots.

Aboard *Pieter de Hoogh* damage to the boiler room and a wounded gunner brought stoker George Evans up on deck where the ship's bosun helped strap him to the *Oerlikon*, Evans manning the gun, the bosun loading the ammunition. The enemy torpedo bombers were coming directly at the stern with the sun to their backs. The blinding glare in the sailors' eyes made the difficult task of firing at targets flying at lightning-fast speeds well nigh impossible. As the attackers zoomed in Evans gave it his best shot then, swinging his gun around, he continued to shoot as the planes swooshed past overhead in a matter of seconds, so fast he couldn't claim a single strike. Frustrating. But at least the gun crew had earned the satisfaction of knowing that not a single missile struck the ship. And, even though the explosion from a stick of bombs splashed the destroyer with water amidships, the only damage was a thorough dousing.

After nearly eight hours of incessant bombing and strafing, at approximately 7:45 the last PQ Convoy 16 casualties to fall victim to the German aerial onslaught were two cargo carriers. The crews were quickly rescued by two destroyers. The first, the British merchant ship *Empire Purcell*, took a direct hit from one of the bombers; the hit started a fire on the forward deck so volatile it was impossible to subdue. The crew had no choice but to go over the side posthaste. The other freighter, SS *Lowther*, fared no better. Five minutes later a Heinkel torpedoed it from 4,000 yards. The hit was so accurate it blew a hole on the port side. The water began filling it so quickly it began to sink immediately. That crew wasted no time jumping over the side either.

The aerial siege continued unabated but without further sinkings and only minor shipping damage for another four hours. That was the Luftwaffe's signature to the most disastrous assault from the air to befall a convoy in such a concentrated period of time in naval history. George Evans was motivated to later write what amounted to a somber epitaph of that long, unforgettable seafaring aerial abattoir: "the enemy left us in peace," though inevitably the Blohm and Voss float planes circled on the horizon like vultures gloating over the remains.

PQ 16 had sustained raids by approximately 280 Junkers 88 and Heinkel 111 dive and torpedo bombers flying at least four times that number of sorties during the afternoon and evening dropping as many as 1,200 missiles. That eight-hour bombardment brought the convoy's total losses up to over 20 per cent since leaving the Denmark Strait. It was impossible to calculate a precise tally of punishment exacted by the defenders due to climatic conditions of intermittent haze over the fleet, although five Junkers 88s had been seen crashing into the sea in flames. And there was absolutely no way to determine with any degree of accuracy the damage inflicted on other enemy aircraft due to the problem of deflection shooting from a slow-speed surface platform at a high-speed target. However, radio monitors throughout the fleet picked up SOS messages from German aircraft returning to their bases in Norway, indicating that casualties aboard were severe with many of the planes badly battered from return fire.

By far the most serious affliction of the day's battle burdening the convoy was the shortage of ammunition resulting from the constant expenditure throughout the non-stop raid. With two more days left before reaching Murmansk, any repetition of such an attack could spell disaster. The only answer was strict conservation of 1,000 rounds per ship, impossible for some that were reduced to far less. Hardly a retaliation to be taken seriously by a protagonist, at best a show of bravado on the part of the defender and a pretty soft one at that. Such a probability gave the crew of the particularly vulnerable *Pieter de Hoogh* not inconsiderable cause for concern. It had absolutely no ammunition left and was carrying several tons of TNT and other high explosives. It would have been hard to find a more volatile target. But, according to Evans, the men took it all in stride and continued their duties "with an outward calm."

As it neared its destination, next night the convoy was joined by three Russian destroyers. The following morning, when a squadron of 18 JU88s and HE111s attacked the fleet, the crews were treated to an astounding performance of versatility and ingenuity by the newcomers to the flotilla. As the bombers zeroed in, the destroyers took no evasive action but maintained their exact course while the ships' gunners let fly with everything they had. Then, as the attackers flew right over the columns of the convoy, with an astounding dexterity of speed and maneuver the Russian ships chased them out to sea and, with unbelievable accuracy, began bouncing their 37 millimetre Bofors shells off the water right into the bellies of the torpedo planes. One of the intruders flew away damaged; two others crashed to a fiery death into the sea, all without the slightest damage to the convoy. Small wonder the crews let out a hearty Hurrah! Well merited—there were no more Luftwaffe attacks that day, no more, for that matter, for the remainder of the Murmansk run.

Next day, May 30, 1942, however, when PQ 16 finally sailed into the port of its destination, the largest within the Arctic Circle, once been a peaceful little fishing village, up the Tuloma River from the Barents Sea, the ships came under more bombardment. Although Murmansk was protected by air cover from Russian Stormovik and Royal Air Force Hurricanes stationed at a nearby fighter field, it could not entirely prevent the Luftwaffe bombers, escorted by Messerschmitt fighters, from bombing the docks and railway cars loading the badly needed cargos arriving by sea to Leningrad. And the ships came in for their fair share as well. As she came in to dock, a bomb landed on the forward deck of *Pieter de Hoogh*. While damage to the Dutch freighter was minor, it had to moor outside when other bombs smashed the dock to pieces.

Evans continued to serve in some of the subsequent convoys to Russia, only one of which, in July, rivalled the hell of PQ 16, when aircraft and U-boats sunk 23 merchant ships out of 36. By war's end 720 ships got through, delivering more than four million tons of cargo to the Russians; the cargo included 5,000 tanks and 7,000 aircraft. During both the outgoing and the homeward voyages, losses to the convoys were 18 warships and 98 merchant ships. Losses to the Germans were three destroyers, the battle cruiser *Scharnhorst* and 38 boats. In addition, some 550 Luftwaffe planes were probably shot down or damaged.

RefScs: TTCOH HOTSWW 392–93

Between Haiti and Cuba
August 27, 1942

KING Clarence Aubrey
LAWRENCE Harold
POWELL Arthur Joseph

"Caribbean U-boat Depth-Charged and Rammed, But Lost as Booty"

Just before midnight, in brilliant warm moonlight, corvette *Oakville*, part of the escort to Aruba-Halifax tanker convoy TAW-15, was steering a northwesterly course when a United States Navy Canso flying boat swooped overhead. Spotting a U-boat in front of the ships, the plane dropped 2,600 pounds of depth charges, their explosions clearly indicating the submarine's position. Immediately *U-94* crash-dived. But *Oakville* already had an asdic fix, and Clarence King, commander of the corvette, quickly gave chase.

King was a Royal Navy veteran of World War I, who had earned the Distinguished Service Cross in that conflict for sinking one U-boat and "probably" destroying two more. His German adversary, Otto Ites, known as "Onkel Otto," was himself no slouch. A U-boat veteran of four years, he had sunk over 100,000 tons of Allied shipping. In April of the previous year, Hitler had decorated him with the Knights Cross of the Iron Cross. A bold and competent submarine captain, Ites was as respected as a fighter as he was popular with his crew.

Convoy TAW-15 presented Ites with his juiciest target yet—29 tankers, with no more than normal escort. In addition to *Oakville*, there were three other corvettes, two Canadian, one Dutch; *Lea*, a slow USN destroyer; and three small American patrol boats, more for show than effectiveness.

King raced to the U-boat's position, where he dropped a pattern of five depth charges. Minutes later the black prow of *U-94* pierced the surface. "Ho Ho!" beamed King from *Oakville*'s bridge (hardly one of those turns of phrase of which naval leg-

Hal Lawrence and Arthur Powell of Oakville, *who boarded* U-94. *(G.A. Lawrence/DND/PA 106526)*

ends are made, Hal Lawrence, the officer in charge, would later jocularly complain). Much more dramatic were the two fiery rockets that *Oakville* shot, hissing across the convoy to signal a submarine sighting.

With the U-boat fully surfaced, King prepared to ram. On the first attempt the corvette missed. King wheeled his ship around for a second run, this time with guns blazing. They could not be sufficiently depressed to hit the target, however; they fired over it. In frustration, one observer recalled that, as *Oakville* closed, the crew pelted the submarine with empty soft-drink bottles. But once again the corvette failed to score a strike.

On his third attempt King was successful, ramming at right angles as his ship's machine guns raked the submarine's conning tower. *Oakville* reversed engines and King ordered a boarding party into action. Gathered on the forecastle, the delegated 12 seamen were knocked silly as *Oakville*'s gunner opened fire with the 4-incher hard alongside them. Only Hal Lawrence and his petty officer, Arthur Powell, recovered quickly enough to begin boarding.

Climbing over the gunwale, they dropped eight feet to the deck of *U-94*. As Lawrence landed, the belt of his tropical shorts snapped, leaving him pantless; then a wave swept him overboard. Powell helped him back up, and the pair advanced on the sub's conning tower. They intended to control the bridge before the enemy crew of about 30 began to climb out the hatch, and before they could scuttle the craft.

Meanwhile, *Oakville* had pulled away to inspect the damage caused by the collision and to lick her wounds. From half a mile away her gunners continued to ricochet bullets off *U-94*'s hull. The Canadians went over the side—it was safer in the water. When the firing stopped they scrambled back on deck and, finally, climbed to the bridge, just as the Germans came swarming out of the hatch onto the deck.

Lawrence ordered them to stand back, but both he and Powell had to shoot to kill to stop their advance. Leaving Powell to hold prisoner what was left of the German crew, Lawrence skirted the bodies and descended through the hatch into the engine room. Well versed in German instrument reading, he was nevertheless powerless to salvage the situation. Water began pouring in until he stood waist deep. As waves began to engulf the deck, Powell shouted down the hatch for Lawrence to get out; the ship could go under any minute. (He was also fearful that the Germans might have set a scuttling charge.) Reluctantly, Lawrence abandoned his dream of seeing the U-boat towed into port with the Canadian ensign flying above the German swastika.

Oakville had been badly damaged in the ramming. Much of the bottom of her hull had been ripped away. The asdic compartment was flooded, as was the forward boiler and, because the lights were blown, all was in darkness. Thus when Lawrence signalled by flashlight "PSB" (please send boat), his ship could only reply "MRU" (much regret unable). A request from Clarence King brought the USN destroyer *Lea* to the rescue.

When *Lea* pulled alongside the submarine, Lawrence and Powell were waiting, along with 20 prisoners. But the American crew was unable to differentiate between them—they treated them all as prisoners. Lawrence roared, "Gangway for an officer. We can't all be saved. I'm Canadian!" When the gobs shrugged off his protestations (after all, how much respect could one soaking, pantless sailor command), Lawrence gave them a vituperative mouthful—that finally convinced them.

Harold Lawrence, born in Victoria, B.C., reached the rank of Lieutenant Commander. He is the author of several books on the Royal Canadian Navy in World War II, including *A Bloody War* and *Tales of the North Atlantic*.

LTCOMM
RefScs: ABW 94–105 RAR 112–13 TOTNA 153–66
TSIAOG 115

EVEN CLOSER TO HOME
MAY–SEPTEMBER 1942

*A*t 11:00 p.m. on May 11, 1942, German U-boat U-533 surfaced off Percé Rock, in clear view of the shore of the Gaspé Peninsula. She fired off two torpedoes, striking a 5,000-ton British freighter amidships. The freighter began to sink immediately. Two hours and forty-five minutes later, U-533 struck again, this time sending Leto, a Dutch merchant ship, to the bottom of the St. Lawrence River.

The explosions rocked the shipping villages in the vicinity, and the fires they set off as the ships sank could be seen for miles. Close to the shore crowds gathered to watch and help survivors climb ashore—coated in oil, some wounded, others in shock. The war had been brought home to Canada. The "Battle of the St. Lawrence," as the Ottawa Journal *coined it, had begun. In reality, however, it was a mere tangent, an extension of U-boat operations begun in the western North Atlantic at the beginning of the year.*

The next day Naval Minister Angus Macdonald issued a cautious statement in the House of Commons, advising that a ship had been sunk in the Gulf of St. Lawrence, and that no reports would be made of further such incidents for fear of divulging pertinent strategic and tactical information to the enemy.

The statement was greeted with outrage by the Gaspé populace. They knew that two ships had gone down, not one, and they knew their identity. So why the hush-hush? The press had already given the Germans most of the information they needed: time of sinking, number of ships, position of attack, the weather, among other details.

And it was for that precise reason that a censorship clamp was imposed. The explanation did nothing to assuage the inhabitants along the far reaches of the St. Lawrence, however. They felt humiliated and in danger—the whole situation looked like a cover-up. In fact this initial domestic action, and the furor and embarrassment that followed, helped initiate the formation of the Gulf Escort Force: two corvettes, five Bangor minesweepers, three Fairmile motor launches and an armed yacht.

It also raised a call for air cover. Three Royal Canadian Air Force Catalina flying boats moved to Gaspé, and another detachment was set up at Mont-Joli. A squadron of Hudson bombers flew out of Chatham, New Brunswick, and Summerside, Prince Edward Island. Training aircraft from Charlottetown flew over the threatened area and, although they were not equipped to do battle, they did force the U-boats to dive and reduced their mobility somewhat. Barry German, a graduate of the first RCN cadet class in 1910, took charge of the force as Naval Officer in Charge (NOIC).

Over the next few months, U-boats sank 18 merchant ships, mostly unescorted, two naval vessels and a passenger ferry, all within the area of the St. Lawrence. From their submarine pens at Kiel, Wilhelmshaven, St. Nazaire and Lorient, they had stretched across the Atlantic to carry the war as far as Rimouski, on the south bank of the St. Lawrence, within 200 miles of Quebec City.

Canadian authorities closed the river to deep-sea shipping from October 1942 through 1943, allowing only small coastal convoys and warships in or out.

Off Cap-de-la-Madeleine
July 6, 1942

FRASER James Philip

"Near Miss"

B y July, escorts were being provided for all Quebec–Sydney convoys. On this bright, moonlit night the German submarine *U-132* spotted one such marine covey sailing along the south shore near the mouth of the St. Lawrence. Despite damage sustained in an earlier encounter with a Royal Navy destroyer, the U-boat attacked on the surface, sinking three merchant ships within half an hour.

RCN escort *Drummondville*, a Bangor minesweeper, closed in on the submarine and prepared to ram. As the U-boat dived and the Canadian ship passed over its position, Skipper James Fraser ordered depth charges dropped. Shifting water layers in the river prevented the U-boat from going deep; *Drummondville* bracketed it with three more depth charges.

Though badly damaged, the submarine managed to escape. Fraser's claims to having sighted the U-boat on its side, bottom up, or with the conning tower blown, and his shipmates' claims that they had seen wreckage after the submarine dived, were discounted by the British Assessment Committee in deciding whether or not *Drummondville* should be awarded a kill.

It was later confirmed that the submarine had, in fact, escaped. Nevertheless, *Drummondville* and Fraser deserve credit for a bold attack, in which his ship and crew had inflicted not inconsiderable damage to *U-132*.

RefScs: TSIAOG 117 UBAC 102–03

Between Anticosti Island & Gaspé off Cap Chat
May 7, 1915–September 11, 1942

BATES Cecil
BONNER Willard
BOWSER Donald
CHURCHILL Winston
COATES Bill
DILLON Frank
DILLON John
DUFF Russ
GARLAND John
GRAND Bill
HARTWIG Paul
HITLER Adolf
HOFFMAN Kurt
JEFFREYS Dave
LADE Harold
LAMB James
MacAULEY Ray
MacDONALD Tommy
MARTIN Gerald
McCONNELL Russ
MOORS George
ROBINSON Edmund
RUSH Fred
SKINNER Ed
SMITH John
TODD David
WILLIAMS Norm

"The four-minute demise of corvette Charlottetown"

Prelude

On December 13, 1941, when HMCS *Charlottetown* was commissioned at Quebec City—the 69th "cheap and dirty," as Winston Churchill labelled corvettes, to be built that year—there were those who predicted an omen of bad luck would sail with her: too many 13—13 of the month, 13 letters in her name. Lieutenant Willard Bonner, who took command of the ship, scoffed at any such suggestion. The only bad luck it augured, he assured his crew, was for any U-boats they encountered. Bonner meant it and he appeared to be just the one to make his boast come true. Commander of the marine division of the Royal Canadian Mounted Police before the war, he was an outstanding RCNVR officer and one of the finest commanders in the Navy.

Six and a half months later in August 1942, *Kapitanleutnant* Paul Hartwig, commander of the German submarine *U-517*, arrived in the St. Lawrence River intent on sinking 80,000 tons of Allied shipping. Such a feat would earn him the Knight Commander's Iron Cross and make him a U-boat ace. He had his sights set on the embryo Gulf Escort Force that, as a result of later successes Radio Berlin would scathingly report, was "composed of requisitioned fishing boats, coastal ships, and luxury yachts, of which the Canadian Navy is obliged to create an escort system. This service comprises a third of the threatened maritime route between Canada and the British Isles."

If anyone could pull it off, Hartwig was certainly the likely candidate. A thorough professional in the Prussian tradition, born of a military family, he was a graduate of *Grosadmiral* Karl Donitz's school of *Rudeltactik* wolf-pack attacks. A pre-war naval officer, he was also a veteran of the battles in the Atlantic.

It did not take long for Hartwig to establish his presence in the Gulf. On the night of August 27, *U-517* shadowed an American convoy on its way to a United States Air Corps airfield being built at Thule in Greenland. The convoy was escorted by a single US Coast Guard cutter. Hartwig singled out a Canadian transport, *Chatham*, carrying construction workers. A torpedo sent her to the bottom, but most of the crew and passengers managed to abandon ship for the rescue boats.

A good start in his quest for the Iron Cross, but in his haste for official commendation and recognition he blew his cover. When he sent off a signal to Berlin notifying them of his first-ever triumph at sea, it was duly intercepted by the Royal Canadian Air

Force radio station at Harbour Grace, Newfoundland, and gave away his position. The RCAF dispatched a Hudson bomber to investigate. It was a close call but Hartwig got away with it. As soon as the submarine sighted the aircraft it crash-dived.

That same afternoon Hartwig teamed up with *Kapitanleutnant* Kurt Hoffman, commander of *U-165*. That evening they joined forces to attack a convoy from either side, each successfully torpedoing a merchantman, SS *Arlyn*, which sank immediately, and SS *Laramie,* which, though badly damaged with a hole in her side, managed to make it to port.

Shortly afterwards, past midnight on August 28, Hartwig brought his submarine to the surface to attack a northbound convoy in the Straits of Belle Isle headed for Goose Bay in Newfoundland. Tom Colby, captain of one of the escorts, *Weyburn*, spotted the wash from the U-boat's conning tower and at full speed shouted orders to ram. At precisely the same moment Hartwig spotted the corvette—a coincidental surprise to both skippers—and went full ahead himself. The closing speed was so great that Weyburn's gunner said: "You could have hit her with a deck-scrubber." But when he fired off a round from the 4-inch forward gun he missed. At that same Hartwig crash-dived, but not before letting off a torpedo in the direction of the convoy. Colby dropped a couple of depth charges, too late to do any damage to *U-517* but enough for the concussion to shake up the crew.

The torpedo from the submarine struck the *Donald Stewart*, a transport loaded down with cement and volatile high-octane aircraft fuel. *Trail*, another corvette, was nearby. Along with her sister ship, *Shawinigan*, she had gone to the rescue of survivors of the *Chatham* sinking the night before. Both were now southbound to meet a home-coming convoy. James Lamb, aboard *Trail*, gave this vivid, horrifying description of the moment of impact: "She exploded like a bomb and burned like a torch, the flames lighting up the water for miles around, with a roar that appalled all of us."

Weyburn lost contact with the U-boat in the swirl caused by the depth charge explosions and turned his attention to picking up the survivors lucky enough to escape the blaze of the old lake steamer, the flames quickly spreading over the surface of the sea. Lamb wrote: "White-faced and horrified—we watched a trapped crewman calmly turn to face the flames before the inferno consumed him."

The sinkings sent alarm bells ringing all the way up to RCN Headquarters. Extra ships were assigned to the river patrols and convoy escorts. In addition, RCAF reconnaissance flights were increased. One of them came close to cutting short Hartwig's promising career. A Hudson that caught *U-517* on the surface dropped a bomb so accurately it landed aft of the conning tower and penetrated the submarine's metal outer skin. Luckily for the U-boat, due to a faulty fuse, the bomb failed to go off. And while it left a jagged hole in the outer upper structure, the crucial water-pressure hull beneath was undamaged. Holding their collective breath, the crew carefully lowered the missile overboard. The hole in the hull was soon repaired, mostly at night while the U-boat silently drifted on the surface with engines stopped to avoid radar detection.

Underway once more, Hartwig moved his theatre of operations upriver, at one point only 250 miles from Quebec City. On September 6, he rendezvoused with Hoffman's *U-165* to set up a patrol line opposite Cap Chat, both submarines setting up station on opposite sides, trimmed down on the surface to make themselves invisible against the shoreline, then settled down to wait.

Around 10:00 p.m. a heavily escorted slow-moving convoy bound for Sydney, Nova Scotia, came into sight. It consisted of a corvette, a Bangor class minesweeper, an armed yacht and two Fairmile motor launches. The escort group was under the direction of Commander Ed Skinner, skipper of the corvette *Arrowhead*. Skinner, a veteran of the Atlantic convoy runs, adhered to his own dogmatic homespun methods of dealing with the U-boat threat in the St. Lawrence. Distrustful of the Canadian radar, and with thermal layering in the river rendering sonar virtually useless, he urged an instant shoot-from-the-hip cowboy style for dealing with an enemy submarine—charge straight ahead with guns blazing. To counter crash-dive evasive action, don't waste time with sonar contact—unreliable anyway—just dump the depth charges right over the diving point.

Other ship captains in the convoy included volunteer officers Bill Grand and Norm Williams, in command of the Fairmile motor launches, *Q-64* and *Q-83*. Both captains had considerable river convoy experience. John Smith, another naval reserve officer, was skipper of the armed yacht *Raccoon*. In his book, *On the Triangle Run*, James Lamb's comments on these luxury-vessels-cum-warships is entertaining to say the least. "She was more a yacht than warship, but armed yacht crews could adapt to anything; one such yacht, HMCS *Renard*, bereft of charts, had once navigated herself from Pictou Halifax with an Imperial Oil map!"

Hoffman struck first. He maneuvered directly into the incoming path of the convoy and fired. His aim was true. His torpedo struck the starboard side of *Aeas*, a small Greek steamer, just under the bridge, exploding a large hole that killed the fireman and wireless operator. The rest of the crew abandoned ship, climbing into the life rafts. The U-boat silently withdrew astern towards the safety of the hilly shoreline as the convoy escort rushed to the rescue. But *U-165* was far from through.

Before reaching its refuge, *Raccoon* crossed the sights of the U-boat's periscope. Hoffman fired off two torpedoes at almost point-blank range, claiming the Gulf's 14th U-boat victim of the year. "Coon" simply disappeared with her full complement of 39 men. It wasn't until three days later that the body of well-known McGill University footballer, Russell "Russ" McConnell, along with wreckage from the armed yacht, washed ashore on the south coast of Anticosti Island, the only trace of the ship's sinking. Explosions from both sinkings, which lit up the sky, could be heard for miles around; windows of houses close to shore were rattled by the detonations.

Paul Hartwig's turn came next. The ensuing 24 hours amounted to a field day for *U-517*'s *Kapitan* but very nearly resulted in his demise and that of his submarine. About the same time that Hoffman was busy making his score, Hartwig was closing in on one of the merchantmen head-on towards the oncoming convoy when suddenly *Arrowhead* appeared on a collision course. Hartwig dived for safety. A frustrated Skinner, deprived of a sure kill, obeyed his precept of shooting from the hip and, without waiting for sonar contact, unloaded a full packet of 10 depth-charges right over the site where *U-157* crash-dived.

Hartwig seems to have been blessed with a charmed life. His U-boat survived with only superficial damage. Nevertheless it was the most nerve-racking attack he and his crew had ever experienced. Explosion from the depth charges rocked the submarine, knocking the men off their feet. The lights were blown out; they had to work to stem the water spraying from fractured pipes and make other repairs in semi-darkness illuminated only by feeble emergency lighting. But like a boxer stunned but never out, Hartwig rose to the occasion, displaying that resourcefulness under fire that distinguished him as one of the greatest of the German U-boat commanders.

Even before the impact of the depth charges going off, Hartwig had the presence of mind, almost by instinct, to release a *Pillinwerfer*, a deception device consisting of a small perforated tin can filled with a chemical that on contact with the water discharged a cloud of bubble, which acted as a solid sonar echo to any probing and, in this case, totally befuddled the corvette's sonar operator. (And perhaps helped confirm, if somewhat exaggerate, Skinner's refusal to rely on such uncertain equipment.) Licking its wounds, which were easily remedied, *U-517* slipped away undetected to fight another day—and what a day!

After a short respite for repairs, the next evening, September 7, Hartwig set out determined to score against the target that so far eluded him, the sitting-duck, slow-moving Sydney-bound convoy, now short one of its escorts thanks to Hoffman's sinking of the *Raccoon*.

It had just turned dusk. Hartwig was lying doggo, lurking, waiting for night to fall before making his move when, beyond his wildest dreams, he sighted three merchant ships arriving from Cape Gaspé on the south shore of the St Lawrence to join the convoy. Two groups of freighters! A veritable shooting gallery! But one that called for the utmost skill and daring as well as perfect timing—and luck. Hartwig was about to fuse all three into the high point of his career.

Submerged, he sailed straight into the middle of the assemblage undetected. Surfacing between the two groups, he found targets port, starboard, fore and aft. With not a moment to lose he fired off both bow tube torpedoes and the single stern projectile at point-blank range. A dream come true—every one of them found a mark.

All three victims—the Greek freighter *Mount Taygetos*, her sister ship *Mount Pindus* and an old lake steamer, *Oakton*, went to the bottom almost immediately. *Mount Taygetos* lost five of her crew in the engine room when the torpedo exploded. An engineer and a fireman aboard *Mount Pindus* were killed when the torpedo struck. *Oakton* suffered the loss of an oiler and two firemen when the missile exploded in the engine room. The ship's St. Bernard mascot survived, but drowned when the ship sank.

Amazingly, 78 crewmen survived the sinkings and lived to tell the tale. Bill Grand's Fairmile motor launch *Q-83* picked up the shivering water-soaked survivors. His crew surrendered their own blankets to keep the shipwrecked seamen warm and deposited them at Cape Gaspé. On later retrieving their covers, Grand like to joke, "We eventually became expert in getting rid of crab lice."

It was Hartwig's finest hour, his greatest triumph. But his notorious success quickly turned the hunter into the hunted. RCAF Hudson and Canso search planes dogged *U-517*'s trail every waking hour. Each time the U-boat surfaced to recharge her batteries, she had to dive to escape an aerial attack. Flushed from his triple victory, however, Hartwig now more than ever was determined to pursue his relentless personal vendetta with the "United Sates enemy" until he'd expended the last of his ammunition. (For all their thoroughness in gathering intelligence and their efficiency, the Germans had failed to recognize the Canadian Navy's part on the Gulf Escort Service home waters as their chief protagonist and instead identified their nemesis in the Gulf as American escorts.)

Whether or not he realized it—and he might well have rejoiced had he learned of it—Hartwig's remarkable exploit brought to an apex the Canadian war cabinet's growing concern over the increasing carnage created by German submarines in the St. Lawrence and the likelihood of even worse to come. Afraid it might become a political issue and yielding to pressure from the British to divert 17 corvettes for the planned—but still under-wraps—Allied landings in North Africa, two days after the triple sinking the government closed down the river to all future over-seas shipping. But the decision came too late to spare Hartwig's next victim.

The Deadly Demise
September 11, 1942

The morning dawned dark and dirty, with fog and swirling mist making it almost impossible to see beyond a few hundred yards—conditions that fouled asdic reception. But Hartwig, his adrenalin flowing, lay in wait in eager anticipation off Cap Chat.

Having safely delivered the westbound convoy SQ-35 to Bic Island off the shore of Rimouski, the Bangor class minesweeper *Clayoquot* and corvette *Charlottetown* made an about-face and set off towards the Gaspé Peninsula. Sailing abreast of each other a mile apart, they ignored the standard precaution of zigzagging in enemy-infested waters—the sonar was useless in the usual thermal layering conditions of the river anyway—confidently relying on the safety of their near full speed of 11.4 knots and the poor visibility.

Just before eight bells, peering through his periscope, Hartwig could hardly believe his luck. Before his eyes, as large as life, despite the early morning mist, was *Charlottetown* cutting right across his bow. So close a target—he could see the depth charges on the quarterdeck—it was impossible to miss. He fired off two forward tube torpedoes, which struck the corvette within 14 sec-onds of each other with such impact that the ship spun right around, headed back west. The first one hit the starboard quarter-deck, the second one, according to *Charlottetown*'s executive officer, First Lieutenant George Moors, struck close to either the engine-room or No. 2 boiler room. Miraculously, the explosion killed only one man, Chief ERA (Engine Room Artificer) David Todd, as well as destroying a single Carley float.

After an unappetizing breakfast of "red lead and bacon," *Charlottetown*'s torpedo telegraphist, Gerald Martin, and Leading Telegraphist Edmund Robinson were in the wireless shack checking to see that all the books were locked up when they heard a loud explosion. "Rob shouted that we'd been hit by a torpedo," Martin recalled. "Everything went dead. I fell against the transmitter. We headed for the wheelhouse. Then the second one hit." They went out on deck and were trying to release the port lifeboat, which was jammed, when they heard the skipper, Willard Bonner, shout from the bridge, "Abandon ship!"

As the stern started to sink and the ship began listing to starboard, Bonner soon realized that the port lifeboat would be useless and shifted his attention to the one on the other side. With members of the crew rushing up from belowdecks and the ship sinking fast, Bonner yelled to them, "Jump for it boys; we're not going to make it," at the very same moment that Martin and Robinson, who had rushed over to starboard when the port lifeboat refused to budge, leaped into the water. "I grabbed a line that was hanging from the lifeboat," Martin said, "and pulled myself into it."

The explosions jolted coder Russ Duff out of a sound slumber in his hammock. "The blast was so extensive," he said later, "that it made a shambles of the mess deck and caused panic in the mess." With others he made it up the ladder to the upper deck "in record time." Without bothering to put on one of the life jackets being dispensed by rating John "Judy" Garland—nicknamed after the American singer who made famous "Somewhere over the Rainbow"—when he saw a Carley float hit the water, Duff jumped in and swam after it. "The water was oil covered and icy cold," he remembered and the float drifted out of reach. Treading water, he watched as the corvette reared on her stern, the bow facing straight up, and sank down almost vertically. Less than four minutes had elapsed since Duff rolled out of his hammock.

Leading seaman Bill Coates also refused one of the out-of-date Mae West life jackets Garland was handing out: "All they would do is keep your head out of the water." Standing near the lumber rack where the staging planks were stored, he grabbed one, threw it over the side and jumped in after it. "When I got hold of it," he recounted, "I paddled away from the ship before it sank."

When the torpedoes struck, Lieutenant David Jeffreys, survivor of two merchant ship sinkings, reacted instinctively. By the time he reached the boat deck the vessel's stern was level with the sea and men left and right were leaping into the water. Jeffreys jumped overboard "dressed in pajamas and 'nowt' else" and swam for the safety of a Carley float.

When rating Ray MacAuley reached the lifeboat it was so crowded he was told to make for a nearby Carley float. By the time he reached it *Charlottetown* was gone. During those harrowing four minutes only one of the two lifeboats got free, but all the ship's Carley floats had been cut loose and dumped in the sea. At almost the same instant that HMCS *Charlottetown* disappeared below the surface there was a tremendous explosion from the ship's depth charges, either set on safe or preset to go off at a certain depth. The blasts killed most of those closest to where the corvette went down, including the captain, Willard Bonner, the last man to leave his ship. Many others were badly wounded. And although *U-517* was by this time some distance away, the explosives went off with such force that the blast rocked the U-boat.

The ship's coder, Russ Duff, had just about caught up with the Carley float he'd been chasing downstream when the concussions drove sharp pains down his back and into his abdomen. Despite the agony he managed to clutch the float after a couple more strokes and climbed into it.

Hanging on to another Carley float, Dave Jeffreys said, "I felt a shudder on my legs as the charges went off." He added, "The lads lying on their tummies in the water suffered badly."

Frank Dillon, the ship's stoker, was swimming side stroke when the explosion blew him right out of the water—"right up and down." He had no idea how high. "It could have been five feet or five hundred feet," he reported, but doubted it was 500 feet, probably nearer to 25 or 30. He dropped back down into the water and went under, then swam back up to the surface, fully conscious. He remembered that he'd swallowed a lot of oil. In considerable pain, he nevertheless managed to climb into a "crowded" Carley float. What happened next is best told in his own words: "We sang. I don't know if from the battle or being scared or what it was. We sang songs. Maybe we'd seen it in a movie somewhere. I don't know where we got the idea."

Clutching the plank he'd retrieved Bill Coates suffered a fractured hip and stomach pains. "I was lucky," he said afterwards, "the plank kept most of my body above the water." Finally he was pulled into the lifeboat.

Charlottetown's telegraphist torpedo operator, Gerald Martin, remembered pulling seaman Donald Bowser into the lifeboat. But because the man was dying he pleaded to be pushed back into the water.

As senior surviving officer, First Lieutenant George Moors took charge of the lifeboat, directing such rescues, collecting men in the water here and there, taking aboard the severely wounded, transferring others to the Carley floats and generally trying to keep those in the water together. In their two-hour search for survivors the only body they found was that of the ship's captain floating upright wearing his life jacket, his face contorted from the torture he must have suffered when the depth charges exploded. It was a traumatic moment for the executive officer, the loss of his friend and skipper whom he revered and held in the highest respect. They tied the jacket of his lifeless body to the rudder of the boat with a piece of rope and towed it astern at the end of its tether. However, his weight pulled the rudder from the boat, and with it the dead captain's body. Author James Lamb, in what amounted to a eulogy, wrote: "Willard Bonner, his last service done, disappeared into the mists forever."

The morning had been replete with heroics. Like telegrapher Fred Rush, who gave his life jacket to a shipmate even though he couldn't swim himself, then jumped overboard to take his chances in the icy St. Lawrence waters. Cecil Bates, a sick-bay attendant who, though badly wounded himself, insisted on treating the injured aboard the lifeboat. And Tommy MacDonald, also wounded when the depth charges went off, who tried to retrieve a drifting float for his floundering mates.

Then there was the ironic episode and end to "Judy" Garland, who had been handing out life jackets, including his own, even though he couldn't swim. The bow was at an almost 45-degree angle, rising out of the water, and he was still hanging onto the gun platform. "We that were close to him," Bill Coates later revealed," told him to jump." But instead he shouted that he was going back for Screech, the ship's mascot, a mongrel picked up in Newfoundland. Garland was never seen again until his body was recovered from the wreckage caused by the depth-charge explosion. But Screech was rescued by John Dillon, who tossed the dog to his twin brother, stoker Frank Dillon, on one of the Carley floats. Two other incidents, one bordering on the bizarre, the other somewhat incredulous: a seaman about to jump from the rapidly sinking corvette who decided to return belowdecks for a picture of his girlfriend he left behind. His body was later found floating in the sea. Then there was the entrepreneurial rating who must have been born under a lucky star. When Garland ran out of life jackets, he went over the side clutching an empty bully-beef container that proved buoyant enough to keep him afloat.

The survivors of *Charlottetown* were eventually picked up by *Clayoquot* but not before her sister corvette nearly plowed right into them. "...she came in steaming through the mist at top speed," Ross Duff, aboard one of the rafts, related. Pursuing a sonar contact, she was bearing down on *U-517* and about to drop depth charges when, at the sudden sight of so many rafts in the water, the captain, Lieutenant Harold Lade, aborted the attack and veered away. Hartwig, who could count his lucky stars once more, dived to the bottom of the river where he lay undetected. After a futile search of two hours for the elusive U-boat, *Clayoquot* returned to pick up the survivors from the lifeboat and Carley floats and deposited them ashore at Gaspé. The bodies of six men, including the captain, Willard Bonner, were never recovered. The four others who perished were buried ashore. There were 54 survivors out of a ship's company of 64.

Aftermath

Another survivor was *Charlottetown*'s mascot, Screech. The hardy mongrel weathered many a long hour aboard one the rafts without wail or whimper. Frank and John Dillon took him home to Montreal and sent him to "Judy" Garland's mother in Gallagher Ridge, N.B., who "…was very happy to receive him," according to the Dillons.

The tragedy brought to the surface the saga of two of the victims, Willard Bonner, the corvette's skipper, and Donald Bowser, who died after being taken aboard the lifeboat. One would never have guessed, a shipmate later recalled, that their pre-war pursuits put the two at loggerheads—Bonner as skipper of an RCMP patrol boat chasing Bowser the rum-runner. "Whenever the captain was on the bridge for action stations, or anything else," Frank Dillon said, "Bowser was always in the wheelhouse with the coxswain."

But the most incongruous irony to the entire scenario concerned its architect, Paul Hartwig. After a few close shaves he accounted for a total of 31,000 tons of Allied shipping in the Gulf, far short of his goal of 80,000 to qualify him for the Iron Cross, although Hitler personally conferred the coveted award upon him all the same. His career came to an end in the Gulf, where he had made such a name for himself, when the submarine he was piloting was brought to the surface by a British destroyer and he spent the rest of the war in a Northern Ontario prison camp. After the war, as one of the few surviving U-boat aces, he joined the West German Navy, rising to the rank of admiral. As a NATO representative, on a subsequent visit to Canada, the former protagonist was made welcome as an ally.

The sinking report that officially registered finale to the nine-month career of the corvette *Charlottetown*, christened with 13 letters to her name on the 13th of the month she was commissioned, was dated September 13. The ultimate irony.

RefScs: CCAN 153–160 FDS 119 TSIAOG 117–119 OTTR 110–125

THE MID-ATLANTIC
JULY–DECEMBER 1942

*B*y mid-summer 1942, the responsibility for 40 per cent of the commercial convoy escort work in the North Atlantic fell on the decks of the Royal Canadian Navy. By that time, Canadian warships had escorted 65 million tons of cargo. July, August and September saw some successes against the U-boats. What counted most, however, was not submarine kills, but getting the convoys through.

Mid-Ocean
July 14, 1942

DOBSON Andrew

"Spirited Chase—U-boat Sunk after Fourth Try"

Late in the afternoon a lookout aboard *St. Croix*, one of seven destroyers donated to the RCN by the US Navy, spotted a surfaced U-boat several miles distant. Skipper Andy Dobson ordered "Action stations, full speed ahead," a chase that took *St. Croix* 10 miles away from Halifax-bound convoy HX-193. During the pursuit, the quarry stayed well out of asdic range and, as the destroyer closed to within 6,000 yards, *U-90* suddenly dived out of sight.

St. Croix held course, anticipating the submarine's moves, and gradually closed distance until finally making asdic contact. "Dobby" Dobson steered over the U-boat's position three times, dropping a pattern of 10 depth charges on each attack. When oil and wreckage appeared on the surface, Dobson was not satisfied he had scored a kill—it was more likely the usual German ruse of releasing flotsam through the submarine's torpedo tubes.

To make sure, Dobson promptly ordered a fourth barrage. This time there was no doubt. The explosion split the U-boat wide open; *U-90* spewed a litter of oily timber, food provisions, personal effects, and that most certain, gruesome and literal evidence of a kill—gulls swooping to devour pieces of flesh. Further poignant evidence: among the remnants, *St. Croix*'s crew found a flimsy brassiere, labelled "Triumph Paris."

RefScs: FDS 131 TSIAOG 124

700 Miles East of Newfoundland
July 31, 1942

DYER Kenneth
WALLACE Dickson Carlile
WINDEYER Guy

"Biblical References Initiated Closely Coordinated U-boat Search and Sinking"

For five days German U-boats had been trailing westbound convoy ON-115. Several contacts had been made by the escort, comprising two Canadian corvettes and five destroyers under the command of Dickson "Debby" Wallace—all of them without result.

Early on the morning of July 31, the destroyer *Skeena*, Ken Dyer in command, secured a solid enough contact to begin a detailed U-boat search. But Dyer needed help; an effective hunt could be conducted only in pairs, so he sent a signal by lamp to Guy Windeyer, captain of the corvette *Wetaskiwin*, with whom he had cooperated in an earlier submarine search. Reckoning that he could also use a little spiritual assistance as well, Dyer decided to invoke the Good Book in his signal, quoting Acts 16, Verse 9:

> "And a vision appeared to Paul in the night; there stood a
> man of Macedonia and prayed him saying, come over
> into Macedonia and help us."

After a quick thumb-through of their own ship's Bible, *Wetaskiwin* flashed back in kind, citing Revelations 13, Verse 1:

"And I stood upon the sand of the sea and saw a beast rise up from out of the sea having seven heads and ten horns, and upon the horns ten crowns, and upon his head the name of blasphemy."

In less ecclesiastical prose: "We're with you all the way! Let's go!"

For the next five hours the two ships made a relentless, systematic search over the area where the contact had been made, signalling now in much more secular language. The precision of both the search and the signals virtually doomed *U-588* from the start.

Somewhere around 5:00, a signal came from *Wetaskiwin*: "Contact bearing 260 degrees, 1,900 yards. Contact is firm... Contact bearing 280 degrees, 600 yards."

From her own position, *Skeena* acknowledged: "Contact bearing 040 degrees, 800 yards...Contact bearing 070 degrees, 4,000 yards." But *Skeena* had been misled by a false asdic echo, which could have been anything from driftwood to a shark. "No sub," she affirmed.

Now *Wetaskiwin* signalled again: "Contact bearing 200 degrees. Attacking." Another disappointment: "Lost contact at 600 yards. By my plot you are over sub. Contact bearing 210 degrees, 1,900 yards."

Skeena, in reply: "Contact bearing 345 degrees, 1,600 yards. Attacking. Please keep to port." *Skeena* dropped her pattern of depth charges, and then waited for *Wetaskiwin*'s report.

It wasn't long in coming: "Confirmed right spot. Contact bearing 300 degrees, 1,000 yards. Attacking." After dropping her depth charges, *Wetaskiwin*'s report was terse: "Lost contact."

Skeena signalled a new point of contact: "Echo bearing 120 degrees, 700 yards."

Wetaskiwin: "Okay. Let me attack now."

Skeena: "Unable to gain contact."

Wetaskiwin: "I will try to help you by directing."

Skeena: "Attacking."

As *Skeena* dropped a pattern of depth charges for the second time, there was little doubt about the fate of *U-588*. *Wetaskiwin* flashed a congratulatory "Excellent" to her sister ship—if signal lamps could blink exuberance they would have lit up the Atlantic Ocean. A laudatory pat on the back was in order. Signals had played the key role in the U-boat's defeat from start to finish. A few more flashes completed the memorable signal exchange.

Skeena: "Did you hear that underwater explosion?"

Wetaskiwin: "Yes. Definitely.... Plenty of wreckage over this way."

Skeena: "I am lowering a whaler to pick up the guts." Then, in a general signal to the escort and convoy, Dyer flashed: "U-boat considered sunk by HMCS *Wetaskiwin* and HMCS *Skeena*. Floating wreckage and human remains recovered."

A fitting sign-off to the episode might have been a reverential "Amen."

RefScs: FDS 131–34 NAR 133–34 TSIAOG 124

500 Miles East of Newfoundland
August 1, 1942

EASTON Alan Herbert

"Scored One Probable Kill, One Damaged U-boat in Single Night"

Skeena's and *Wetaskiwin*'s success in sinking *U-588*, thereby reducing U-boat strength in the vicinity of convoy ON-115 by one, meant no let-up in the wolf packs' relentless pursuit. On the following evening, just as fog started to roll in, *Sackville* sighted a surfaced U-boat and immediately gave chase. But a snowflake flare bursting above the convoy signalled that one of its ships had been torpedoed, and the Canadian corvette was forced to break off pursuit to render whatever aid and protection it could give.

In the glow of the burning vessel and the white light of the flares, the outline of another submarine was clearly seen silhouetted against the merchantmen. Before *Sackville* could

attack, the U-boat slid deftly into the middle of the convoy, torpedoed another freighter and raced away from the scene.

Wheeling around to zero in on the attacker, *Sackville* fired off
a series of star shells to illuminate the area—instantly the submarine submerged, leaving a frothy swirl in its wake. Riding
across the bubbling vortex, captain Alan Easton ordered depth
charges dropped. The first explosion brought the U-boat back to
the surface, its bow sprouting at such an acute angle almost the
entire length of the submarine heaved into sight. Then, as the
other charges detonated around it, the sub made another fast exit
below the surface.

Easton again maneuvered his ship over the spot where the U-
boat had gone under, dropping 10 more depth charges—oil
seeped to the surface, followed by a heavy underwater explosion.
Based on this evidence, *Sackville* was later credited with having
scored a "probable kill."

Another hour went by before the corvette sighted her third
submarine of the night, again fully surfaced—and cruising just
125 yards off her port bow. But it was just as quickly lost from
view in the soupy fog that shrouded the convoy. Another half
hour and lookouts reported what was presumably the same U-
boat, 200 yards dead ahead, cutting across *Sackville*'s course.
Easton instinctively gave the command to ram—"Full speed
ahead."

Abruptly, the German submarine turned directly towards the
Canadian corvette, driving in so close it rendered *Sackville*'s 4-
inch gun useless. An eerie chase in the murky darkness ensued,
the two vessels zigzagging side by side only yards apart. Unable
to open fire, *Sackville* continued trying to ram while the U-boat
swerved and weaved. Suddenly Easton got the break he had been
hoping and waiting for. For an instant, as the two ships swung
apart, the U-boat came within the scope and firing range of the
corvette's 4-inch gun.

One shell was all it took to shatter the base of the submarine's
conning tower. *Sackville*'s machine gunners opened up, spraying
the tower, bridge and decks at point-blank range. Scrambling
from the bridge, the U-boat commander barely made it to the

hatch. He pulled the lid as the U-boat went into a crash dive. Certain that the submarine had been put out of action, at least temporarily, *Sackville* claimed and was awarded a "damaged."

The Third Canadian Escort Group had performed nobly. More important than the destruction of one U-boat and putting two others out of commission was the fact that those gallant efforts, and the vigilance of the escort, allowed the sinking of only two convoy ON-115 merchant ships. The outcome was, in every sense, a victory.

RefScs: FDS 134–35 TSIAOG 125

Off Newfoundland
August 6, 1942

BERNAYS Max Leopold
HENNESSY Ralph Lucien
STUBBS John Hamilton

"Deadly Destroyer/U-boat Duel"

L ate in the afternoon, a lingering fog began to lift over the northwestern Atlantic, revealing a surfaced U-boat—*U-210*—six miles distant from convoy SC-94 bound from Halifax to the UK. *Assiniboine*, an escort vessel captained by John Stubbs, gave chase in a wild, weaving half-hour game of cat-and-mouse in and out of fog banks. Fitted with an outdated, perfectly useless radar, the destroyer had to depend on visual contact. To his credit, despite this handicap, Stubbs never once lost his quarry.

Assiniboine closed range and was greeted with a hail of 20-mm incendiary shells from the U-boat, which its captain had skillfully maneuvered into the "blind" spot: close enough that the destroyer could not lower its heavy guns to bring them to bear, yet sufficiently distant and at a sidewise angle to prevent ramming.

But Stubbs was a ship-handling master, and he now began a series of maneuvers to upset that juxtaposition. Over the next 35

Ralph Hennessy salutes Winston Churchill aboard Assiniboine. *(Ken Bell/DND/PA 140559)*

minutes, a nautical dogfight ensued—each vessel parrying and thrusting, snarling with every weapon at its command.

In the early stages of this fierce free-for-all, *Assiniboine* came out second best. The incendiary shells had smashed into the starboard side of the destroyer, setting fire to fuel drums stored alongside the wheelhouse. The ship's Number One, Ralph Hennessy (who would later captain the *Assiniboine*), took charge, leading a fire brigade into action.

Inside the wheelhouse, Max Bernays, chief petty officer, ordered his helmsman and telegrapher outside to help the firefighters. He then locked himself in, knowing full well that if they didn't succeed he would roast. Yet, with incendiary shells crashing against the bulkheads and spattering splinters in his face, he calmly and stoically carried out engine-room and helm orders as the battle raged outside. As Hennessy and his fire brigade brought their blaze under control, fresh fires broke out on deck.

On the bridge Stubbs, too, set an example of unruffled composure under fire. Standing fully exposed as gunfire riddled the woodwork around him, he kept careful watch to hold *Assiniboine* firmly in place beside the weaving submarine. The range was still too short to bring the main guns to bear. The crew relied on small arms—rifles, machine guns, even revolvers—to sweep the submarine's decks and tear holes in her hull. A sudden turn for the better—the opportunity the gunners had been waiting for—for a brief instant, they were able to bring the destroyer's 4.7-inch gun into play. The first shell hit the sub's conning tower square on, killing the U-boat commander.

Now Stubbs attempted to ram, but the U-boat successfully eluded each pass. Deciding not to press her luck, the submarine prepared to crash-dive. She had begun to tilt forward when *Assiniboine*'s prow made contact just behind the conning tower. It was merely a glancing blow, however, and Stubbs steered the destroyer clear for another try. If nothing else, the German submariners were plucky—*U-210* was full of fight right to the end. As *Assiniboine* bore down, she was making some 10 knots and firing vainly, defiantly.

Her final fate came quickly. Ramming at full speed, *Assiniboine* cut broadside into the U-boat. At the same time, a pattern of shallow-set depth charges was thrown overboard—they literally blew the submarine out of the water. For the *coup de grâce*, several shells from one of the heavy guns were discharged into the sinking hull. Within two minutes, *U-210* was swallowed by the sea.

Assiniboine had paid a heavy price. Her bow was buckled and leaking, and her crew were busy tending the wounded as she returned to St. John's to lick her wounds. It would take until the following year, 1943, before she was refitted and back in action.

Ralph Hennessy was born in Scotland in 1918 and moved to Ottawa, Ont., with his parents two years later. In 1936 he enlisted in the RCN, but took his training with the Royal Navy. As a midshipman aboard HMS *Resolution*, he took part in non-intervention patrols in Spanish waters. At the outbreak of World War II, he joined *Assiniboine*, serving with her for the next three years. For his part in the sinking of *U-210*, Hennessy was awarded the DSC. In 1943 he came ashore as executive officer of HMCS Kings, a shore-based facility in Halifax. Hennessy returned to sea in 1944, taking command of *MicMac* a year later.

In 1947 he was appointed Chief of Naval Personnel and Director of Training. In 1952 he returned once again to sea, as executive officer of *Quebec*. He held several senior appointments between 1956 and 1958 at RCN Headquarters in London, England. Hennessy was promoted to Vice-Admiral in 1966, and made Controller-General of Canada's Armed Forces. In 1968 he became Chief of Personnel. He retired two years later.

VADM DSC CD KStLJ Born September 15, 1918
RefScs: DHist bf FDS 135–37 NAR 143–45 TSIAOG 124–25

Mid-Atlantic
September 10–14, 1942

DOBSON Andrew Hedley
HENDRY George
PULLEN Thomas
RUTHERFORD Clark Anderson

"Catastrophe in the Black Pit—Demise of the Destroyer Ottawa*"*

September to December 1942, entering the Black Pit—that 600-mile killing ground where there was no air cover—convoys were losing as many as 16 ships in the three to four days it took to cross the gap. Convoy ON-127, leaving Lough Foyle in Northern Ireland on September 5, escorted by the Fourth Canadian Escort Group under Dobby Dobson, was no exception. As the ships entered the "naked" corridor, the German wolf pack *Vorwarts*, made up of 13 U-boats, was lying in wait.

At this critical stage, aboard *Ottawa*, one of six escort ships and the only destroyer in the group other than Dobson's *St. Croix*, two crewmen came down with acute appendicitis. With a heavy sea running, conditions for performing a pair of appendectomies were far from ideal. With help from *Ottawa*'s Number One, Tom

Pullen, surgeon George Hendry managed to execute the operations despite the roll of the ship. But the incident hardly augured an unremarkable voyage.

Over the next two days U-boats were everywhere. They had sunk seven merchant ships and damaged four others when Hendry's medical expertise was called upon again. One survivor pulled from the sea by *Ottawa* had taken a rivet deep in his gut. With Pullen again assisting and the wounded seaman strapped to the captain's dining table, four hours of painstaking surgery weren't enough to save him. The burial at sea with full naval honours as the sun set on the evening of September 13 seemed to portend more tragedy; ON-127 seemed jinxed.

Close to midnight, *Ottawa* was steering well ahead of the convoy when a torpedo struck. Pullen immediately went below to survey the damage—chaos, a shambles; wreckage was everywhere, and where once the bow had been there was a gaping hole and the dark raging sea. Then a second torpedo struck.

It shattered what was left of the destroyer, and the crew quickly abandoned ship, diving and lowering themselves into the freezing water. Pullen and *Ottawa*'s skipper, Clark "Larry" Rutherford, were the last to leave the bridge. Satisfied everyone left alive had gotten off safely, they grappled their way down the side of the ship and jumped into the sea.

In the icy waters many of the men, struggling to stay afloat, bitterly cold and in deep shock, seemed to give up. They let go of the Carley floats and drifted off into the night—100 men were lost; among them Hendry, the doctor who had carried out his duties so admirably, and Larry Rutherford, who had given his lifebelt to a seaman.

Convoy ON-127 held the dubious distinction of being the only convoy that winter of 1942-43 on which all the U-boats engaged were able to fire their torpedoes. Not without justification, the RCN blamed this fact—along with the Germans' success in sinking seven merchantmen, damaging four others, and destroying an escort destroyer—on early interception, a lack of air cover and poor equipment. In fact, only one ship had radar—and it didn't work.

But this reasoning did nothing to dissuade the Admiralty's view that the underlying cause was lack of proper training.

Clark Rutherford entered the RCN as a cadet in 1933 and was trained in the Royal Navy, his first ship being HMS *Frobisher*. As a midshipman he served with five different British vessels. In 1937, having completed his training with the RN, Rutherford returned to Canada. His first RCN ship was *Fraser* and he later transferred to *Skeena*. He assumed command of *Ottawa* in July 1942.

LTCOMM KIA September 14, 1942
RefScs: DHist bf FDS 138 NAR 159–65 TSIAOG 126

Mid-Atlantic
October 29–November 5, 1942

AUDETTE Louis de la Chesnaye
PIERS Desmond William

"Devastation of Convoy SC-107"

By the late fall of 1942, 40 U-boats were at sea in the North Atlantic, the largest number so far deployed. And they were equipped with a new cipher code, which British Intelligence had yet to crack. By the same token, *Befelbshaber der U-boote* headquarters (*BdU*—commander-in-chief of U-boats) were able to receive intercepted Allied shipping signals via *Bdeinst* (German Naval Intelligence). To complicate matters further, by this time the Royal Canadian Navy had donated 17 corvettes to Operation Torch, the Allied offensive campaign in North Africa; the RCN was operating with undertrained personnel and outdated equipment. The *Untersee Kriegsmarine* held a distinct advantage.

Eastbound convoy SC-107 from Halifax suffered drastically from these handicaps and shortcomings. And, during a four-day battle without let-up, it also had to wrestle with the worst Atlantic winter weather in 30 years.

The convoy consisted of 42 merchantmen, formed in 10 columns spread across an area three miles wide by a mile deep, protected by the Fourth Canadian Escort Group. They had just rounded Cape Race, at the southern tip of Newfoundland, when signals intercepted and decrypted by *Bdeinst* revealed their presence and direction. On October 29, this intelligence was confirmed and relayed to *BdU* by the German submarine *U-522*, which ascertained SC-107's position, speed and course.

The convoy's senior escort officer was "Debby" Piers, captain of the destroyer *St. Croix*. Piers had been on convoy duty almost since war's outbreak. At age 25, he was a relative youngster, and very much a junior officer among his naval peers. But in his capacity as SEO of seven previous convoys, he had never lost a ship. It was an enviable, remarkable record at this stage of the war, one that was soon to be lamentably and ignominiously shattered—SC-107 would prove to be Piers's *bête noire*.

In addition to *St. Croix*, the escort consisted of three RCN corvettes, *Amherst*, *Arvida* and *Sherbrooke*, and one RN corvette, *Celandine*, the best-equipped, most modern of the four. Tagging along were two other corvettes, *Algoma* and *Moose Jaw*, on their way to support the Torch landings. A rescue ship, *Stockport*, rounded out the escort.

SC-107 steamed eastward, closely shadowed by enemy submarines. Before the convoy reached the Black Pit, a Royal Canadian Air Force twin-engine Hudson bomber managed to sink *U-658*. It was hardly enough to shake off the rest, but for the merchantmen and their escorts, it was a cheering sight in the face of the somber reality that, within hours, they would be unprotected by air cover. Meanwhile, just inside the western perimeter of the Black Pit, *Gruppe Veilchen*, a patrol line of 17 U-boats, lurked, ready to pounce.

As a foretaste of the misfortune that loomed ahead, *Celandine*'s radar broke down; before too long visual scanning equipment on two of the Canadian ships quit as well. In consolation, however, *Restigouche* and *Stockport* were both equipped with new high-frequency direction finding (HF/DF) equipment, with which they were able to audibly track the shadowing wolf pack. During November 1, a total of 25 enemy signals were intercepted by the two vessels, and the submarines' positions were pinpointed. While, with only one destroyer available, it was impossible to chase them down, at least the escort was successfully thwarting initial U-boat attempts to press home attacks—until the sun went down. Then all hell broke loose.

As soon as darkness fell, the wolf pack stormed in and snowflake illumination rockets burst over the convoy like a fireworks display. The first blow fell when *U-402*, captained by Baron von Forstner, broke through *Arvida*'s radar screen on the starboard beam (she was just one of the escorts whose radar was out of commission) and fired a torpedo into *Empire Sunrise*, striking the merchantman amidships. As the crippled cargo ship wallowed astern, *U-381* finished her with another torpedo from 1,800 yards, in the process narrowly missing *Restigouche*, whose zigzag course saved her hide.

Predictably, the twin-pronged attack split up the convoy, sending the escorts off in all directions in search of U-boats and conveniently opening up the target area to fresh assaults. Forstner thus bypassed *Celandine*, busy protecting *Stockport* as the rescue ship fished survivors out of the sea, and zeroed in on the very heart of SC-107, sinking three more merchant ships and damaging another.

One of the targets was an ammunition ship that exploded with such a thundering blast it could be heard, and felt, miles away. Crews belowdecks in vessels well distant from the detonation were so stunned they thought their own ships had been hit. Like *Empire Sunrise*, the merchantman was forced to limp astern, a sitting duck.

Simultaneously, *U-522*, which four days earlier had made the first submarine contact with SC-107, was also making a commendable accounting for itself. In two attacks it sank a pair of ships and damaged another, which its companion, *U-521*, quickly finished off.

Eight ships were lost in a single night, a bitter pill for Piers and his escort to swallow, and the cause of almost intolerable anguish and despair for the convoy itself—and there was still more grief to come. However, during the following day

(November 2), stormy seas and strong wintry gales very nearly shut the battle down. While weather conditions made the convoy almost impregnable, they also rendered it impossible for the escort to take offensive action against the wolf pack—an ironic twist that terrible weather, any ship's worst natural enemy, actually provided the convoy with some relief.

The weather did not, however, stop *U-522*. Just to rub the enemies' noses in it, under these most adverse conditions, the elusive U-boat managed to slip through the screen and sink a merchant ship, bringing *Gruppe Veilchen*'s tally to nine. Mercifully, by later afternoon the weather had deteriorated still further; it was so bad, in fact, that *Veilchen* lost all contact, giving SC-107 and its escort, now reinforced by the British destroyer *Vanessa*, a night of respite.

By morning, visibility had improved sufficiently to enable nine U-boats to regain contact with the convoy. Bearings secured by HF/DF allowed the British ships *Vanessa* and *Celandine* to make depth-charge attacks effective enough to damage four submarines, but even that failed to deter *Gruppe Veilchen*. At noon, *U-521* maneuvered into the midst of the convoy and sank a merchantman in broad daylight—number 10.

Towards dusk the convoy took evasive action by steering to port, but the wolf pack hung on tenaciously. As soon as it turned dark, *U-90* sneaked into the convoy between *Moose Jaw* and *Vanessa*, escorts unfamiliar with each other's procedures, and scored a prize kill—the commodore's ship *Jeypore*, at the head of the convoy. Once again the search for the assailant split SC-107 wide open, leaving it vulnerable to further assaults. This resulted in the loss of three more ships, all torpedoed by a single U-boat, *U-132*, which had slipped into the middle of the convoy unnoticed.

At this point *Amherst* closed in on *Daleby*, one of the torpedoed freighters, to search out her assailant. The corvette was almost immediately rewarded by a solid asdic signal—ping ping ping—a submarine. *Amherst*'s skipper, Uncle Louis Audette (all RCN captains over age 30 automatically earned the sobriquet "Uncle"), ordered a depth-charge pattern readied and prepared to cross over the target. But just as the corvette was about to drop its lethal load, *Daleby*'s survivors, struggling in the icy sea, could be seen and heard from the bridge. The moment of decision rested solely with the ship's captain. The dilemma: attack, in which case at least 40 men would meet a ghastly death from the explosions, or let the submarine go, leaving it free to kill again.

The fact that there really was no choice could in no way lessen Audette's agony in having to make it. With an aching heart he gave the order to attack. Then, at the precise moment the depth charges were about to be launched, the asdic's power failed. The signal was lost. No target. The incident can only be described as phenomenal, as if a miracle had occurred in answer to Audette's dilemma—Solomon could not have solved it better. Audette instantly countermanded the attack signal, no doubt with a profound sense of relief. By the time the power returned, the submarine had disappeared. *Amherst* wheeled about, left free to pick up survivors.

Daleby was a blazing hulk. *Amherst* had already written her off as abandoned. But as the corvette neared, three men still on board could be heard screaming for help. As if in atonement for the earlier decision he had been forced to make, Audette now broke one of the longest-standing rules in the book—he ordered the engines stopped in enemy-infested waters and a lifeboat lowered to effect a rescue—an act of moral fortitude, if indeed one of naval disobedience.

By the morning of November 4, *Stockport* and the two US Navy tugs helping her were overloaded with survivors—300 aboard the rescue ship alone. Having fulfilled their task, they proceeded to Iceland, escorted by *Arvida* and *Celandine*. Later that day the absence of the two escorts was filled by the arrival of three American ships, but not before *U-89* claimed one last victim.

The night passed without incident. U-boats were still hovering about, waiting for an opportunity, but, fortunately for the tattered and bedraggled convoy, none arose. On November 5 the enemy submarines were finally driven off by long-range Royal Air Force four-engine Liberator bombers, directed from HF/DF bearings received by *Restigouche*.

SC-107 lost 15 ships, the worst RCN convoy disaster since the battle of SC-42, 14 months earlier. This catastrophe was symptomatic of a rapidly deteriorating situation in the North Atlantic, a situation for which the Canadians shouldered the major share of the blame. At a time when Britain's reserves were being eaten up by the offensives in North Africa, SC-107 was the straw that broke the Admiralty's back. While Canadians would play escort to several more convoys that winter, the decision to withdraw them from that duty had already been reached, and was soon to be promulgated.

Louis Audette was born in Ottawa, Ont. He began practising law in Montreal in 1931, prior to joining the RCN in 1939. He retired from the Navy in 1945 with the rank of Commander, Royal Canadian Naval Reserve. Following the war he held various posts in civilian life, including chairman of the Canadian Maritime Commission; chairman of the Preparatory Committee; with the Intergovernmental Maritime Consultative Organization of the United Nations, and president of its first assembly. He also served as chairman of the Tariff Board and administrator of the Maritime Pollution Fund.

COMNDR MID Born 1907
RefScs: FDS 139 NAR 177–80 RCNIR 127 167 215 366
TSIAOG 126–28 205

1200 Miles North of the Azores
December 25–30, 1942

BECK Frederick
FREWER Frederick
WINDEYER Guy

"The Convoy that Nearly Died"

Before it even left Lough Foyle, Northern Ireland, on December 19, westbound convoy ONS-154 was already doomed. Pre-sailing exercises for the First Canadian Escort

Group, under *St. Laurent* skipper Guy Windeyer, were aborted due to lack of proper available equipment, as was the preparatory conference of captains. Worse still, *St. Laurent*'s companion destroyer, a British naval vessel, had been ruled unfit for sea duty. Her absence would severely limit any offensive action by Windeyer's ship, the fastest one in the escort, which included five corvettes—*Battleford*, *Chilliwack*, *Kenogami*, *Napanee* and *Shediac*, as well as the rescue vessel *Toward*.

A few other deviations from standard procedures spelled further peril. Convoy ONS-154, consisting of 47 merchantmen, would be routed just north of the Azores. This meant crossing the Black Pit without air cover at its widest possible point. Of small consolation—very small, in fact—was the addition of the British service ship *Fidelity*, carrying two catapult-launched float planes. And—as an experiment—the tanker *Scottish Heather* would tag along to refuel the escorts at sea.

As the convoy steamed into the air gap on Christmas Day, it caught the tail end of a hurricane. Unwittingly, its course also set it directly south of two hovering German wolf packs—*Spitz* and *Ungestum*—a total of 20 U-boats, hungrily waiting for just such a tempting target. Although the British had by this time broken the new enemy submarine code, the formula had not been in place in sufficient time to plot new submarine positions. On the other hand, by Boxing Day, *Spitz* had easily picked up a firm fix on ONS-154's whereabouts and had calculated its speed and direction. Based on this intelligence, relayed through *Bdeinst*, Donitz ordered an immediate attack.

Eight U-boats closed in and began to shadow the convoy, which was beset by strong, blustery gales and waves rising to 12 feet. Many of the ships were damaged and driven apart; the escort had its hands full, coping not only with the host of submarine warnings and sightings pouring in, but trying desperately at the same time to round up the meandering merchantmen.

At 2:00 a.m. the following morning, in poor visibility, drizzle and a heavy mist, *U-356* cut inside the convoy, making two expertly executed surface passes during which it sank three ships—*Empire Union*, *Melrose Abbey*, *King Edward*—and left

Soekaboemi with a gaping hole in its stern. Windeyer bore down on the attacking U-boat, raking it with 20-mm shells.

Napanee joined the fracas, taking potshots with the corvette's 4-inch gun and lobbing a star shell to light up the area. As the submarine crash-dived, both *Napanee* and *St. Laurent* dropped shallow depth charges. Then Windeyer unloaded a 10-pack pattern. Oil spread in a large slick over the water—a sure kill. (Not to be confirmed, however, until after the war when German records revealed the loss of *U-356* that night of December 26/27. Only then was the escort given credit for its destruction.)

Over the next 30 hours the convoy enjoyed a comparative lull, broken only by a single attack from each side: *U-225* mangled the tanker *Scottish Heather* (she managed to limp safely back to the Clyde, leaving the escort without means for replenishing fuel on a particularly long run), and *Chilliwack*, which caught a U-boat on the surface with her 4-inch gun, then depth-charged when the sub went under. (She reported an enormous explosion. Although there was no evidence of a kill, there was every possibility that the submarine had at least been sidelined.)

The next morning, December 28, the wolf packs re-established visual contact; they spent the day preparing for an assault as soon as darkness fell. After studying reports coming into the Admiralty on U-boat activity near the Azores, the Royal Navy ordered two of its destroyers diverted from the Torch landings in North Africa to provide extra escort support. But it would take until the following day for them to arrive.

As night fell, Windeyer, in desperation, ordered *Fidelity* to launch one of its float planes for reconnoitering, a measure that resulted in a minor calamity. *St. Laurent* laid down an oil slick carpet to calm the sea for the plane's return landing. But the aircraft struck the destroyer's wake, crashed and sank. At least both the pilot and observer managed to get out before the plane went under.

At 7:20 p.m. *St. Laurent* was busy picking the flight crew out of the water when, in the growing darkness, Fred Beck, captain of *Battleford*, spotted U-boats neatly arranged abreast of each other, a mile apart, steering straight for the convoy. As soon as they knew they were sighted, one of the submarines dived. *Battleford* lost visual contact with a second one, except for a blip on the radar screen. Beck decided to chase the third and fourth raiders, bringing his 4-inch gun to bear and illuminating the scene with a star shell. In the chase that followed, however, he not only lost his quarry—he lost the rest of the convoy as well. It took him until the next morning to relocate them.

The Germans, on the other hand, had no problem finding ONS-154, and at 8:00 they began to lay into it with a will. *U-519* made the first attack, putting *Norse King* out of business. *U-225* drove torpedoes into *Melmore Head* and *Vile de Rouen*. As the three badly crippled vessels drifted astern, on the opposite side of the convoy *U-260* sank *Empire Wagtail* while *U-406* mortally damaged three more freighters—*Baron Cochrane*, *Lynton Grange* and *Zarian*. Completing the night's destruction, *U-225* destroyed *President Francequi* as well as the commodore's ship, *Empire Shackleton*.

A naval battle royal, one that those lucky enough to survive would never forget. Ships burned to the waterline. Explosions burst with a ferocious suddenness that could be heard and seen miles away. Battleship foghorns whooped loud blasts as the escorts weaved between ships, searching out and fending off the undersea raiders. Torpedoes swished through the water in all directions. The air crackled with displays of white tracer shells from the U-boats mingled with the red pencil lines of bullets fired from the merchantmen. A cacophony of sounds and sights as snowflake bursts and star shell flares lit up the sky.

By the light of dawn, driftwood, flotsam, wreckage and bodies floated everywhere. Survivors cried for help. It had taken only five U-boats less than two hours to destroy nine ships. The subs spent much of the morning scavenging through what was left of the chaos they had created.

That afternoon they added one more casualty to the carnage. *Fidelity* had been straggling behind with engine trouble. As she fell farther astern, she was attacked repeatedly by *U-435*. By late afternoon the submarine finished her off, sending her to the bottom with all 334 of her crew aboard.

Close to dusk, the U-boats finally retired over the horizon, though still within the escorts' radio direction-finding range. As darkness closed in, ONS-154 and escorts stayed alert to the imminent possibility of a renewed onslaught. But, for some inexplicable reason, the attack failed to materialize. To all intents the night passed peacefully for the Allied crews, but this did little to calm the jitters.

A victim to the nervous pressure was the escort's senior officer. After three sleepless nights and the relentless demands and responsibilities of command in combat, the four-day naval battle had taken its toll. Guy Windeyer was a nervous wreck. *St. Laurent*'s ship's surgeon ordered him to bed, and his command was taken over by First Officer Fred Frewer, who later described the engagement as a "terrible nightmare."

By mid-afternoon of December 30, thankfully—the two British destroyers arrived. They helped chase off the shadowing U-boats just in time—the situation had become desperate; total disaster threatened. The U-boats had come through the struggle virtually unscathed. The convoy was still a long way from the protection of air cover—and it had already lost 14 ships and 486 lives. Her escort had been depleted of its "aircraft carrier" and its tanker. And now four of the escort ships were so low on fuel they had to sail south to the Azores. (In fact, en route *Battleford* had to take *Shediac* in tow. The other two vessels, British destroyers *Meteor* and *Milne*, made it to port under their own steam.)

On December 31 a new escort took over and, for once, providence smiled on ONS-154, for the remainder of the voyage passed without further incident. But the raw facts were unchanged—the mission had been an absolute disaster. And it could have been far worse had the wolf packs continued their assault (that they did not has never been explained).

The fate of ONS-154 served to underline the fundamental weaknesses of Canadian escorts. First, lack of coordination. While individual crews performed admirably, they failed to act collectively as a team. Clearly, better group training was needed. Second, lack of leadership. With few exceptions, Canadian escorts did not have experienced hands at the helm.

In fairness, however, the basic flaws in the Canadian escort service should be judged in relationship to the overall situation. To begin with, there was a serious shortage of escorts. And, although it was true, as the RN's anti-submarine director pointed out, that "80 per cent of all ships torpedoed in trans-Atlantic convoys in the last two months were hit while being escorted by Canadian groups," the Admiralty also generously acknowledged that "the Canadians have had to bear the brunt of the U-boat attacks in the North Atlantic for the last six months, that is to say, about half of the U-boats operating at sea." It also conceded that the RCN's small ships, manned almost exclusively by reservists, had "put up a good show...immensely to their credit."

The British now offered to the Canadians the use of a group training unit, with facilities being established at Londonderry. While the RCN's most active and important phase of participation in the Battle of the Atlantic was over, its great days in the battle at sea still lay ahead.

RefScs: CCAN 173–74 FDS 140–43 NAR 206–13 TSIAOG 129–31

THE LOW NOTE
NOVEMBER–DECEMBER 1942

*A*s *1942 drew to a close, Canadian ships were still badly under-equipped, although some improvements were in the works. Radar was gradually being installed. Ships were also being fitted with a new weapon known as the Hedgehog, a device that threw explosive charges ahead of the attacking vessel, to strike at a submarine while still maintaining asdic contact.*

These few advantages aside, some bare facts remained: Canadian crews were sorely undertrained due to the RCN's rapid expansion (yet, fortunately, morale was kept at a consistently high level). Eighty per cent of merchant ships hit by U-boats were those escorted by the Canadian Navy. And now, with merchant ships along the eastern seaboard and in the

Caribbean under escort, Donitz had shifted his weight into the mid-Atlantic, testing RCN escorts even further—beyond their capabilities. Nor did it help that 17 RCN corvettes had to be sent to the Mediterranean to assist in North Africa, depleting an already understrength force.

The RCN's predicament came into bitterly clear focus during the five-day battle of SC-107 in November—seven RCN ships and an RN vessel pitted against 17 U-boats. The outcome: one of the worst convoy disasters of the war—15 of 42 merchant ships lost; only one submarine sunk, and that purely by accident.

The debacle brought matters to a head. The RCN was temporarily withdrawn from escort duty until it could be reorganized and retrained. The situation was so serious that the directive had come straight down from the bridge. On December 17, 1942, Mackenzie King, prime minister of Canada, received a message from Winston Churchill:

A careful analysis of our transatlantic convoys has clearly shown that in those cases where heavy losses have occurred, lack of training of the escorts, both individually and as a team, have been responsible for these disasters.

I appreciate the grand contribution of the Royal Canadian Navy in the Battle of the Atlantic, but the expansion of the RCN has created a training problem which must take time to resolve.

MEDITERRANEAN DUTY
NOVEMBER 1942–FEBRUARY 1943

*N*ear the end of October 1942, two giant armadas set sail, *the greatest invasion fleets of the war up to that time. One, made up of 102 ships including 29 troop transports, sailed directly from the United States—its target, Casablanca, in French Morocco on the northwest Atlantic coast. The second left Great Britain 250 merchant ships strong, among them some*

40 troop transports. Its objectives were Algiers and Oran, on the northern Mediterranean coast of Algeria.

Together they comprised Operation Torch, and represented the turning point—from defensive to offensive action—for the western Allies in World War II. The strategy for the landings had been affirmed by Churchill and Roosevelt in July. Their objective was to link up with the British army in the western African desert, bring the North Africa campaign to a close and make the Mediterranean safe for further Allied movements.

Early on the morning of November 8, both in Morocco and along the beaches east and west of Algiers, Canadian landing craft ferried in American and British troops. Initially, the only opposition came from Vichy French forces: mostly snipers, some shore batteries and naval vessels; it was light, and few casualties resulted. In the ensuing week, Canadians continued ferrying in reinforcements and supplies, almost without incident. The flotilla suffered its heaviest casualties when the ships carrying returning and wounded men were torpedoed on the way home.

In addition to the Canadian flotilla, many Canadians serving with the Royal Navy also played an important part in the Torch landings. One of these men—the country's most prominent naval officer and, according to naval historian F.J. Blathewick, "possibly the bravest Canadian"—distinguished himself in a gallant action that won him the Victoria Cross.

Oran Harbour, North Africa
November 8, 1942

PETERS Frederick Thornton

"Hero of 'Finest British Naval Engagement Since Trafalgar'"

To pave the way for a United States 6th Armored Corps landing party, and those American troops to follow, the Royal Navy's objective was to immobilize Oran Harbour and force the surrender of the town itself. That meant capturing or taking out

14 well-armed Vichy French warships, ranging from a heavy cruiser to submarines, in the face of firmly embedded shore batteries. On the plotting table it looked feasible enough, if highly hazardous. In execution, it was almost inviting self-destruction.

If there was one person equal to such an assignment it was Frederick Peters. A native of Charlottetown, P.E.I., "Fritz" Peters had already made his name legend in World War I, winning both the Distinguished Service Order and the Distinguished Service Cross. In World War II he had already accounted for two German submarines in the North Atlantic. Small wonder he had been picked as the perfect candidate to lead such a suicidal mission, with the incongruous designation "Operation Reservist."

The plan called for several motor launches to lay down a smoke screen; *Walney* and *Hartland* (two former US Coast Guard cutters acquired by the RN under the lend-lease agreement) would ram a boom lying across the 200-foot mouth of the harbour, breaking it. Both ships were slow, lightly armoured and mounted with only two 4-inch guns apiece, but—with a lot of luck—they were considered to be up to the task. Once inside the 3,000-yard-long breakwater, with *Hartland* drawing fire, *Walney*, captained by Peters, would steam up to the quay and unload four canoe teams equipped with self-propelled mines—they would take the French warships by surprise, commandeering them. Meanwhile, *Hartland* would secure the jetties and ships near the harbour entrance. Then, with port and vessels in British hands, surrender of the town would be a mere formality—the stuff of which dreams are made.

Allied Intelligence was counting heavily on shaky German-Vichy relations—they may have been love/hate, but they were much stronger than the Americans and British had been led, or wanted, to believe. Expecting, at the most, passive resistance from the French (which was about all they had encountered at Casablanca, Algiers and on the beaches), Oran was another matter—it was *the* key Axis naval port in western North Africa. And, despite an uneasy pro-Nazi allegiance (out of necessity or otherwise), Oran was held by the *French* fleet manned by *French* crews, still smarting from the British sinking of their major battleships in these same waters after the fall of Dunkirk (to prevent them from falling into German hands).

That action in the summer of 1940 had created a friction in Anglo-French relations that would last for a decade. In the meantime, further hostile action by the Royal Navy against the French fleet would be regarded as an affront to the glory of France itself, and by French sailors as *"une affaire d'honneur."* British Intelligence apparently overlooked (or conveniently ignored) the at times frenzied Gallic sense of duty. At any rate, they certainly did not expect the fierce and spirited defence of the harbour they faced from their former ally once the assault was actually underway.

The British seem to have also given short shrift to the matter of timing (perhaps generating from the same illusions that downplayed the possibilities of French resistance). How else can it be explained that Tom Troubridge, the task force commander, had been instructed to give orders for the assault to take place two hours *after* American and British troops had already landed elsewhere, thereby effectively scratching the element of surprise?

As a result, at 2:45 in the morning darkness of November 8, when *Walney* and *Hartland* approached the port (backed by the RN light cruiser *Aurora* and a flotilla of destroyers), a reception committee of alerted French gunners was ready and waiting. Searchlights flooded the two cutters, followed by a flurry of small-arms fire. Peters responded by bellowing *en Français* over the ship's hailer (portable loudspeaker) a demand to surrender.

This served only to ignite and inspire the defenders. Their shore batteries and warships opened up at point-blank range. Nevertheless, at 3:10 a.m., partially screened by smoke and with motor launch outriders on either side, *Walney* broke through the boom, only to be faced by the French destroyer *La Surprise*, desperately trying to break out. Peters tried to ram, but missed. The French sloop raked *Walney* with fire, damaging both engines and massing casualties in dead and wounded. Badly crippled and listing to one side, *Walney* managed to limp further into the harbour, towards *Epervier*, an enemy destroyer that Peters now intended to board and further use to embark his canoe teams.

But his ship was forced to drift through a relentless gauntlet of shell fire and steel—submarines berthed to the north, *Epervier* on the south. *Walney's* boiler room took a direct hit and exploded. Another shell struck the bridge, which burst into flames. Peters was one of only 17 to survive when, wounded in the shoulder and blinded in one eye, he was blown clear of the bridge. *Walney* was a blazing wreck; most of her crew and the landing troops were dead or wounded. Some of the soldiers had found their way above decks to lob hand grenades at the submarines and spray them with small-arms fire. The injured were carried below to the wardroom, but a shell exploded in that confined space, killing them all.

The carnage continued. The ammunitions stores blew up. Depth charges belowdecks were hit and exploded. Half blinded, suffering horribly from the wound in his shoulder, Peters persisted nonetheless. Driving his disabled, virtually unmanned vessel forward into the jetty, he pulled it alongside *Epervier*. As those troops who were still able to disembarked from *Walney*, they came under yet more fire from French gunners.

To help put mooring lines ashore, Peters moved forward, then aft. But, realizing he could never get his cutter berthed, he gave the order to abandon ship. *Walney* drifted away from the pier, explosions detonating from the hold. Finally, with all hands overboard, Peters jumped into the water and swam for shore. Between 9:00 and 10:00 that morning the stricken vessel rolled slowly onto her side and sank, part of her hull protruding from the shallow water, a grim reminder of a gallant battle lost.

Hartland suffered a similar fate. Groping her way through the harbour entrance after *Walney* had shattered the boom, she came under intense shell fire; and once inside, she became the point-blank target of a French destroyer, *Typhon*. A brief broadside brought her to a standstill. Attempts to berth alongside a trawler were in vain and, ablaze from stem to stern, the battered cutter drifted to the centre of the harbour. With no alternative, she anchored, under constant shelling from ships on both sides of the inlet. By 4 a.m. most of those aboard had either been killed or wounded. Survivors abandoned ship as best they could. At dawn, *Hartland* blew up and sank to the bottom.

Casualties were frightful. Between the two ships, 270 men were killed and another 157 wounded; 77 survived and were taken prisoner—among them, Peters.

His feat did not go unrecognized. The United States Army awarded him its Distinguished Service Cross, the highest US decoration awarded to a foreigner, proclaiming his "extraordinary heroism in action." The British awarded Peters the Victoria Cross, the first VC bestowed on a Canadian sailor in World War II. The commendation described his action as "a forlorn hope of the highest gallantry." And, as usual, Winston Churchill had the last word, sanctifying the award by describing the overall action as "the finest British naval engagement since Trafalgar."

But the honour that might have delighted Peters the most came from the French population of Oran. Two days after his capture, Peters was freed from a French prison hospital by Allied troops liberating the town. In the parade that followed, he was borne through the streets on the shoulders of its citizens, hailed with flowers as tribute from a grateful populace.

Frederick Peters didn't live to receive his Victoria Cross officially. He was drowned five days after the Oran raid. A Sunderland flying boat, carrying him back to England, crashed into Plymouth Sound while making its landing approach in dense fog.

Born in 1889, Frederick Peters was the son of the attorney general and first Liberal premier of Prince Edward Island, as well as the grandson of one of the founders of Confederation, John Hamilton Grey. In 1905, at age 16, he joined the Royal Navy as a cadet, the start of a remarkable naval career. Peters spent most of the pre-Great War years with the China Station, aboard gunboats patrolling the Orient to protect British interests.

His bravery was first recognized by the Italians, who decorated him for leading rescue parties to evacuate a populace threatened by the eruption of the Mount Messina volcano, just before the outbreak of World War I.

In 1915, he was awarded the Distinguished Service Order, the first Canadian to receive the honour (and rare for a first lieutenant, a junior officer), for valour aboard HMS *Meteor* in an engagement in which his ship was severely disabled by German naval guns. Later in the war, Peters received the Distinguished Service Cross.

Following the armistice, Peters retired from the RN with the rank of Lieutenant Commander. After stints at various civilian occupations, he took a job on Africa's Gold Coast. When World War II began, he worked his way to England via a steamer and re-enlisted in the British Navy. Within a month he was given command of an anti-submarine flotilla made up of small ships, whalers and trawlers, operating out of the Orkneys and the Shetland Islands off the coast of Scotland. Between October 1939 and June 1940, Peters was credited with sinking two German U-boats and awarded a bar to his DSC.

He was later posted to the Directorate of Naval Intelligence, where he worked with Guy Burgess and Kim Philby who, unbeknownst to him or anyone else at that time, were soon to become the most famous spies/traitors in British history. Then, in 1942, Peters was given the "top secret" assignment of capturing Oran.

Peters's Victoria Cross was never awarded ceremoniously. His family received the Commonwealth's highest decoration for valour through the mail, accompanied by the standard bureaucratic letter of acknowledgement (Peters is the only native of Prince Edward Island to ever receive the honour). On the other hand, Dwight Eisenhower, Supreme Allied Commander in Europe, dispatched two of his senior officers to Nelson, B.C., to formally present Peters's American Distinguished Service Cross to his mother in a private ceremony at her residence.

Peters, who died at the age of 53, has no known grave, but his name appears in the Naval Memorial at Plymouth, England.

VC DSO DSC & Bar DSC (Amer) CAPT Born September 17, 1889 KIA November 13, 1943
RefScs: CVC 174–75 CWMC&F NAC STS 12/91 IL 6/43 TM&ME Vol IV 148 TSOTVC 370–71 VM 174–75

BATTLING THE U-BOATS, MEDITERRANEAN STYLE
JANUARY–FEBRUARY 1943

*G*erman Intelligence had had ample warning of Allied preparations for Torch. They were fully aware of the operation's overall purpose—to clear the Mediterranean. But their calculations had failed to put a finger on the Allies' immediate military objectives. The Wehrmacht believed that landings would take place at Dakar, on the coast of Senegal 1,600 miles south of the American-British convoy routes. And it was to that spot that U-boats were dispatched. The Germans were thus caught completely off-balance when the Allied fleets sailed into their appointed beachheads, securing them quickly and unmolested—and without interference from the sea.

That was mistake number one, a purely tactical one; the next error in judgment had strategic significance. Over Donitz's protestations that the Atlantic represented the win-or-lose battlefront for his U-boats, Hitler responded to Torch in November 1942 by ordering his submarines into the Mediterranean in hopes of fending off the Allied invasion forces. But it was too late. The Americans and British had already established firm footholds inland by the time the submarines arrived and, more significant, their resupply convoys were by this time strongly protected, even though the route stretched from the United Kingdom to Gibraltar, and as far east as Bon, off Tunisia. Meanwhile, the North Atlantic convoys were enjoying what amounted to a milk run.

When the 17 RCN corvettes assigned to the theatre began sailing from Canada in various stages, some to the United Kingdom, others directly to Gibraltar, none of them had any idea where they were heading. Senior officers in charge were just as much in the dark. Everything was hush-hush and in a hurry. To make up the composite, most of the ships had been withdrawn from North Atlantic convoy duty, and the Pacific fleet had been divested of all five of its corvettes. On arrival at their destinations, most of them were refitted with 20-mm guns and *new 10-cm radar sets, with wider range, extended depth vision, better night capability—and they could not be intercepted by the U-boats.*

The corvettes needed all the help they could get. U-boat warfare in the Mediterranean was a different cup of tea than that in the Atlantic. For starters, it was a smaller sea, and the enemy was closer. Escorts were subject to air attack, mostly at dawn and after dark, particularly on moonlit nights (by daylight they enjoyed strong Allied air superiority). The U-boats attacked singly rather than in packs. And they were joined by submarines of the Italian Navy, which multiplied the underwater forces with which the Allies had to cope (of some consolation was their lack of élan compared with their German counterparts).

Although Torch had initially been a walkover, its objectives reached with little or no resistance and footholds quickly established, by January 1943, when the U-boats arrived in the Mediterranean and German reinforcements began pouring into Tunisia from the Italian mainland, it had ceased to be a picnic. Matters quickly settled down into a hard-fought campaign— keeping the Allied supply lines open became crucial work.

90 Miles off Algiers
January 13, 1943

COLEMAN Robert

"Record Time from Contact to Kill"

Prior to sailing for North Africa to take part in Operation Torch, *Ville de Quebec*'s longest sea voyage had been the convoy run between Boston and New York. But she had quickly proved her mettle in her first test under fire. Late in 1942, on her way to the United Kingdom to be refitted with new radar equipment and 20-mm guns before proceeding to Gibraltar for Mediterranean convoy duty, she had taken part in a ferocious fight with German U-boats, distinguishing herself by rescuing 54 survivors from a torpedoed merchant ship. And her finest hour was yet to come.

On the afternoon of January 13, 1943, only days after arriving in the Mediterranean theatre, *Ville de Quebec* was assigned to help escort convoy TE-13, en route from Gibraltar to Algiers. She was mere hours from her destination when the ship's asdic operator made a solid submarine contact off the starboard bow. Captain Robert Coleman gave the order to fire depth charges. Almost simultaneously with their detonation, *U-224* shot to the surface, bow first.

Ville de Quebec's gunners opened fire with the ship's newly acquired Oerlikons as Coleman signalled full speed ahead and turned the corvette to ram. Within two minutes of making contact, *Ville de Quebec* hit the U-boat squarely amidships between the forward gun and the conning tower, throwing *U-224*'s first lieutenant out of the hatch and into the sea. It had all happened so fast that the ship's crew belowdecks were unaware of the success they had helped to score, until they heard *Ville de Quebec*'s hull grinding over the submarine, followed by a numbing blast astern.

The sub tilted upward before the weight of water rushing through two jagged openings in her side dragged her to the bottom. She disappeared from view within four minutes. Something of a record had been established—from contact to kill, only 10 minutes had elapsed. The only survivor was the Number One, who had been thrown clear when the Canadian corvette smashed into his submarine.

In the collision, *Ville de Quebec* had two forward compartments torn open and the asdic dome sheared off—nothing serious enough to prevent her from rejoining the convoy under her own steam. The convoy's merchantmen hailed her conquest with a crescendo of boat whistles in tribute. That was only the start of her elevation to celebrity status.

While the ship was undergoing repairs in Algiers, RCN Chief of Naval Staff Percy Nelles publicly proclaimed *Ville de Quebec*'s victory. The battle-scarred "veteran" then played host to British naval top brass. Among those inspecting the ship's company were such luminaries as Dudley Pound, First Sea Lord and

Admiral of the Fleet; Andrew Cunningham, Commander-in-Chief of the Mediterranean; Louis Mountbatten, Chief of Combined Operations; and John Dill, Chief of the Imperial General Staff.

But the *pièce de résistance* was an inspection by the King and Queen when the pride of the city of Quebec berthed in the United Kingdom in February.

RefScs: CCAN 181–83 FDS 153 TSIAOG 133

North of Bougie, Algeria
January 18, 1943

SIMMONS Edward Theodore

"Crew Shared $1,000 in Victory over Luckless Italian Submarine"

It could be said afterwards that the Italian submarine commander, who met his demise against an experienced Canadian corvette skipper with one German U-boat kill already to his credit, had more guts than brains, and very little luck to go with either. During preliminary tests shortly after she left Cagliari on her first patrol, *Tritone*'s engineering officer determined that her diving gear was not operating properly. He urged his captain to turn back.

The obstinate Italian captain refused. Shortly after dawn the next day, the 950-ton submarine reached its destination off the northern Tunisia coast. Almost immediately, *Tritone* sighted convoy MKS-6, westbound for Gibraltar. Despite being unable to dive effectively, the skipper closed to within 5,000 yards at periscope depth. He should have heeded his E/O's advice—as he readied a torpedo launch, the boat suddenly lost its equilibrium. It sank out of control to 60 feet.

All hell broke loose inside the sub—recriminations, near panic. Though, somehow, the captain managed to bring her back up to periscope depth, her balance was still out of kilter, making it impossible to fire the torpedoes. Ignoring, or perhaps ignorant of, the proficiency of asdic and radar, with a calm sea and visibility at 100 per cent, he decided to press on.

Port Arthur, a convoy escort, picked up an asdic contact at 1,400 yards. The Italian commander could not have met up with a tougher antagonist. Ted Simmons was no stranger to submarine warfare. Back in September 1941, he had headed up the boarding party that spelled the doom of *U-501* during the battle of SC-42. Simmons signalled full speed ahead. As the Canadian corvette closed to within 400 yards, the ship's hydrophone picked up the sound of *Tritone*'s propellers, and Simmons ordered a pattern of 10 depth charges dropped.

They exploded before the submarine could submerge, blowing out *Tritone*'s fuses, damaging the electric motors, fracturing the pressure system pipes and puncturing several fuel tanks. The stricken vessel heeled over and sank sidelong, finally settling at a depth of 400 feet.

To all intents—game over. But, through some quirk of fate, the ear-shattering explosions had failed to damage the submarine's electrical system, usually the first apparatus to break down from the force of concussion. This was not sufficient salvation, however, for *Tritone*'s skipper to want to continue the fight. His bravado and recklessness deserted him—he turned to his engineering officer for help and advice. The answer was direct and simple: surface, surrender and save the crew before the dwindling air supply ran out altogether.

In hindsight, *Tritone* might have been better off to stay submerged. The depth-charge explosions had put *Port Arthur*'s asdic out of business. And, although the British destroyer *Antelope* (which the corvette had summoned for assistance) had already arrived on the scene, she was equally unable to establish contact right away due to the disturbances created by the detonations.

As it happened, *Tritone* came bursting to the surface, and *Antelope* let go from 700 yards with everything she had—4.7-inch guns, Oerlikons, 2-pounder pom-poms—setting the submarine aflame. *Port Arthur* swung about to ram, but abandoned the attempt for fear of getting in *Antelope*'s line of fire. Apparently summoning a second wind, *Tritone*'s captain decided to go out in a blaze of glory. He ordered his crew to man the guns and fire all torpedoes in a last-ditch stand.

But the Italian sailors had had enough. As they began to scramble out of the conning tower hatch to surrender, most of them were killed—the tower took a direct hit from *Antelope*. *Port Arthur* had also opened up but, hearing the enemies' cries for help and seeing the survivors leaping into the sea, Simmons gave the order to cease fire. Minutes later the ill-fated submarine sank out of sight. *Port Arthur* was given credit for sinking *Tritone*, despite *Antelope*'s last-minute participation. Ted Simmons was awarded the Distinguished Service Order, to add to the Distinguished Service Cross he had received for his part in the sinking of *U-501*. But there was a more tangible prize: *Port Arthur*'s crew shared in a purse of $1,000. The sum was subscribed when the ship was commissioned on May 26, 1942, by the citizens of the community after which the ship was named, donated for distribution in the event of its first victory.

RefScs: CCAN 182–87 FDS 153–56 TSIAOG 133

8 Miles off the Algerian Coast, 60 Miles East of Oran February 6, 1943

CAMPBELL William
CORNELL James
MacDONALD Gordon
MERRYWEATHER Hugh
PAIN Ernest
PARKS Budd
TINGLEY Hall
WILLETT James

"First Canadian Warship Lost in Mediterranean—Sunk by Italian Air Force"

It had been a rare evening of serenity for wartime shipping so close to the North African shoreline. Then, just before darkness descended with its usual tropical suddenness, reality abruptly intruded. The tranquility was shattered by the thunder of cannon fire, and the crew of HMCS *Louisburg* spotted gun flashes spouting from HMS *Laforey*, nearly a mile away.

Noisy, but nothing particularly unusual. Firing practice, in all probability. Not worth a second glance. Then three great fountains of water erupted astern of the ship—bombs, dropped by high-flying German bombers. Throughout convoy KMS-8, bound for Bone (Annaba), Algeria with eight Canadian corvettes and two British destroyers, the signal went out—action stations! Full alert!

Screened by the setting sun, three Italian Savoia Marchetti SM-78 torpedo bombers swooped over the Atlas Mountains and flattened out. Crossing the sea at deck level, they singled out *Louisburg* for attack. Their tactics, timing and accuracy were phenomenal.

Warning came from the ship's crow's nest too late. The Oerlikons were rendered useless in any case—their 20-mm cannon couldn't be lowered below the guardrails, and the *Regio Aeronautica* bombers, with perfect precision, flew just below that level as they zeroed in. One Savoia bombardier released his torpedo—it splashed into the water, aimed directly amidships.

The plane banked across the corvette's bow, giving the gunners one fleeting, clear, close shot—the tracers sped well wide of the mark. At that instant, the torpedo exploded, with a blinding flash and bellowing roar. Flames and smoke billowed from the ship's innards, blasting out the engine-room's skylights—steam seared its way across the deck, scorching everything and scalding everyone in its path.

Broken in two, the ship filled quickly. First the bow lurched upwards, then the stern. On the bridge and amid the chaos, *Louisburg*'s captain, William Campbell, calmly gave the order to abandon ship. By that time, most of those who were able had already jumped overboard or grabbed onto a Carley raft. Others had been blown off their feet; some, like most of those in the engine room where the torpedo exploded, had been killed where they stood or were immediately drowned.

There was no time to man lifeboats. *Louisburg* sank fast, going under in less than four minutes. The carnage didn't end there. Under water, the boilers blew up. Then the depth charges, pre-set to detonate at shallow depths, erupted. Some 40 crew members perished, among them the ship's captain. And though 50 miraculously survived the torpedoing, some died of their injuries several days later.

Budd Parks had been thrown into the air by the explosion. He tumbled down a ladder from the bridge deck to the deck below, banging his head against a steel ammunition locker. With several others, he managed to unhitch a Carley float—it got away from him when he jumped into the water. After swimming through the oil-drenched sea, he reached the raft, and was later rescued by the British destroyer *Lookout*.

Another survivor picked out of the water by the British ship was Ernie Pain. He had been knocked unconscious by the torpedo's blast. He came to, tangled in the ropes of the mast. He'd been unable to free himself before the ship hauled him down with her. He was lucky—he was blown to the surface when the boilers exploded. Swimming desperately to avoid being sucked down by the ship's vortex, he swallowed so much oil and salt water he was sick for a week. But, seeing others dying of bends on *Lookout*'s mess-deck tables, Pain considered himself fortunate.

Gordon MacDonald was standing behind the ship's 4-inch gun; he was hoisting a shell onto his shoulder when the torpedo struck, and he was still holding the charge when he was slammed to the deck. Struggling to his feet, he ran for the lifeboats—by the time he got there he was knee-deep in water. The ship was sinking, and MacDonald with it. Then, like Pain, he was suddenly blown clear by an underwater detonation. He found himself only feet away from a Carley float. It wasn't until he was taken aboard *Lookout* that he realized his shoulder had been broken when he hit the deck.

For gunnery officer Hall Tingley it was another story: he knew damned good and well he was injured from the word go. Directing the Oerlikons' cannon fire from the "bandstand," he was standing directly over the engine room when it was blasted.

Tingley was thrown "arse over teakettle," breaking a knee joint and cracking a heel bone. He pulled himself upright, nevertheless, and spying a Carley float 100 yards distant he dived into the sea. Though at that point the damage to his leg was of secondary consideration, it was far more serious than he had realized. Tingley recuperated for a month in a British army field hospital in Algiers.

James Cornell, a sick-bay attendant, was the last to scramble up from belowdecks, which were completely awash by the time he reached the main deck. He was also the last man to see his captain alive. Literally running into Campbell, the able seaman assured him that no one remained belowdecks. The captain insisted on having a final look for himself, and wasn't seen again.

Cornell made it over the side, and was another of *Louisburg*'s crewmen delivered from a date with Davey Jones's locker because of the underwater explosions. He was a strong swimmer, but the pull of the sinking vessel was still too much for Cornell; it kept sucking him under. Lungs bursting, resigned to being a goner and about to pack it in by gulping a final "breath" of sea water, he was suddenly propelled back to the surface. Cornell was rescued, hanging onto a piece of matting blown from the ship, after four hours in the oily water and darkness.

Jim Willett owed his life to Hugh Merryweather, who had given up his life preserver to save his shipmate. Both Willett and Merryweather were sucked under when *Louisburg* sank. Willett lived to tell his tale; the explosions had lifted him back from the depths. Merryweather was never seen again. The blast fractured Willett's skull and deafened him. He spent the rest of the night in the sea; in the morning he and several others were picked up by a Royal Air Force flying boat.

On their return to Canada, *Louisburg*'s survivors were rich in their praise for the crew of *Lookout*. Though the British crew was unable to provide the bedraggled Canadian seamen with fresh uniforms, they'd given up their underwear to clothe them. And they'd done their best to tend the wounded, and feed them all with limited rations aboard. To reward the British jack tars for their hospitality, *Louisburg*'s survivors sent them the ship's remaining canteen fund, amounting to a couple thousand dollars.

RefScs: CCAN 183–90 FDS 156–57 TSIAOG 133

North of Philippeville, Algeria
February 8, 1943

FREELAND Harold

"Night Duel Ends in Italian Sub's Surrender"

The Canadian corvette *Regina*, a Royal Navy minesweeper and two merchant ships made up the second section of convoy KMS-8, plodding east from Gibraltar to Bône. It was nearing midnight when *Regina*'s radar operator noticed a faint blip on his screen, indicating a submarine three and a half miles away.

Though skipper Harry Freeland altered course immediately, the radar image disappeared. In almost the same breath, however, asdic picked up a contact 1,000 yards dead ahead. Lookouts sighted the foamy wake of a surfaced vessel—the Italian submarine *Avorio*, cruising at seven knots to recharge its batteries. *Regina* chased at full speed; the quarry dived fast and the corvette dropped a 10-pack depth-charge pattern. Freeland circled impatiently for an agonizing 10 minutes. He need not have fretted—*Regina*'s charges had done their work well.

The blasts blew holes in the ballast tanks and jammed the submarine's steering gear. A portion of her bow had split open, and the forward torpedo tubes were out of action. The magazine where the scuttle charges were stored was swamped. On deck, the chief surface armament, *Avorio*'s 3.9-inch gun, had been rendered *hors de combat*. The Italian commander had little choice other than to surface his battered 600-ton craft and fight it out as best he could.

The opening round went to *Regina*, whose 4-inch gun scored a direct hit at the base of the conning tower, killing the captain, his first lieutenant and navigator, along with 16 of the crew. Rather than raising their hands in surrender, the remainder of the crew fought back gamely. Limited to awkward S-turns due to the damage to her steering, and lacking a cannon, the Italians had to content themselves with spraying the bridge and wheelhouse of the zigzagging corvette with machine guns and rifles.

Though sporadic and comparatively weak in the face of *Regina*'s firepower, their resistance was lethal and formidable enough to keep a few heads down. But, in the end, it was really no contest, and it was over in minutes. *Regina* had fired eight shells from her 4-inch gun, 20 rounds from the pom-poms and 635 20-mm shells, all to deadly effect. After a 15-minute search to make sure no other submarines were lurking about, Freeland dispatched a boarding party to pick up prisoners and assess damage, with an eye to possibly salvaging the craft. The report came back that, while the sub was sinking slowly and steadily, it was still navigable, although not under its own power.

Regina's radar had been wrecked by the depth-charge blasts. Freeland didn't dare risk taking the sub in tow for fear of possible further submarine attacks. He therefore requested a tug be sent from the nearest port to tackle the job under his ship's protection. Around 4:00 a.m., *Jaunty* arrived, albeit grudgingly.

Within an hour, the submarine had swallowed so much water the tug had slowed to a crawl. Without warning, *Jaunty*'s crew cut the tow line—the boarding party was marooned on *Avorio*'s upper deck, in water up to their knees. They shouted for help. Without replying, the tug chugged away, happy to be making its exit from the danger zone, and apparently content to be leaving the boarding party to fend for themselves. *Regina* launched a lifeboat. As Alexander and his mates clambered aboard, in a final *gesto magnifico*, *Avorio*'s bow rose straight up, and the vessel sank below the surface.

Postscript: Many World War II warships carried the names of Canadian cities and towns. Few who served on those ships had ever seen (and some had never heard of) the places for which their vessels were commissioned. By the same token, it was often the case that most citizens of those same communities had never seen the sea—let alone a battleship—other than through newspapers and film clips.

Yet, a deep and warmhearted affinity developed between those at sea and those ashore sharing that loose but common bond. Men aboard the ships welcomed and were heartened by the encouragement and kindnesses of the citizens for whom they served and the occasional gifts of knitted sweaters and socks, cigarettes, candies and cakes. The sailors responded to the best of their ability with letters, postcards, photos and visits while on shore leave. In turn again, "their" communities took a fierce pride in the achievements of the crews who served them.

The sinking of *Avorio* serves as an example. Following official announcement of the victory, the mayor of Regina wired a telegram to Captain Harry Freeland. It read:

> Citizens of Regina very proud corvette named after our city. Please convey to officers and crew our congratulations and hope this is the first of many similar victories. Good hunting and a safe return to port.

RefScs: CCAN 190–93 FDS 157–58 TSIAOG 133

Gibraltar, 7 Miles from Cap Spartel
February 22, 1943

GARRARD William
GOLBY Thomas

"Operation Sheer Guts"

To this day there lies in the annals of the Royal Canadian Navy a tragic sense of irony regarding the manner in which *Weyburn* met her doom, leaving in her swell a display of intestinal fortitude seldom, if ever, seen in maritime history. It seems a cruel twist of fate that the prairie-sponsored corvette, commissioned on November 26, 1941, came to such an untimely end. Having first met the enemy during the summer of 1942 in the Gulf of St. Lawrence, then weathering the tense, turbulent convoy runs in the Mediterranean, besieged by submarines and torpedo boats, and subjected to air raids, she came to grief when she struck a mine leaving the port of Gibraltar en route to the UK.

She had set sail late and, in an effort to catch up with convoy MKS-8, Tom Golby, *Weyburn*'s captain, had ordered full speed ahead. His ship was just pulling into her escort position when she struck the mine on her port side, exploding amidships. The blast tore a hole that buckled the deck, split the funnel in two and flooded the engine room.

Steam pipes burst. Metal and wood flew in all directions. The situation was catastrophic, and it might have gotten a lot worse had it not been for the cool presence of mind of an officer and rating who removed the firing pins from depth charges gnarled in the upheaval. Still, two of the explosives were so badly jammed in the wreckage it proved impossible to yank the detonators free.

The ship was listing badly, yet it gave no indication of being in immediate danger of sinking, and those of the crew who had survived the shock were already preparing her to be taken in tow. Shielded by a sloop from the convoy escort, British destroyer *Wivern* pulled alongside to take off the wounded and pick up survivors in the water. In the transfer, William "Hip" Garrard, who had emerged otherwise unscathed from the disaster so far, severely mangled a foot and ankle between ships. Though in agony, he made it to the safety of the rescue vessel.

Twenty minutes had elapsed since *Weyburn* collided with the mine, and all seemed comparatively shipshape for the badly damaged corvette, when she suddenly lost her stability. The bow reared up, and with fearful finality, the stern plunged down. In only seconds the entire ship went under, taking Tom Golby, the skipper, and all those on the bridge with her. The two depth charges still set in "fire" mode exploded only moments apart.

Wivern's medical officer, who had been trying to transform the mess decks into a makeshift operating theatre, was blown off his feet and had both ankles broken. The chaos created by the detonations now made that venue untenable. The wardroom—cramped, narrow and definitely a poor second choice—had to make do. But, with the ship's M/O incapacitated, it was the surgery itself that demanded the maximum degree of improvisation.

Unable to stand and throbbing with excruciating pain, the ship's doctor had no alternative but to lie back on a bunk and deliver instructions to his sick-bay attendant on the intricacies of wielding a scalpel while, to their everlasting credit, a random selection of deckhands carried out his subsidiary orders to the letter—bandaging, cleaning, stitching.

At his own insistence, "Hip" Garrard's turn came last. For half an hour, his mangled leg torturing him, he had refused treatment until all his men had been attended to. He then wrestled his way aboard the operating table and, in lieu of anaesthetic, received a stiff shot of 110-proof Pusser rum, normally guaranteed to tear the guts out of even the saltiest guzzler to go before the mast. Not so *Weyburn*'s indomitable Number One—it only hardened an already obstinate resolve, and lent an inebriant euphoria to fortify him somewhat against the agony and the apprehension of having a leg chopped off by an amateur apprentice guided by a disabled mentor.

Fortuitously, Garrard's alcohol-induced sense of well-being worked two ways. Besides bolstering his courage, it also reinforced his qualities as a leader and his understanding of human nature. Before succumbing to semi-consciousness, Garrard—admittedly, in his own best interest—wanted to put the fledgling surgeon and his pain-riddled tutor as much at ease as possible. Prepared to go under the knife, grinning through gritted teeth, he gave the order: "Hack away, boys! It's all yours!"

British officers witnessing the scene called it "a magnificent example of sheer guts." One, in fact, that made Garrard's name an RCN legend in his own lifetime.

Sixty-eight crew members survived *Weyburn*'s demise. There were 11 fatalities, the last combat casualties suffered by the Canadian Navy during Operation Torch. By March, 1943, the

North African campaign had finally stabilized. One by one, the 17 RCN corvettes in the theatre were withdrawn for duty elsewhere, chiefly for convoy duty in the North Atlantic.

RefScs: CCAN 193–94 FDS 158–60 TSIAOG 133–34

GIVE & TAKE, "MAN & CHEER" 1943

1943—the year the Allies overcame the U-boat menace. Not only was it fitting and timely that the Royal Canadian Navy should at last come of age—it was no accident. Even with the limitations imposed upon her by circumstance—inferior equipment, untrained personnel, organizational problems and a multifarious jumble of RCN, RN and USN commands—she had performed admirably.

The problem of inexperienced crews was overcome in short order. Even as Churchill was issuing his order to withdraw Canadian escorts in December 1942, an intensive training program was being instituted by the Royal Navy and implemented at Londonderry.

The RCN had stuck to her guns—not only at sea, but across the conference table as well. By the early part of the new year, 48 per cent of all escorts assigned to North Atlantic convoys were Canadian, and she had every right to show her colours. The RCN deserved and demanded unilateral control over her own destiny, in her own sphere of operations—and she got it. On May 30, Leonard Murray was named Commander-in-Chief Canadian North West Atlantic, the only Canadian ever to command a naval theatre in wartime.

At sea, the Battle of the Atlantic had been neither quick nor easy, nor without cost. It had evolved into a drawn-out seesaw, a titanic tug-of-war that, during the first four months of 1943, could have been lost to the Allies at almost any given time. At one point, in fact, the feasibility of dropping the convoy system altogether came under serious consideration.

The conflict called for all the strength, the resources, ingenuity and integrity that either side could muster, in what each knew was an ultimate life-or-death struggle. New methods, equipment, weapons and countermeasures brought anti-submarine warfare to a highly scientific and sophisticated state of the art.

In January, round one went to the Kriegsmarine *when Hitler fired Erich Raeder as Commander-in-Chief, replacing him with Karl Donitz—heart and soul, a submariner. Now the U-boat took priority at sea and in the shipyards. In any case, Donitz already had 400 submarines available, 40 of which were roving the Atlantic. And vicious, turbulent weather—the worst of the war so far—favoured them that winter. While their crews were no more comfortable than those manning surface ships, the con-voys were so split up by storms and gales it made escort protection almost impossible. In January and February 141 merchant ships were lost. Apart from the U-boats, the elements themselves caused plenty of damage. In January alone, four merchant ships went aground, 18 foundered and 40 needed extensive repairs.*

Then, on March 1, the Germans introduced a new signal code that took British Intelligence three weeks to crack. Another setback, and a critical one. During this period the wolf packs scored their greatest successes—97 merchantmen sunk. Twenty per cent of the merchant ships that sailed the Atlantic in con-voys—one in five—never reached their destination: the highest interception and loss ratio of the war. To make matters worse, during those same three weeks, foul weather severely restricted air support as well. Truly the winter of discontent—at sea, and over it—for the Allies.

Now for some good news! By March, several developments were in the offing that, along with a change in the weather and a break in the German cipher code, were about to spell a change in fortune.

The first of these developments involved a change in tactics. Basically the role of the escorts was a defensive one. But pro-tection in and of itself could never beat the U-boats. Without some sort of threat of attack, the Battle of the Atlantic could well be lost. Fast ships were needed, fast enough to skirt around the outer fringes of the convoys, intercepting submarines before they could penetrate the escort screen.

By late March, five such "Support Groups"—in effect, strike forces—had been formed and deployed. Each group consisted of five or more destroyers with (to all intents) a roaming commission. In concert with the escorts they made an ideal anti-U-boat partnership. The Royal Navy took on the responsibility of search-and-sink, to work in tandem with the RCN's role of detect-and-defend (although it should be noted that Canadian destroyers did work within RN squads and, later, two solely Canadian support groups were commissioned). Augmenting this already effective combination, merchant and USN aircraft carriers lent still further potency to both defensive and offensive functions (the need for aerial reconnaissance and support was so critical that space was cleared on some merchant vessels to accommodate float-plane launches).

By May, the United States had provided the RCAF with 40 long-range, 4-engine Liberators, operating out of Newfoundland, Labrador and the Maritimes. In addition, the RCAF had six squadrons flying out of the British Isles, and American aircraft were flying from Iceland and the eastern seaboard. By the end of the month, the Greenland air gap—the notorious Black Pit—was closed.

And there was another big plus as well. For attack and escort vessels, a revolutionary refinement in sub-killing had been introduced—an innovation known as the Hedgehog. It was a contraption that resembled a forward-bent metallic sprout of broccoli, and it completely reversed the traditional method of laying depth charges. The main drawback had been the temporary loss of asdic contact as the attacking ship passed over a U-boat, dropping its charges astern. The new device, positioned forward of the bridge, threw 65-pound bombs 230 yards ahead of the ship—24 charges, spaced 12 feet apart, in a prescribed circle 100 feet in diameter. It changed the entire attack procedure—with disastrous results for the attacked.

But the Germans were not lacking ingenuity in the destruction department either, and, until a countermeasure was devised, their acoustic torpedo was anathema to Allied surface vessels. The "Gnat," as it was aptly named, put an end to aiming—a U-boat could even launch it from abeam of the intended target and the missile would home in on the sound of the ship's propellers.

Fortunately, within weeks a counterdevice was developed. Known as the "Cat Gear" (for Canadian Anti-Torpedo), it consisted of two large metal noisemakers towed a safe distance behind the ship. It drew the Gnats away from the propellers, detonating them out of harm's way.

Gradually the Allies were gaining the upper hand. In May, 47 U-boats were sunk (as opposed to 18 in February). With the air gap closed, convoys could now sail the shortest, fastest routes. By September the wolf packs were making their last concerted effort—even then, the merchant ships steamed on, unmolested for the most part. Then, in October, Portugal granted the Royal Air Force use of its bases in the Azores—une pièce de résistance—effectively allowing the air umbrella to be spread over the last unprotected segment of the Atlantic battlefield.

During 1943, the tallies were at last favouring the Allies. Losses in shipping were reduced to 800,000 tons, and construction exceeded losses by 10 million tons. The Germans lost 237 U-boats that year. Statistically, a submariner was lucky to survive three patrols. It had taken over four years—but, in the longest, fiercest battle ever fought at sea, the submarine threat to the East-West lifeline had finally been bested.

Even so, the U-boat fleet was by no means beaten; it was, in fact, still very much alive and kicking. Germany was producing larger and faster submarines, and they could stay at sea longer than ever, thanks to the introduction of the Schnorkel (snorkel). A periscope-like device, the Schnorkel allowed a submarine to take in air without surfacing, thereby reducing the risk of detection. And so the U-boats continued to harass convoys (short of putting them in any real peril) from as far north as Murmansk,

*to the Mediterranean in the south, and west to the Gulf of St.
Lawrence. However subdued, the* Kriegsmarine *was scarcely
ready to cry "Kamarade!"* *

*But for the Allies, nothing could shake the assertion that
1943 represented victory in the Atlantic theatre. And it was a
victory in which Canada had played a remarkable part for her
size and resources. The role of RCAF planes in providing air
coverage was a dominating influence. And, by year's end, the
RCN loomed as a formidable force among world navies. From a
niggardly 13 vessels and fewer than 2,000 personnel at the outbreak of war, Canada now stood on line with 306 operational
ships of war, 71,549 men and 4,453 women, at sea and ashore.
And it had fought against the Axis in every combat theatre.*

*In the best naval tradition, it was perhaps a proper moment
for a "manning and cheering" celebration—though not quite
yet the time to "splice the main brace!" For even greater days
lay ahead. To add to its other achievements, the Royal
Canadian Navy would, by year's end, become the primary
guardian to the convoys crossing the Atlantic. It was a lonely
and thankless task, carried out under the most gruelling and
inhumane conditions, and often at fearful risk.*

Mid-Atlantic
May 12–15, 1943

PICKARD Anthony Frederick

"First Coordinated Air-Escort-Hedgehog Victory"

By May 1943, convoy protection had grown into a sophisticated, multi-source enterprise, combining shore- and
carrier-based aircraft with close-escort and support-group
seacraft. And it was paying off. Convoy HX-237 had left New
York on the first day of the month. On May 5, a close escort,

---

* A German colloquialism for "We give up!"

including Canadian corvettes *Chambly*, *Drumheller* and *Morden*, was having difficulty finding the mid-ocean meeting point due to intermittent fog. An aircraft from the American escort carrier *Biter* found the ships and homed them in on the convoy. And that was but a foretaste.

Whenever the fog cleared out, long-range Liberators were patrolling the seas along the convoy route. On the ocean surface (around and about, but out of sight of the convoy), the support group was constantly on the hunt for the enemy. On May 12, a Liberator sank a U-boat. Two days later, a bomber sent a second submarine to the bottom and attacked five others. This was a new experience for the merchantmen—here they were, the centre of the action and the real enemy target, yet blissfully unaware of the battles raging around them.

Then at dusk on May 15, *Chambly*, captained by Anthony "Hank" Pickard, spotted a U-boat and gave chase, but she was no match for the speed of her quarry. Before the change in convoy tactics, that might well have been the end of the affair. But now *Biter* dispatched one of its Wildcats to take up the pursuit. Spotting the submarine, it attacked with depth charges in the face of heavy anti-aircraft fire. The U-boat quickly dived. The Wildcat dropped a marker, then circled the area until *Chambly* arrived on the scene. *Chambly* held an asdic fix and waited for the support group to take over.

What occurred next was a breakthrough attack on a submarine. Instead of depth charges, the British destroyers opened fired with their Hedgehogs. The result was awesome. After 16 seconds, an enormous explosion erupted, spewing oil, wreckage, bits of flesh and clothing—an emphatic kill, and a turning point in safeguarding the convoys.

RefScs: FDS 172–74 TSIAOG 140–41

Mid-Atlantic
May 17, 1943

DENNY Leslie Permain

"Second Score for the Multi-Escort and Hedgehog"

As HX-237 proceeded to its destination, a straggler from the convoy fell victim to a torpedo. *Drumheller*, captained by Leslie Denny, had pulled 15 survivors out of the water when a Sunderland flying boat began circling above. It signalled by Very light that the corvette was almost on top of a submarine. It took only 10 minutes to establish a visual contact, by which time the U-boat was running away at top speed.

A brief donnybrook broke out—the *Sunderland*, a suddenly arrived Wildcat from the carrier *Biter*, and the Canadian corvette closed in. As *Drumheller* opened fire the U-boat crash-dived. *Drumheller* obtained a quick asdic contact and dropped depth charges. Denny then regained a fix in time to guide a British frigate into position for a Hedgehog attack.

The sea erupted with a devastating roar, churning up the normal evidence of a kill, along with an immense bubble—60 feet in diameter—rising from the submarine's shattered pressure tanks. Chalk up another win for the new teamwork approach to U-boat control.

RefScs: FDS 174.75 TSIAOG 141

Mid-Atlantic
September 19–23, 1943

DOBSON Andrew Hedley
RANKIN Angus
TURNER William

"'Battle of Battles'—the Last Major Wolf Pack Attack"

Relying on a new "secret weapon," Donitz launched his "battle of battles" in mid-September, a fresh U-boat offensive calculated to regain the *Kriegsmarine*'s North Atlantic supremacy. The success of that "secret weapon"—the acoustic torpedo—was, in fact, short-lived. And while the four-day struggle between German submarines and two convoys was costly—four escort vessels and seven merchant ships lost—the losses were much lower than those suffered in earlier engagements. In fact, Donitz's "battle of battles" would be the last major wolf pack attack of the war.

The Allied plan was to merge two convoys, a combined assemblage of 63 merchant ships, in mid-ocean. ONS-18, a slow flotilla, left the United Kingdom on September 12. By the 19th, ON-202, a fast group, had begun to catch up. A newly formed Canadian support group was on its way to reinforce ONS-18's close escort. It was made up of the destroyers *St. Croix* and *St. Francis*, and corvettes *Chambly*, *Morden* and *Sackville*, along with the British frigate *Itchen*.

As the convoys closed their gap a day later, the escorts were picking up U-boat signals. There was no doubt they were gathering in large numbers, maneuvering into position for a night attack. As darkness fell, the convoys had yet to form into a cohesive unit; the merchant ships were spread out in such disarray it was impossible for the escorts to properly organize.

The U-boats moved in, but they made only two minor attacks on merchant ships—their main focus was the escorts. Making her way back to contact the support group, *Lagan*, an ONS-18 escort, sighted a sub on the surface and gave chase. But as the British frigate prepared to close in, a torpedo from another U-boat blew away a 30-foot section of her stern.

Meanwhile, *St. Croix* had detached herself from the support group to investigate an aircraft sighting. Commissioned three years earlier, under the spirited command of Andy Dobson, she had sunk two submarines. The acoustic torpedo held no respect for age or achievement, however. Two missiles struck from behind. *St. Croix* listed immediately and uncontrollably. Dobson gave the order to abandon ship. He then signalled *Itchen*: "Am leaving the office."

He didn't make it. Seconds later, a third electronically directed "Gnat" struck astern of the ship. There was a tremendous explosion, flames shot into the air, and within three minutes the destroyer sank, taking with her the captain and all aboard.

Forced to choose between picking up survivors or hunting down the U-boats, *Itchen* opted for the latter. She signalled *Polyanthus* (from the ONS-18 escort) to take on the rescue work. But the British corvette never arrived. She too fell victim to the "secret weapon." It blew a hole in her stern and she went down, leaving a sole survivor.

In the foggy daylight of September 21, *Itchen* picked up *St. Croix*'s crewmen, who had somehow managed to stay alive in the freezing water for 13 hours, as well as *Polyanthus'* solitary survivor. It was a rescue that proved to be ironic, with a fateful turn of events.

That night the U-boats renewed their attack, making nine assaults. Even though one was rammed and sunk, and two were hit by gunfire, something of their old vigour had returned. After another foggy day, the night of September 22 was ideal for the subs—black and clear, with a low ceiling. At 11:30, *Morden*, captained by Bill Turner, sighted a surfaced U-boat and shot off a star shell for illumination. *Itchen*, in the vanguard of the pursuers, switched on her searchlight, revealing the U-boat 300 yards dead ahead.

She had just opened fire with her Oerlikons when an acoustic torpedo smashed into her from astern. *Itchen* exploded with an ear-splitting roar, then vanished into the sea. Three men were picked out of the water—one seaman from *Itchen*, another from *St. Croix*, and the lone survivor from *Polyanthus*.

By morning the U-boats were finally driven off by RCAF Liberators from Newfoundland. While searching for survivors, *Sackville* did establish a radar contact—a surfaced sub. As she closed in she let go with her 4-inch gun, but the submarine quickly dived out of sight. Captain Gus Rankin ordered depth charges dropped, then turned to make a second run just as the charges exploded. The concussion rocked the corvette, shook rivets loose in the hull and cracked a boiler. On reflection, Rankin was certain it was a torpedo that had been detonated by his depth charges, not the submarine itself, which he was sure had escaped.

The existence of a new acoustic weapon had been clear to the Allies for some time. But its exact nature and impact had remained a mystery until these attacks on the double convoy. In the post-mortem, a salient fact stood out. All four escort vessels had been hit astern—normally, the easiest, surest, most logical attack posture was from abeam. The answer was apparent—the torpedoes homed in on the propellers. An antidote—the Cat Gear, dragged behind to lure the Gnats away from the props—was quickly fashioned. Donitz's new Excalibur had been snapped off at the hilt.

RefScs: FDS 179–81 TSIAOG 149–50

BATTLES IN THE BAY
JULY–DECEMBER 1943

While the bitter U-boat battles were being fought in the mid-Atlantic, another war was being waged in the flat Bay of Biscay—north of Spain, off the west coast of France. Here, in a generally calmer climate, Allied naval forces played a multiple role. Their first objective, protect the convoys shuttling between Great Britain and Gibraltar. Second, smash submarine flotillas setting out to sea from their bases at Brest, Lorient, Le Palais, St. Nazaire, La Rochelle and Bordeaux. Third, attack German shipping supplying the coastal garrisons, thereby forcing the enemy to use more road and rail traffic, which are highly susceptible to aerial harassment.

Another exercise, albeit a disagreeable one, was to clear the bay of Spanish fishing ships. It was strongly suspected that these "neutrals" often acted as lookouts for German submarines. The orders stated: remove the fishermen and sink the vessels.

Though, relatively speaking, sailing conditions were less inclement in the Bay than in the North Atlantic, the risks were to some extent even greater. In addition to the ever-present U-boat threat, powerful Elbing and Narvik class destroyers were lurking in the French coastal ports. Proximity to France meant enemy air attacks were a constant threat. Long-range, four-engine Focke-Wulf Kondors were a daily menace. Allied ships were also within range of speedy German tactical bombers—Dornier 215s and Junkers 88s. These twin-engine aircraft subjected their victims to an eerie new weapon the sailors nicknamed "Chase-Me-Charlies"—radio-directed glider bombs, launched from the bellies of the Dorniers.

Over the full course of 1943, the Allied navies managed to successfully meet their objectives on all three accounts. And, by early 1944, a protective umbrella of heavy and medium Allied bombers blanketed the length and width of the Bay.

300 Miles West of Portugal
July 19, 1943

HOLMS William

"Tribal Baptism by Fire"

On July 9, *Iroquois* set sail for Gibraltar from Plymouth harbour, part of an escort to three troop carriers—*California, Duchess of York* and *Port Fairey*. The Canadian vessel was the first of the new, formidable, heavily armed Tribal class of destroyers emerging from the Dominion's shipyards.

Manned by a crew of 300, *Iroquois* bristled with firepower. Fitted with six 4.7-inch guns in twin mountings, two high-angle 4-inch anti-aircraft guns, a quadruple-pom-pom gun, six 20-mm Oerlikon cannon and four torpedo tubes, she was also equipped with the latest in radar-controlled naval gunnery.

Two days out of port, at 8:30 p.m., a Focke-Wulf Kondor was sighted, shadowing the convoy just out of firing range. Half an hour passed; two more Kondors appeared, and all three fell into attack formation. As the first bomber swept in from down sun and down wind, it was met with a fierce barrage of fire from the five escorts and three troop vessels—not enough to prevent it from hitting *Duchess of York* squarely with two bombs, setting her ablaze.

The second attack followed the first by four minutes, and was just as successful. The target was *California*, and she erupted in flames and smoke after being bracketed by a stick of bombs. Now it was *Port Fairey*'s turn. She was luckier—the explosives fell short by a narrow margin.

One Kondor pilot now turned his attention to *Duchess of York*, intending to polish her off. The other two concentrated on *Iroquois*. But a fusillade from her 4-inch ack-ack and pom-pom guns drove the first bomber away and so upset the aim of the second that its bomb load fell harmlessly, 200 yards short of the destroyer.

The bombers retreated. Shepherded by two British escorts, *Port Fairey* proceeded to Casablanca. *Iroquois* and two other destroyers took aboard survivors from *California* and *Duchess of York*—the troop carriers were hopelessly aflame. Nearly 600 personnel (all but 57) were saved. The crew of *Iroquois* had acquitted themselves nobly. They deserved the highest praise. Instead, any such notion was dashed by subsequent events, provoked in part by the destroyer's captain, Bill "Scarface" Holms, and his militant disdain, if not utter disregard, for the sensitivities of his men.

On the return voyage to Plymouth, *Iroquois* picked up three survivors of a U-boat sunk the day before, one of them an officer. While their oil-saturated uniforms were being laundered, someone pinched the badge from the officer's tunic. Obviously the handiwork of an eager souvenir hunter, it was nevertheless a breach of the Geneva Convention. The German *leutnant*, only too well aware of his rights, demanded not only the return of his emblem, but that the perpetrator of the "crime" be caught and punished.

Ignoring the fact that the ship's company had just survived a gruelling and dangerous mission and that, after a short stay in port, they were about to go back into action, Holms chose to go by the book. He cancelled all shore leave, pending the return of the missing emblem. After several days, the badge had still not been produced; with orders to sail the night of July 19, that same morning the crew refused to report for duty.

Again, by the book, this was mutiny. In reality, it was more a protest. In any event, an already nasty confrontation was "fortuitously" averted from advancing further when Holms suffered a heart attack and had to be taken ashore. His first lieutenant was placed in temporary command.

That evening, the unpleasantness behind her, *Iroquois* set sail with a sister ship, *Athabaskan* (the second Tribal class destroyer built in Canada), to cover a support group in the Bay.

Refscs: FDS 188–93 TSIAOG 157

25 Miles off the Northwest Coast of Spain
August 24–28, 1943

MILES George Ralph
O'BRIEN Barry

"Introduction of the 'Chase-Me-Charlie'"

Shortly after 10:00 on the morning of August 24, a boarding party from the corvette *Snowberry* had finished checking out two Spanish freighters—possible blockade runners—when a Focke-Wulf Kondor, which had been circling warily over support group EG-5, decided to take a closer look.

Snowberry let fly with her 20-mm Oerlikons. *Landguard*, a Royal Navy destroyer from the same group, joined in with heavier armament. Neither vessel did any damage, but the brief action was a portent of things to come. That afternoon and evening, and early the next day, flights of Focke-Wulfs kept constant watch on EG-5, which, in addition to *Snowberry* and *Landguard*, included another Canadian corvette, *Edmundston*, two more RN destroyers and two British frigates, *Nene* and *Tweed*. The aircraft stayed well out of harm's way and, without mounting a direct threat, they nevertheless forced the seagoing crews to remain on continuous alert.

At 1:30 p.m. on the 25th, an American Liberator, making towards Gibraltar, popped out of the clouds to telegraph a brief alert: "21 enemy planes heading this way," and then climbed back into the overcast. Twelve minutes later the marauders loomed dead ahead at 4,000 feet—seven Dornier 217s and 14 Junkers 88s.

The naval gun crews readied themselves for a dive-bombing attack, while the German aircraft split into seven formations— each bomber flanked by two Junkers escorts. They swept to the starboard side of the group, then turned in towards the ships as if to make a low-level attack abeam. But no—this was something entirely new. Crossing over to port, they flew a course parallel to the ships for several minutes. Suddenly small gliders, approximately eight feet long with eight-foot wingspans, dropped from the bellies of the Dorniers. They shot forward 200 feet, leaving white vapour trails behind them.

As the gunners opened fire, the missiles banked sharply in towards the vessels—and then dived, at over 400 miles an hour. By now there was no mistaking—these were flying bombs! The ships took immediate and violent evasive action, but no matter how strenuously they fishtailed, the missiles, controlled by radio from the Dorniers, followed. It was as if they were being reeled in on a fast line—a capability that, right there on the spot, earned them the nickname "Chase-Me-Charlies."

This introduction of the 500-pound glider bomb was far from successful, however. In their first test under fire, the German crews had no experience with the new technique under combat conditions. Only two ships were damaged, and those came via incidental near misses. At the outset of the assault, *Nene*, the senior ship in the group, had hoisted the flag signal for all vessels to "avoid action" individually. More than anything else, this thwarted the bombers' efforts. It had been a shattering experience for the Navy crews nonetheless, particularly for *Snowberry*—it was Captain Barry O'Brien's first experience leading her company into action.

The gunners, especially, had a frustrating time of it. With the ships weaving and dodging—and the bombs changing direction—it was almost impossible to take effective aim. It had been no picnic for those on the bridge or in the engine room, either. They were hard-pressed to coax the most from their ships. At one point during the attack, *Tweed* had signalled *Snowberry*, "Your best speed?"

O'Brien replied, "Fifteen knots."

Back snapped a retort. "Don't give us that stuff. We're doing 18 and you're still keeping up!"

Snowberry's chief engine room artificer later admitted that he had urged 10 more revolutions per minute out of the "old ice cream freezer" than he'd ever thought possible.

The Germans' first attempt with their new weapon had been a failure. But they learned quickly from their mistakes, and two days later it was quite a different story. Meanwhile, informed of the glider bombs, the minds at the British Admiralty were apparently so taken aback with surprise that the best they could offer were: (a) shoot down the missiles with anti-aircraft guns (...*and did their Lordships think that the gun crews had taken the afternoon off?*), and/or (b) plug in all electric razors on board in the hope that they might match the radio wavelength of the bomb guides, hence jamming the signals.

The first suggestion, of course, had certainly already been given a good try, and it had failed for reasons that were soon to become even more obvious. The second suggestion—certainly an interesting twist on simple wishful thinking—was actually implemented, though it could hardly be taken seriously.

Shortly after noon on August 27, the Dorniers returned in force—20 of them. They had obviously been doing their homework. Their aim had improved, and dramatically so. One

Chase-Me-Charlie utterly demolished a British sloop. It disappeared in a miasma of black smoke and flame.

Another glider bomb struck *Athabaskan*, which was some miles distant from *Snowberry*'s support group. Entering below the bridge, it knifed through the hull and exploded, igniting fires. As she drifted to a stop, *Athabaskan* became a wallowing target for two Dorniers, whose missiles fortunately went awry.

Five men had been killed; 12 were wounded. The central armament control system had been knocked out—all guns would have to be fired manually and individually. But this calamitous state of affairs was nothing new to her skipper, George "Gus" Miles.

He had seen it all before when, three years earlier, he had brought *Saguenay* home to port after she had been torpedoed in the Atlantic. Under his inspired leadership, all hands worked around the clock to douse the fires and make repairs. And, although *Athabaskan* was a lame duck—easy prey to further aerial attack and a sure target for U-boats—by skillful seamanship, Miles navigated her safely back to Plymouth harbour (during the four-day voyage, the destroyer twice ground to a halt, and it was only through the energetic efforts of her engine-room crew that she managed to get under sail again).

With all due respect to the Admiralty, only hard-bitten experience under fire could determine the most effective means for dealing with the elusive and deadly glider bombs. The first raid had come as a surprise. The second had been so quick and decisive that the ships, many of them new to the game entirely, had little time to properly retaliate. It was soon discovered that the best method was to attack the source (i.e., aim at the Dornier with long-range anti-aircraft guns, and hold fire against the missiles themselves until they came into the closer range of the Oerlikons and pom-poms). Even then, only practice made perfect, but in the final analysis, the only real way to cope was to fight fire with fire—and that meant proper air protection.

RefScs: CCAN 206–10 FDS 196–97 TSIAOG 158

500 Miles off Cabo Finisterre, Spain
November 21, 1943

DUNN James Alexander
ORR Mac

"Action in the Azores"

Portugal's action, allowing the Royal Air Force to operate from bases in the Azores, precipitated running battles—German aircraft and U-boats on the one hand, Allied planes and surface ships on the other. The Admiralty dispatched naval reinforcements, among which were a group temporarily diverted from Biscay Bay duty. It included RCN corvettes *Calgary* and *Snowberry*, as well as the RN frigate *Nene*, all veterans of the initial Luftwaffe glider bomb attacks.

The group was moving rapidly into position at night in support of a convoy that had been shadowed by U-boats and attacked by Chase-Me-Charlies when *Nene* made a radar contact with surfaced submarine *U-536*. She steamed full ahead, joined by *Calgary*. A star shell showed the U-boat to be right within range. Both ships opened fire from two miles, scoring hits on the sub's casing.

The U-boat commander retaliated, setting off a torpedo that *Nene* barely dodged; the submarine then dived to safety. For a solid hour, *Snowberry*'s skipper, James "Hamish" Dunn, and Mac Orr, *Calgary*'s first lieutenant, directed depth-charge drops, but without result. It took a double-pattern explosive from *Nene* to bring the U-boat to the surface.

She rose between ships, and was greeted by a hail of fire from all three. Hits from 4-inch guns, Lewis guns and Oerlikon cannon battered the submarine as it tried to wend its way forward, barely making three knots. The conning tower was damaged; crewmen were gunned down on the deck. But she fought bravely on, banging up against *Snowberry*'s side in an attempt to ram.

In the end, most of the crew went down with the submarine, or were drowned. Only 18 were captured. According to

Snowberry's report, not one of them gave any evidence "to make us believe that they were members of the Master Race."

RefScs: CCAN 211–12 FDS 198–99

500 Miles off Cabo Finisterre, Spain *December 26–28, 1943*

GRANT Harold Taylor Wood

"Greatest German Destroyer Action in the Bay in Late '43"

On December 26, 11 German destroyers left Bordeaux and Brest to meet a German merchant ship carrying cargo from Japan and escort her through the Allied blockade. The *Kriegsmarine* vessels were well-equipped for such an assignment. Five of them were Narvik class, the other six Elbings, all of them formidably armed. Their officers and crews were confident they could handle any enemy warships that stood in their way—and with good reason. The Narviks boasted five 5.9-inch guns, more than a match for the British and Canadian Tribal class destroyers, and the Elbings packed four 4.1-inch guns.

By December 27 they were well out of the Bay of Biscay, sailing in two columns for a rendezvous that would never happen—at four o'clock that afternoon, aircraft from RAF Coastal Command had already sent the blockade runner to the bottom.

Almost simultaneously, aerial scouts reported spotting the destroyers, still well east of their rendezvous point. The Admiralty ordered HMS *Glasgow* and HMS *Enterprise* to intercept them. The latter vessel was commanded by a veteran Canadian sea dog. Harold Grant had served in World War I, and *Enterprise* was the second RN ship the RCN officer had been commissioned to command in World War II. Collectively, the German destroyers outnumbered, outweighed, outmanned and outgunned the British cruisers. But, even with the addition of air support, they would prove poor rivals against the experience, determination, wiles and aggression of the Haligonian skipper.

Glasgow and *Enterprise* had joined forces at 3:00 a.m. on the 28th, 300 miles northwest of Cabo de Finisterre, and set out on a course to block the German ships from their French bases. By daybreak, the Germans were still sailing west, unaware that the blockade runner had been sunk, and the British cruisers were sailing due east, 45 miles to the south. At nine o'clock they altered course to northeast, placing themselves between the Germans and France.

At eleven, the destroyers received a recall signal from German Naval Command—reverse course and make for base as fast as possible. The order had come too late; *Glasgow* and *Enterprise* were now strategically positioned. At 1:13 p.m. the cruisers broke out their battle ensigns. Thirty-five minutes later the German destroyers appeared on the horizon. At 1:46 *Glasgow* opened fire from 18,000 yards, and two minutes later *Enterprise* followed with her own salvo from 20,000 yards. Now the battle was joined.

In rough seas and the gloom of an overcast afternoon, the Germans came directly ahead, determined that nothing would stop them from reaching their bases. Throwing out smoke floats to set up a screen, they were full of fight, sending shells bursting around the two British cruisers—they also presented clear targets themselves. The duel progressed, all sailing parallel, now on a southeasterly course. The British cruisers held the navigating edge in heavy seas but, while they were certain they were inflicting heavy damage on the destroyers, the amount of that damage was hard to assess through the smokescreen.

Then, at 2:25 p.m., a glider bomb crashed into the sea near *Glasgow*. Two minutes later, *Enterprise* was hit by a shell from a destroyer—and another glider bomb struck the water 400 yards off her port quarter and exploded. But the air attack was a feeble one, impeded by the weather, and the cruisers had little difficulty fighting off the enemy marauders.

The German destroyers now changed course, heading north to make their getaway. Harold Grant ordered *Enterprise* in close to stop them. Through the smokescreen he could make out one direct hit. Then, drawing nearer yet, he found himself engaged by two destroyers, one on either side, bracketing his cruiser with fire. One shot knocked out his aerial. *Enterprise*'s return fire inflicted its own damage—one destroyer had her funnel blown away.

The action was too much for the Germans. Seven destroyers, those that were able, broke off the battle and scurried north, leaving the others to fend for themselves. One of the abandoned ships escaped by limping south behind a heavy smokescreen. Another was stopped entirely, dead in the sea. The remaining two fought to the bitter end. It was four o'clock before *Glasgow* and *Enterprise* sank them both.

With a darkening sky, and both cruisers low on ammunition, Grant and *Glasgow*'s skipper decided to call it a day, breaking off pursuit on the last lame destroyer. It was a solid victory for the cruisers—three enemy destroyers sunk, a fourth heavily crippled, and the seven that had made it back to port no doubt also suffering some damage. It was the last major sea engagement of 1943 in the Bay of Biscay, a year during which the Allied navies—the RCN prominent among them—made possible the eventual strangulation of German garrisons and ports along the coast of France.

Harold Grant was born in Halifax, N.S., and attended the Royal Canadian Naval College in 1914. He first served as a midshipman aboard HMS *Leviathan* in 1917. Before the Great War ended in 1918, he had served aboard three other Royal Navy ships. In 1919 he was aboard HMS *Warwick*, which took part in the North Russian Relief Fund during the Bolshevik revolution.

Serving aboard several Royal Navy ships between wars, he was also Director of Naval Plans and Director of Naval Reserves in 1934 and 1935, consecutively. At the beginning of World War II, Grant was made Chief of Naval Personnel and Third Member of the Naval Board of Canada. In 1942, he became Captain (D) Newfoundland. The following year he was given command of HMS *Diomede* before being named captain of HMS *Enterprise*.

Immediately after the war, Grant became Chief of Administration and Supply, and served as Chief of the Naval Staff from 1947 to 1951, retiring with the rank of Vice-Admiral. Grant died in 1965.

VADM CBE DSO MID BSM(US) Born March 11, 1899
Died May 1965
RefScs: FDS 200–03 MMN 22

POLICING THE PIPELINE TO INVASION
JANUARY–MAY 1944

*O*n January 8, 1944, the Canadian corvette Camrose *shared
credit with a British frigate for the sinking of German submarine U-757 while acting as escort to the combined convoys
OS-64 and KMS-38. Eight depth charges sent the U-boat to the
bottom of the Atlantic, leaving only an oil slick, pieces of flotsam and a uniform cap as mute testament to the kill.*

*Likewise in February—only one submarine sunk along the
northern convoy route. On the 24th of the month,* Waskesiu, *the
first Canadian-built frigate, assisted by a British counterpart,
forced a U-boat to surface, and then sank it with gunfire in a
five-hour action.*

*These singular sinkings were characteristic of convoy
operations at the start of the new year. In January, the eastward
movement of ships, equipment, troops and supplies for the Allied
invasion of Europe had begun—a long and plodding chore that
continued throughout the winter and early spring until, by June,
ships of the Royal Canadian Navy were providing all the close
escorts to trade convoys plying the seas between the New World
and the Old, and a portion of the support groups as well.*

*Convoys had grown to enormous proportions—as many as
150 ships, spaced out over a vast 100-square-mile swath of
ocean. Now totally protected by air cover, the task of the escorts
and support groups was a tedious, almost routine sentinel duty.
The job remained, nevertheless, as difficult and potentially perilous as ever before. The mammoth armadas made protection and
maneuver awkward, often downright dangerous. Their monstrous
size magnified susceptibility to collision in fog, storms and darkness. And the sea itself was no less cruel. Ships were still battered
in the fierce winter weather, became lost and often sank.*

The U-boats could no longer strangle the steady flow of ocean traffic, and they no longer held the status of strategic menace they had earlier enjoyed. But they were still around— everywhere—bigger, faster, more formidable and just as harassing as ever. Armed with 22 torpedoes and equipped with their schnorkel (known as the "snort"), their range and duration at sea were virtually limitless. There were no more big U-boat battles. But they were still a deadly aggravation, and their presence called for constant alert. They refused to go away, and at times they put up a very stiff fight.

Mid-Atlantic
March 5–6, 1944

COUGHLIN Clifton Rexford
DAVIS James Sinclair
GROOS Harold Victor
MOFFAT William Purvis

"Marathon 32-Hour Sub Hunt"

At approximately 10:00 a.m. on March 5, *Gatineau*, commanded by Harold Groos, made asdic contact with a submerged German submarine, *U-744*. With *Gatineau* were another Canadian destroyer, *Chaudiere*; *St. Catharines*, a frigate; two corvettes, *Chilliwack* and *Fennel*; as well as an RN destroyer, *Icarus*. They formed part of C2 Group, escorting convoy HX-280 eastbound from Halifax to the United Kingdom—quite an alignment against a single U-boat.

The sea was particularly rough, some of the worst weather encountered by North Atlantic shipping since the turn of the year, and the sonar echoes were faint. But Groos signalled *St. Catharines*, the senior ship, that he was going to attack anyway. Thus began a marathon, 32-hour, hunt-to-exhaustion U-boat chase—the longest of the war. It was a relentless pursuit. Before *U-744* was finally brought to heel, 23 different attacks were

Harold Groos (3rd from right), skipper of Gatineau. *(DND/PA 136275)*

mounted; 291 depth charges—87,300 pounds of high explosives—were dropped; countless shells, as well as torpedoes, were expended. Something of a record in ship-to-ship communications was also established; during the action, no less than an astounding 15,000 signals had flashed between the seven surface vessels involved.

Gatineau dropped a pattern of depth charges, to no avail. The German submarine dove deep, to 200 metres, then turned sharply as the charges exploded, swinging around inside the destroyer's turning circle. *Gatineau* lost its signal in the disturbance caused by its own wake. *St. Catharines*, under the command of Jimmy "Foghorn" Davis, had meanwhile picked up the asdic echo. She dropped a second pattern of depth charges. The time was now 10:28 a.m.; half an hour later, *Chilliwack* let go another pattern—still no apparent result.

But *U-744* had not escaped entirely unscathed. Her crew was working in total darkness—the explosions had shattered every light bulb; they had also jarred the hull sufficiently to cause cracks and leaks and broken gauges. Though wounded, the U-boat was still intact, her engines running without interruption.

As darkness closed in, the surface vessels continued to pound away with depth charges. Although they maintained constant sonar contact throughout the night, victory continued to elude them, and the pursuit carried them some 50 miles south of where it had begun. At 8:00 a.m. the attack resumed in earnest. But after a sustained depth charge attack lasting almost four hours, the sub's commander so skillfully maneuvered his craft that all contact was lost with the U-boat for more than half an hour.

This called for a fresh appraisal of the situation. If contact was lost again, the submarine could very well lie "doggo" until dark, then surface and make good its escape. On the other hand, if the U-boat had sustained severe enough damage, it might be forced to surface at any time. The decision was made to wait it out. No further depth charge drops until 4:00.

The call was a good one. At exactly 3:32, *U-744*'s conning tower appeared, just ahead of *Chilliwack*. The sub was in no shape to take any further underwater punishment, and its battery was dead—no choice but to fight it out in the hope of making a run for it on the surface. Both *Chilliwack*, captained by Clifton Coughlin, and *Fennel*, skippered by Bill Moffat, immediately enveloped the U-boat with their fire. An anti-aircraft gun was blown into the sea. The captain, standing on the conning tower and raising his hands in surrender, was killed instantly by a shell. Many of the crew, giving up any hope of manning their guns, slid off the deck into the water. Others were mowed down by *Chilliwack*'s relentless fire.

The corvette bore down on *U-744*, firing as she went, under Coughlin's orders to ram. But it became apparent there was no need—the hull was ripped open, the conning tower torn to pieces, and most of the crew had already abandoned ship. Coughlin ordered "hard aport." The corvette swerved to avert collision, followed hard in her wake by *St. Catharines*. Both vessels lowered boarding parties into the heavy sea.

Through the hatch, they searched the compartments below for anything with intelligence value that they could lay their hands on in a hurry—equipment, records, logs, code and signal books. Time was of the essence—the sub was filling with water, and there was always the danger that scuttle charges had been set. As the men climbed back into their lifeboats, a rolling swell lifted them up against the U-boat. They capsized, and the materiel they had salvaged at such risk was lost to the deep.

Forty of the submarine's crew were rescued; 11, their captain included, were killed. Although *U-744* remained afloat, it was too much awash to be taken in tow. The rescue work completed, at 6:30 *Icarus* sent her to the bottom with one well-aimed torpedo.

Harold Groos was born in New Orleans, Louisiana, and was living in Victoria, B.C., when he joined the RCN as a cadet in 1930. He spent the first five years of his naval career with the Royal Navy, serving aboard several British warships, including *Rodney* and *Warspite*. Returning to Canada in 1935, he served on *Skeena*, and then *Fraser*. In September 1942, Groos took command of *Orillia*; he subsequently commanded *St. Francis*, *Gatineau* and *Huron*.

At the close of World War II, Groos became Assistant Chief of Naval Personnel and served on the staff of the Director of Plans and Operations. Later, he was appointed executive officer of *Naden* and then commanded *Crusader*.

LT COMM
RefScs: DHist bf CCAN 236 FDS 217–23 TSIAOG 151–54

Mid-Atlantic
March 8–10, 1944

STEPHEN George Hay
WATSON John Manuel

"Sally's Day"

St. Laurent had just rejoined EG-9, escort group to convoy SC-158 en route from Halifax to the United Kingdom, after spending a difficult day towing a damaged corvette, when she received orders to go to the aid of *San Francisco*, a Swedish merchant ship whose cargo of flax was on fire, spreading fast. The Canadian destroyer was a natural choice for the assignment. In his four years at war, her skipper, George Stephen, had earned a respected reputation in both the RCN and the RN for his doggedness in salvage and rescue.

By the time *"Sally"* hove to alongside the merchantman, the blaze was practically out of control. Flames and smoke belched from the hatches; the decks were buckling from the heat. Most serious was the fact her pumps weren't working properly, due to loss of pressure.

Stephen ordered *St. Laurent*'s 70-ton pump (70 tons of water per hour) transferred to the merchant ship—no easy assignment in a rough and heavy running sea, and all the ancillary equipment that had to be moved with it. The lifeboat needed three trips to complete the task, and on the last one it capsized, losing its gear. Still, within two hours firefighters had the pump going in full operation. Meanwhile, one of *St. Laurent*'s officers led a fire crew from *San Francisco* into the hold to pitch some of the flax overboard so that hoses could be played on the roots of the blaze. It was gruelling, dangerous work. A man could stand only a few minutes toiling in the scorching heat and choking fumes; the crews had to be spelled on and off. But, after 18 hours, the fire was at last under control.

In the meantime, *Sally* had rejoined the close escort: corvette *Owen Sound*; *Swansea*, a frigate; and an RN destroyer, *Forester*. And George Stephen was about to add to his laurels, this time against a U-boat.

At 4:25 p.m., *Owen Sound*, skippered by "Manny" Watson, sighted *U-845* and immediately chased, though at too slow a speed. When she dropped her depth-charge pattern, she was so close to the explosion it knocked out her asdic and electrical power and engulfed the ship in a great gush of water. It took 10 minutes to repair the damage before she could resume the chase, which was soon broken off when *Owen Sound* was ordered to assist a damaged freighter in the convoy.

At this point, *St. Laurent* took over, joined at nightfall by *Swansea* and *Forester*. At 10:34 the U-boat surfaced, hoping to make a run for it. To prevent an acoustic torpedo attack, Stephen ordered his ship's Cat Gear let out, slowing the destroyer and widening the range between her and the sub. Nevertheless, she scored two hits on the U-boat's conning tower and then began closing range, firing as she went.

U-845 was hurting badly. A fire had broken out inside and her stern was down, though she was still maneuvering ably. *St. Laurent* overtook the sub and was preparing to ram when Stephen changed his mind—why damage his own ship when he could finish her off by pulling alongside and firing with everything from big guns to revolvers?

For a *coup d'état*, Stephen ordered depth charges dropped. The explosions broke the back of the submarine, bringing it to a stop. *St. Laurent* let go a final salvo with her 4.7-inch guns. It blew three more holes in the conning tower, whereupon *U-845*'s crew surrendered—all 45 were taken prisoner. His first submarine kill after four years of rugged rescue work, Stephen was so jubilant he tore the peak clean off his sea-worn captain's cap when he raised it in salute to *Sally*'s victory.

RefScs: FDS 224–27 TSIAOG 154

Mid-Atlantic
Mid-April, 1944

KING Clarence Aubrey

"A Textbook Submarine Attack"

It was almost routine. In fact, while the hunt for the submarine was in progress, *Swansea*'s veteran skipper, Clarence King, casually checked his position with a sun sight, and took his own sweet time about it, too.

Having obtained an asdic contact with a U-boat bent on torpedoing the escort carrier *Biter*, the Canadian frigate immediately maneuvered into perfect attacking position and, with calm

Captains of four escort craft after the safe arrival of Convoy SC-154. (l. to r.) G.H. Stephen, J.E. Harrington, C.A. King, J.A. Burnett. (J.D. Mahoney/DND/PA 137695)

efficiency, dropped a pattern of 10 depth charges. As soon as the submarine surfaced, *Swansea*'s gunfire quickly and effectively dispatched it to the deep.

Later, *Swansea* teamed up with a sister frigate, *Matane*, to destroy another U-boat. These feats made King an "ace"—counting both world wars, he scored a total of five submarine sinkings.

RefScs: FDS 227 TSIAOG 154

South of Cape Race, Newfoundland
May 6, 1944

BARRETT Rafael
BAULNE Rene
BEST Charles
BROWN Donald
BYRON James
DONITZ Karl
EDGAR-BROWN David
ENGLISH Dermot
KAPLAN Irving
MASON Cashman
MUNRO Ed
PATTERSON John
PETERSEN Charles
TATE Ian
WARREN Jake
WOODS Mervyn
ZIMMERMANN Eberhard

"A night of unforgettable misery—torpedoing of the Valleyfield"

On the evening of May 6, 1944, somewhere in the vicinity of 150 miles to the south of Cape Race on the Avalon Peninsula, *Unterseeboot U-548* received a wireless communiqué from *Kriegsmarine* headquarters in Germany: "Zimmermann, for Commander: Daughter born 4 May, Mother and daughter well. Congratulations. Admiral Commanding U-Boats."

Unbeknownst to *Kapitanleutnant* Eberhard Zimmermann, news that he had just become a father (and all other messages he received—and sent) did not escape the attention of staff officers at the British Admiralty "listening in," through the Ultra secret decoding device, to signals the instant the Germans issued them. Ergo: Canadian naval authorities at St. John's, Newfoundland, to whom they were constantly relayed, already aware of *U-548*'s presence, dispatched two corvettes from Escort Group W-2—

HMCS *Timmins* and *Agassiz*—to take necessary action. Meanwhile the Flag Officer bulletined all ships in the area warning them of an enemy submarine in the Cape Race area.

Directly affected, because it was sailing right into the danger zone, was Escort Group C-1 comprising of a frigate, *Valleyfield*, the senior ship, and four corvettes, *Halifax, Frontenac, Giffard* and *Edmunston*. Returning from escorting a westbound convoy and having turned their responsibilities over to a relief group, they were speeding north to St. John's at 13 knots chock full of "Channel Fever," that heady sense of excitement of looking forward to all the delights of shore leave—lights, liqueur and lots of lovelies only hours away. After gruelling weeks at sea, they were hardly in the frame of mind to take too seriously one of the usual U-boat alerts that invariably turned out to be false.

But not neglectful all the same. Despite the euphoria of the promised carefree days ahead, strict naval discipline was preserved, the ships adhering to standard Admiralty formation procedure with *Valleyfield* as the senior ship in the centre, *Halifax* and *Frontenac* to port, *Giffard* and *Edmunston* on the starboard side, each one 300 yards apart from the nearest ship. Watch-keeping officers on the bridges kept their eyes focussed ahead, and the ships periodically zigzagged to prevent any U-boats following from lining them up as a target.

However, conditions in this case called for deviation from normal procedures. Heavy chunks of ice floes, known to the sailors as "growlers" and "bergy bits," as well as fearful, awesome towering icebergs, presented a danger that made keeping formation impossible, and the senior officer decided to cancel the zigzagging.

But by mid-afternoon when the group cleared through the ice there was no order to resume the evasive maneuver. And that was the responsibility only the senior officer, Commander James "the Brain" Byron, who had issued it, could countermand. However, exhausted after 40 straight hours on the bridge, he was asleep in his cabin. No one thought, or dared, to awaken him. Since it meant an earlier arrival at St. John's, the crew liked to joke, irreverently, that "the old man" didn't want to be late for a cocktail party ashore. In fact, in all seriousness, *Valleyfield* was slowly letting her guard down—with fatal consequences.

The captain of the senior ship, Lieutenant-Commander Dermot English, who deferred all major group decisions to Byron, had left the bridge with him for some shut-eye as well. He too was completely tuckered out by two days and nights of constant watch. He left Lieutenants Ian Tate and Cashman Mason in charge and unknowingly about to face difficult circumstances requiring critical attention. And they were not alone.

Ice for one; there were still a number of dangerous growlers and bergy bits about, calling for extreme vigilance on their own part, as well as the extra lookouts the watch officers had pressed into service for safety's sake. But their greatest concern was the new radar equipment *Valleyfield* had been saddled with. The operators simply couldn't get the hang of the cumbersome new-fangled TX-C machine. When Tate failed get a report from the R/O of heavy iceberg he had sighted and called down through the voice pipe to the radar office to check its bearing, the frustrated operator complained he not only couldn't get an echo on that particular bearing but, in any case, with so many bergy bits floating around the ship, it was impossible to tell one from another. Impatiently Tate told him to turn the wretched thing off and go back to the faithful old SWIC.

Back to basics; *Valleyfield*'s fate now rested with the eyesight of human lookouts, which wasn't getting any easier with night falling and a slight haze, and help from the dubious quality of a set ready for an electronic museum. But the frigate was not the only ship in the group so afflicted. On her port beam the corvette *Frontenac* had been without radar serviceability for some time. To all intents, that made it two out of five in the group without radar assistance.

It was some consolation that the other three in the formation had their equipment working satisfactorily, but as far as *Valleyfield* was concerned that protective advantage was only figurative.

At 10:00 p.m. *Edmunston* on the extreme starboard side and *Giffard* on her port beam both reported blips three miles distant.

These however turned out to be the corvettes *Timmins* and *Agassiz* on the hunt for the reported U-boat. Moments later Escort Groups C-1, the hunted, and W-2, the hunter, passed each other a safe distance apart after *Timmins* flashed her running lights in recognition.

An hour and a half later another radar alert—this time a low-flying Royal Canada Air Force Coastal Command twin-engine Canso that caught *Halifax*, on the inner port side of the formation, in the glare of its Leigh searchlight. However, satisfied that its own radar blip was a ship and not a U-boat shadowing the ships, it switched of the light, waggled its wings and flew off westward.

Those exercises acted like an elixir to the watchkeepers on deck, even though they were now approaching the waters where the U-boat had been reported. After all, they weren't merchant ship targets threatening to be torpedoed. On the contrary, they were well-equipped anti-submarine warships, all five of them, a veritable "fleet" ready to take on several U-boats if necessary, let alone a single predator. With St. John's virtually just over the horizon, the calm sea flooded in the bright moonlight and the journey coming to an end, all seemed right with the world. Aboard the flotilla of C-1, watchkeepers, at least, were in a jolly mood.

There was one conundrum to be settled; the problem of whether or not to stream out the CAT gear, the devices designed to counter the Gnat menace, the German acoustic torpedo, which could be fired in the direction of a target and that then homed in on the victim with its microphones from the ship's propeller vibrations. The "foxer" preventative equipment was as simple as it was effective. Consisting of two large metal noisemakers towed on a line a safe distance astern of the ship, it drew the torpedo to itself and exploded it harmlessly. However, the noise from the CAT gear interfered with the radar reception so seriously it rendered it virtually useless. It was therefore decided not to stream them and they remained secured inboard on all five ships. As it turned out, had they been in operation they would not have altered the outcome in the slightest.

So the five ships of C-1 sailed straight ahead, without zigzagging, right into the lion's den—on a collision course with *U-548*, scanning the surface in search of prey. With the senior officer and captain of his ship asleep belowdecks, the only vigilant precaution and protection for Valleyfield in the vanguard rested with the watchful eyes of the lookouts peering over a tranquil sea under brilliant moonlight from a clear sky and the radar operating effectively on only three of the five ships.

That Eberhard Zimmermann was in the right place at the right time to profit from the opportunity on the verge of falling right into his grasp was more pure luck and circumstance than good management and certainly no thanks to Admiral Donitz and the U-boat headquarters' ignorance of the Allies' shipping routes off the Atlantic coast of North America. It was an incredible miscalculation—and after five years of war—that *U-548* should be designated to harass Allied merchant shipping off the port of St. John's when the actual shipping lane was over 100 miles to the north. Moreover, after all those years of operating in the waters off the North American coast, the Germans, both at the command level and that of the U-boat commanders, still insisted on erroneously identifying all Allied warships as American—U.S. destroyers, U.S. ships, U.S. whatever. It seems equally incredible that German headquarters seemed unaware that the area to which they had dispatched Zimmermann was the principal base for anti-submarine warships and aircraft constantly on patrol for U-boats, which the misinformed *Kapitanleutnant* learned to his regret. After a few near escapes, on May 3, 1944, he moved to the vicinity southwest of Cape Spear hoping to find a safer—not to mention more lucrative—hunting ground.

After six weeks in the seas around Newfoundland, never quite sure of his exact location and with the danger of floating ice all about, the experienced commander of one of Germany's newest, largest submarines, Type 1Xc, capable of carrying 22 torpedos, most of them the acoustic Gnats, and with a seasoned crew aboard, had scored a big zero. Two days later he came close to changing his luck when he fired at what he mistook to be an American (of course) destroyer but missed. At the same time an RCAF Canso, which spotted clouds of black smoke billowing from one of the U-boat's diesel engines, had swooped down, forcing Zimmermann to take cover. But the aircraft, which had been sent to look for him, now had a fix on the area in which he was operating, and the message from Berlin congratulating him on becoming a parent confirmed it.

Now on Mat 6 at approximately 11:25 p.m., from the conning tower of *U-548* Zimmermann detected the dim outline of a vessel heading almost directly towards him to port about four nautical miles away. He immediately crash-dived, altering course slightly to place him almost at a converging angle at what through his periscope he wrongly identified (naturally) as an American destroyer and sounded action stations to prepare all forward torpedo tubes for firing.

As he closed in for the kill within three nautical miles, confident in the knowledge that he was still out of range of any approaching radar detection, he was taken aback by his hydrophone operator, who reported strong propeller sounds left and right. Zimmermann rotated the periscope 360 degrees, but with its limited range found nothing. However he was acutely aware of the danger he'd sailed into: a veritable beehive of escort ships. But it was too late. The die was already cast. At exactly 11:32 p.m. he fired off a Zaukonig acoustic homing torpedo at a range of 1,500 metres, aimed at the port bow of the target. At the same instant he put the U-boat into a steep diving turn in the opposite direction to starboard to get clear of his onrushing target at a closing speed of 20 miles an hour.

Seconds before the acoustic torpedo struck *Valleyfield*'s No. 2 boiler room, causing an explosion that sent up a massive sheet of flames and a screaming geyser of water and steam, the routine above and belowdecks, with the single exception of the asdic operator's concern for something out the ordinary, was business as usual. But with the prospect of shore leave only hours away, an aura of anticipated excitement—Channel Fever—pervaded nevertheless. As midnight approached, the next watch was being rousted out of their bunks—"Wakey! Wakey!"—most of them still fully dressed except for boots and coats in case of emergency, but some more comfortably clad for sleeping wearing only shorts. In the petty officers mess, Yeoman Irving Kaplan, the senior signal rating, was taking no chances. He was fully dressed in his warm padded zipped-up zoot suit, his naval-pattern life jacket worn on top of it—ready for come what may. Not so coder Ed Munro, rubbing the sleep out of his eyes for his turn in the wireless office. He was taking his time putting on his shirt and pants over his underwear.

In the engine room the senior watchkeeping officer of that section of the ship was writing up his log, his artificers checking bearings and oil levels. In the oppressive heat of the boiler rooms the duty stokers were mopping the sweat from their brows, monitoring the pressure and temperature gauges. Everything in order.

From the bridge a scene of serenity. The magnificent splendour of the mirror-like calm of a sea stretching in all directions as far as the eye could see, bathing in the magnificence of the light of a bright, shiny full moon, now that the mist had all but dispersed. But war at sea left no time for such awe and wonder. Particularly in U-boat-infested waters. On watch, stay alert at all times. Don't let your vigilance down for a second. Lookouts aboard *Valleyfield*, clad in their fur-lined hooded watch coats, stamping their heavy-sea-booted feet to keep warm, scanning the arc of the horizon through their binoculars for the umpteenth time.

Lieutenant Cashman Mason, stationed on the compass platform passed orders through the voice pipes at the gyro compass housing to the quartermaster in the deck below. Lieutenant Tate, sharing the watch and alternating with him at the conning position, was free at this particular moment to supervise the radar and sonar searches and the vigilance of the lookouts, as well as maintaining a general lookout himself.

It was a little after half past eleven when he noticed that the "captain's pointer" on the compass in which the asdic was transmitting steadied itself on a bearing at "Red 16" broad on the port bow. Apparently the operator was investigating something on that bearing. As the ship's anti-submarine officer, Tate made it his business to find out what was going on. He turned on the bridge loudspeaker to amplify what the operator was listening to.

When the operator switched on the asdic transmissions, everyone on the bridge could hear the sound of a mild ticking, like a watch, moving faster and faster, almost like a hum.

Tate sensed trouble. "Investigate from 250 degrees to 280 degrees," he shouted through the asdic voice pipe, giving the set an arc stretching along the weird underwater noise. Too late. Before the operator could respond, all hell broke loose.

Chaos!

Within moments of the explosion one of the ship's most critical nerves failed.

The ship's power was instantly put out of commission. From the bridge Cashman Mason managed to press the emergency button that sounded alarms above and belowdecks to summon all hands to Action Stations just in time. But Ian Tate was out of luck. To his utter frustration he was about to shout a warning down the engine room voice pipe to clear the lower deck spaces, but it was too late. The lights had gone out; the bells were silenced. However, there wasn't much need for an alert anyway. The carnage had overridden it.

When the torpedo struck *Valleyfield* on the port side to the area of the bridge in the No. 2 boiler room, the impact of the blast sent reverberations throughout the vessel from stem to stern. Men were knocked out of their bunks and off the tops of lockers. Others were numbed by the effects of the explosion, befuddled by what had happened, others just too scared and stunned to even know what to think. But there was no panic. A strong sense of discipline and emergency training immediately came into play.

Thick gooey bunker oil from punctured fuel tanks quickly spread over the icy water, turning it into a glue-like scum. The ship immediately began breaking in two fore and aft from the precise point where the torpedo exploded. The mainmast toppled over from the forefront and crashed into the sea on the port side. The fo'c'sle and bridge tore apart from the after half of the ship and veered over to starboard, the lower space filling with sea water. The watchkeepers on the bridge hung on to the best of their ability, stunned from the shock of the sudden, unexpected (how could it be anything else?) explosion and deafened by the frightful noise of escaping steam and the hideous shrieking of metal tearing apart.

Holding onto the housing of the rapidly listing compass platform below the bridge, Ian Tate was joined by the ship's navigator, Jake Warren, and the captain, Dermot English, jolted from his sleep. Both men had made their way up from the chart room on the deck below. Having sized up the situation, English leaned over the bridge and shouted to the last of the men scrambling up the boat deck: "Man the boats and Carley floats!" Tragically that was the last order—an unintentionally singsong one—issued aboard *Valleyfield*. Time was fast running out. At this point she was no longer the proud RCN frigate senior ship for Escort Group C-1, but a helpless forlorn metal wreck to be abandoned just as fast as it was humanly possible. Life now took precedence over all else aboard the final moments of His Majesty's Canadian Ship. The end was approaching with terrifying haste. The forward section of the vessel was listing more heavily with every passing moment, the fo'c'sle filling with water, the bridge beginning to sink, the bow rising slowly but surely like a giant human arm in a farewell salute, until she was standing on end, members of the crew, trapped in the sealed-off mess decks, suffering their final drowning agonies.

That the captain, Dermot English, so strict about life jackets being worn on duty at all times, was now the only one not wearing one, seemed incongruous but for the fact that he had shed it to give to a seaman who, in his haste to abandon ship, had forgotten his own. As an alternative Tate suggested pulling off the Kisbee life preserver, a canvas-covered cork ring, secured to the bridge dodger for emergencies, but it wouldn't budge. In desperation Tate told the skipper: "It's no use sir, we'll never get it free. Better swim for it!" English, who had come to the conclusion there was nothing more he could do to save his ship, readily agreed.

With Warren he climbed over the ship's railing, now nearly perpendicular to the sea, and jumped in the water among the gaggle of survivors struggling to get as far away from the ship as possible before she went under.

By this time Tate, who had been unable to follow, found himself perched atop the bridge housing and so awash that he flung himself into the onrushing water and hoped for the best. With the forward part of the ship now standing vertically on its end, Tate was frightened it would tumble right on top of him. Unable to swim clear, he was sucked under by the pull of the sinking wreckage and struggled to climb upward against the strength of the vortex encumbered by his heavy overcoat. Luckily, the buoyancy of his life jacket saved him from drowning, and he bobbed to the surface, spluttering and shivering but none the worse for wear. His good fortune held: he found himself only a few yards away from a float net some 20 feet square, which he was able to grab onto along with others. It kept them above water from the shoulders up but that was about all. With most of their bodies immersed in the icy sea, they wouldn't last long. However, as the swell from what was left of the sinking ship subsided, a Carley float came into view, and although there were some men aboard there was room for others, uncomfortable perhaps but better than freezing to death. Tate and the others hanging to the float's net swam over to the raft and climbed aboard. It now supported an overcrowded twenty seamen, some huddling together knee-deep in water, others straddling the cork ring that kept the raft afloat, the rest, Tate among them, clinging to the lifeline around it. To secure his hold Tate, among others, hooked the end of his lanyard from his lifebelt onto one of the clips on the lifeline.

The stern of the frigate was still afloat, but not for long. As the men in the sea watched, the front section of the hulk, weighted down by the water filling it, sank below the surface, lifting the rear of the wreck into the air. Then it too succumbed to the depths, the boilers exploding with a fearful blast, ending the lives of seamen, stokers and artificers left aboard. But the situation might have been a lot worse but for the sacrifice of three torpedo ratings—Leading Seaman Donald Brown, Ordinarily Seaman David Edgar-Brown and Able Seaman Mervyn Woods. Making their way aft, they reached the quarterdeck and frantically set the depth charges to Safe and withdrew the primers. Had it not been for that heroic act the charges would have exploded when the hull sank below the surface, killing every man in the water. The gallant trio were never seen again, sucked down as the last vestige of *Valleyfield* vanished into the sea.

The scene left in the wake of its death throes was heart-rending, men struggling to survive in the sticky oil-covered sea. It was a miracle that so many were even still alive to tell the tale. Signal Yeoman Irving Kaplan, for example, managed to free himself from the flooding officers' mess through the deck-head escape hatch to the gun deck, where he joined two others making a futile attempt to launch a Carley float. When that failed Kaplan climbed on top of a gun shield and plunged into the water. Joined by another seaman who was hanging on to a Kisbee life ring, they paddled away from the sinking ship. But Kaplan had to abandon the life ring when the calcium flare attached to it ignited and began to burn him. After some distance he found the main group and managed to straddle the supporting rung of the Carley float.

In icy water up to his waist, he was fortunate that his "zoot suit" gave him enough protection to help others find places around the raft to clip their life jackets. One sailor, unable to find a space, clung desperately to his leg. Others hung onto the rope net that fastened to one side of the raft, which now joined another Carley float adjacent to it. One of the men holding the net was the captain, Lieutenant-Commander Dermot English.

When English, who, without a life jacket was up to his shoulders in water, saw Kaplan, he called out, "Count the men," an order impossible to obey. There were too many heads bobbing about, making it impossible to arrive at an accurate total, so he ignored the order. In any case there was no way of discerning the dead from the living.

Fortunate to number himself among the living was Coder Ed Munro. Still clad only in his underwear when the torpedo struck, he had grabbed his life jacket, climbed through the escape hatch onto the deck and plunged into the sea. Practically naked, he was numbed by the 32-degree water but still managed to swim away from the sinking forefront of the ship and avoid being sucked under by its final plunge below the surface, relying on sheer, blind instinct to keep him going.

Once out of danger, he found himself in the middle of a lot of oil-soaked flotsam. But his talisman was still bearing with him; practically turned to ice, he was still able to swim to a nearby float where he joined others hanging onto the lifeline around its edge. Submerged almost to their shoulders, they watched, transfixed, as the forefront of HMCS *Valleyfield* succumbed to the depths. From one of the floats a chorus of men began to sing: "For she's a jolly good fellow." An epitaph to the great old lady they had been proud to call home for so long.

In the depths below, the architect of this tragedy noted in *U-548*'s log, "a very loud hollow-sounding detonation." The propeller noise of his target's engines had ceased, replaced by "violent breaking and cracking noises." Immediately after firing the torpedo, Zimmermann put his submarine in a sharp turning dive to starboard, then continued on down before levelling off at a safe depth and shut off the engines. The jubilant crew glued to the hydrophone listened to the results of their triumph. But as the noise grew louder and louder, Zimmermann, fearful that the wreckage might land on the submarine, restarted the engines and got underway again, none too soon. Within seconds the *Valleyfield*'s bow section struck the seabed close behind him. The U-boat kept running "dead slow," safely leaving the scene of the carnage it had created.

Meanwhile, on the surface, through their binoculars, the coxswain and officers of the watch on the bridge of *Giffard*, immediately to starboard of the C-1 lead ship, were suddenly startled at the sight of a huge tower of flame and white spray billowing up from *Valleyfield* 300 yards to port, following a tremendous explosion. One of the officers pressed the alarm buzzer of the voice pipe. But it was the blast that awakened the ship's captain, Lieutenant-Commander Charles Petersen, asleep in his bunk directly below, and brought him to the bridge.

Ironically Petersen was not popular with the officers and men under his command. He was singularly incapable of establishing a rapport with them, a direct outcome of his time as a "China Coaster," a merchant-naval officer with the British Chinese Custom Service, before joining the Royal Canadian Naval

Reserve when war broke out. He was abysmally unequipped to cope with high-spirited, young Canadian volunteers. Petersen simply was incapable of adjusting from ordering "coolies" around to leading "white men." As a result, *Giffard* laboured under an atmosphere of tension when what was needed was *esprit de corps*. However, as a commander of a ship he was diligent and well-meaning, with, in his own mind at least, the best of intentions—if indecisive. This was one of those occasions. *Valleyfield*'s explosion completely frazzled him.

Before taking any action, he wrestled with the probabilities of what might have caused the explosion, an engine or boiler room explosion or both, or an accidental depth-charge detonation aboard ship or in too-shallow water. As precious moments elapsed it seems incredible that the probability of torpedo attack never crossed his mind. At last he gave the order to close with *Valleyfield* whatever the situation. He tried to call her captain, Dermot English, on the ultra-frequency ship-to-ship radio transmitter, but of course there was no reply, a possibility Petersen seems not to have taken into account. Then, when his radar operator reported that the frigate's diminishing blip had completely disappeared, Petersen was beside himself. What to do? Frantically he told the yeoman to contact *Valleyfield* with his signalling-light projector. No acknowledgement, of course.

Giffard by this time was closing towards *Valleyfield*'s last reported position. But there was no sign of her. Then several of the watch officers spotted a blinking light through their binoculars that could only be a calcium flare—a sure sign of distress. Petersen headed the corvette directly towards the spot.

By this time, with no sign of *Valleyfield*, Petersen had at last reached the realization that she must have been sunk. But how? An internal explosion? A mine? A torpedo? He failed to take into account that the other three ships in the group might well be unaware of *Valleyfield*'s mishap or anything else remiss, or, for that matter, their radar operators concentrating so intently on looking for floating ice and other objects that they failed to notice any gap in the line of their formation. Petersen completely overlooked that possibility and neglected to order "Operation Observant" to the group—an immediate square search for a U-boat just in case the senior ship had been torpedoed—a distinct possibility. Had he taken that precaution, with the rest of the group favourably placed to find and sink *U-548* lying on the bottom in the immediate vicinity, *Halifax* on the extreme left particularly well positioned to do so, the enemy submarine might well have been detected and destroyed and a great many lives spared.

Instead the three corvettes, unaware of the tragedy, continued northwards, distancing themselves farther and farther from the scene of the disaster by the minute. And still Petersen procrastinated. As his ship drew closer to the spot where *Valleyfield* went down, the lookouts on the bridge could make out the fearful spectre of men clinging to pieces of floating wreckage, others huddled on life rafts, some hanging onto them for dear life. Sights of men in agony struggling in the icy waters hoping against hope to be rescued. To those wretched men on the verge of drowning, the sudden appearance of *Giffard* looming before them was like a godsend, their salvation. Clipped to a Carley float ring with a seaman pitifully clinging to his leg, Yeoman Irving Kaplan cried out: "There's a ship coming." His words were followed by a chorus if cheers. Then, to their utter rage, the hailer from the bridge of their "rescuer" bellowed, "Have you been torpedoed?" To the men in the water it was incredible. Back came an instant reply from *Valleyfield*'s navigator, Jake Warren. At the top of his lungs he shouted: "No you stupid bastard, we just thought it was a nice night for a swim!" Ironically, if not the sort of answer Petersen would have liked, it was exactly what he wanted to know. Yes, indeed, *Valleyfield* had been sunk by a U-boat, and it forced *Giffard*'s skipper into action, albeit a compromise, one that would plague him for the rest of his life.

It apparently never crossed his mind at this critical juncture to signal the other three ships in the group. He was more consumed with the danger to his ship from the presence of a lurking U-boat. He slowly made his way into the midst of the men clinging to floats and flotsam for dear life and did not consider what the rest of the escort was up to. From what he could learn from his asdic operator, there had been no sound up until the moment of the torpedoing, which meant that the attack must have been at close range. This would put the U-boat still within the immediate vicinity of the sinking, placing *Giffard* in proximate peril. His first duty, therefore, he surmised, was above all to save his own ship, and that meant finding the U-boat and destroying it. That made his failure to notify the other ships in the group all the more inexplicable. One glaring fact existed: Petersen was the only one in charge of the ship nearest to what had happened, and therefore the responsibility for his actions was his and his alone. Reasoning that the perpetrator—still in the area—had to be found and at the same time *Valleyfield*'s survivors in the sea rescued, he faced two options. Start an immediate search for the enemy submarine and temporarily (how long?) abandon the men in the water, which meant many more would drown, or proceed slowly through them, picking up as many as he could before proceeding with the U-boat hunt. Petersen chose the latter. A humane alternative but, as it turned out, an unsatisfactory one.

Giffard made her way slowly into the greatest concentration of the survivors, scramble nets lowered on either side with men climbing down to the level of the water to pull the men out of the sea. Others stood by with ropes to throw lifelines to the men in the sea and on rafts.

An appalling scene unfolded.

As carefully as the corvette proceeded, the movement wasn't sufficiently slow for men to hold onto the net long enough before it was torn from their grasp by the ship's momentum. Coder Ed Munro was clinging desperately to the Carley float he had latched onto when, as it edged against the port side of the ship, the momentum of the vessel capsized the raft, spilling its occupants into the sea. Munro watched in horror as one of them was sucked astern into one of the ship's whirring propellers. Munro held on until his hands were so numbed from the cold he was forced to let go. Ironically, still only clad in his underwear, chilled to the marrow, he somehow managed to swim to another Carley float. He climbed in and promptly collapsed.

By this time Petersen was on the verge of total despair. His rescue attempt was failing. With a German submarine around somewhere his ship was still in jeopardy. He was on the spot. Then it finally dawned on him that he was still part of a flotilla and he needed help. Now, at last, he decided to signal the other three corvettes in the group, something he had, for reasons known only to himself, not done earlier. Out went the message: "Close me." That was all. No why or wherefore. What did it mean?

That was exactly what the irate skippers of *Halifax*, *Edmunston* and *Frontenac*, still plowing their way through ice floes, awakened from their slumber by the cryptic communiqué, wanted to know. And where was the signal coming from? The baffled ship commanders calling each other over the inter-ship telephones tried to puzzle it out. Why had the signal come from Petersen aboard *Giffard* instead of Commander Byron, the senior officer aboard *Valleyfield*? What the hell was going on?

Eavesdropping on the nattering between ships, Petersen finally realized that some explanation was needed to supplement his signal. His second message read: "*Valleyfield* torpedoed." The time was eight minutes after midnight. Half an hour from the time *Valleyfield* had been struck by a U-boat!

Now the recipients were really stunned. An entire 30 minutes wasted since the lead ship with C-1's senior officer and her captain aboard had presumably been sunk, and this was the first they'd heard about it. Someone had a lot to answer for.

That someone had at last come to a decision, though in all fairness it wasn't an easy one for him to make. His rescue attempt simply wouldn't work unless his ship was almost at a complete standstill, and with the threat of another torpedoing that was too risky. It left him with no choice but to hunt down the enemy submarine. It might have crossed his mind that he would never have had to face that dilemma had he called for the other ships in the first place.

In any event, he now swung into action. Abandoning the men still struggling for their lives in the water, dismayed and angry at having been left to their fate, Petersen set a course northward and streamed out the Cat Gear as protection against torpedoing, completely unaware that the object of his search was practically right under his nose.

Down in the depths, Zimmermann was following a northerly course as well, slowly and quietly. Along with his crew, through *U-548*'s hydrophone, he had been listening in on the chatter between *Halifax*, *Edmunston* and *Frontenac*. Though they couldn't understand English they knew there was a group of ships in the vicinity. They could hear the sounds of *Giffard*'s propellers and the shrill of the CAT Gear. The noise indicated they had become the prey of a surface hunt. Zimmermann shut down his engines and lay doggo, slightly above the ocean bed. The last thing he wanted was to tangle with a bunch of "American" anti-submarine destroyers. He'd bide his time, waiting for the right moment to escape.

According to Charles Lamb, author of *On the Triangle Run*, Petersen did not take the predicament in which he found himself, albeit of his own making, lightly. It weighed heavily on him. He felt a sense of utter futility as he searched for an enemy he might never find while men "oil soaked, half paralyzed with cold were real and near, and they were dying," even as he searched vainly for "their vanished attacker."

Petersen's concerns and feelings permeated *Giffard*'s ship's company, sailors shivering, stamping their feet to fight off the bitter cold, acutely aware how much worse off their comrades-in-arms, whom they had been forced to leave to their fate, were, suffering and dying, trying to stay alive in the freezing, unfriendly sea. And yet they knew the search for the submarine had to be made.

It was more traumatic than they could ever have imagined. When Giffard sailed away, the salvation of the survivors of the sinking sailed with her and a pall of gloom descended. Their slender hopes of survival, the slim chance that they might somehow make it, the sheer will to live, quickly eroded. All hope of rescue gone. In Lamb's words: "There was no singing now, no cheerful helping one another secure safer or more comfortable places on the rafts, only a glum silence. The full realization if their situation was brought home to them." Like a vision of death.

There were exceptions. The more hardy among them never lost heart. Navigator Jake Warren kept himself alive, although periodically passing out and coming to, by clinging to pieces of wooden wreckage, anything floating by that he could find. Signal Yeoman Irving Kaplan, more fortunate than most wrapped up in his "zoot suit" that kept him marginally warmer than those less well clad, after taking the precaution of clipping the lanyard on his life jacket to the lifeline of the overcrowded Carley float in which he had been seated, used his advantage to help secure the handholds of others clinging to the raft from time to time.

On the other side of the same float Ian Tate heard the skipper repeat the order he had given Kaplan earlier, "Count the Men!" But like Kaplan he found it impossible to carry out with all the bodies piled up on the raft and heads, some living, some dead, bobbing up and down in the water, and he told the skipper so. Whereupon English calmly replied: "If I don't come out of this alive, Tate, call my wife." This time Tate agreed to his captain's request. "Aye, aye, sir," was his response. "I will."

Tate now began drifting in and out of consciousness but was jolted into fighting to stay awake to avoid the fate of two brother officers clinging to the Carley raft on either side of him. When he awoke from one of his periodic lapses into sleep, he found that they were both missing. He could only conclude that they had unclipped themselves to end their agony and had floated away, never to be seen again.

As an aside: Charles Lamb's comment on the incongruity of seamen wearing beards, a proud naval tradition among all ranks, under these dire circumstances is worth repeating. Matted in the hairy growth, the fast-coagulating oil slick in the water not only added to the already unwanted weight of their beards but added the discomfort of having to hold their heads above water, in many cases a difficulty at best.

In addition to fighting unconsciousness, Tate, *Valleyfield*'s bare-faced anti-submarine officer, faced a much more critical problem. Because there were only three Carley rafts still afloat, they were overcrowded to the point of sinking. Many of those clipped to the raft to which Tate was secured were being dragged below the surface and in imminent danger of drowning. Most were lucky enough to unclip themselves. Tate was not among them. He was unable to reach his clip and, on the verge of being pulled under, he cried out in panic for help. Hearing his shout of distress from the other side of the raft where he was sitting, Able Seaman Rene Baulne unsheathed his seaman's standard knife and, reaching across a pile of bodies, quickly sliced Tate's lanyard in two. His quick thinking and action not only saved Tate's life, it served as a welcome inspiration to others ringing around and huddling in what instantly became known as "Baulne's raft."

On another Carley float, coder Ed Munro was about to live through an experience so hideous he could never forget it. Numbed by the cold, clothed solely in his underwear and life jacket, he was experiencing bouts of nausea and periodic blackouts. He regained consciousness from time to time. On one occasion, as he looked around the rows of men huddled about, sprawled and piled on top of each other, he attempted to strike up a conversation with the body next to him. And that's exactly what it was. A body. A lifeless one, eyes shut. Mouth open, hanging grotesquely agape. Munro looked about him and asked if anyone could hear him. His words were greeted with deathly silence with good reason. He quickly realized with a shudder that he was the only one on the raft still alive. Just before he lapsed back into unconsciousness, a subliminal image formed in his fading vision that he was, in Charles Lamb's words, floating on a "raft of death."

To those in the water it seemed like a lifetime, but in fact only an hour had passed before the other corvettes appeared on the scene in answer to Petersen's SOS to take over the search for the enemy U-boat and to assist *Giffard* in any way possible in the rescue of survivors. Petersen carefully maneuvered his ship to face the moon, to provide as minimal a silhouette target as possible, and slowed his ship almost to a crawl as he sailed ahead amid the men in the water. Her crew did their utmost to help pull the forlorn figures, shivering from the cold, gasping from exhaustion, aboard. Both *Giffard* and *Edmunston* launched their sturdy little sea boats to assist in plucking survivors from the sea. One of the first to be saved by the boats was Jake Warren—just in time. *Valleyfield*'s navigator had become so weakened by his ordeal he was almost at the end of his tether. Tragically, the attempted rescue of the ship's captain, Dermot English, resulted in his demise. One corvette crewman reached out and gripped him by the collar of his uniform. But it was no use; his jacket was so water-sodden it tore apart, and English, who had given his life jacket to save the life of another, lost his own life as he splashed into the sea, drifted off and disappeared.

Others suffered a similar fate, so weak from the agony of trying to stay alive in the bitter cold water they didn't have enough strength left to grab onto the scramble net. Before the seamen could reach them, they drowned from sheer exhaustion.

Ian Tate, by good fortune and providence, summoned just enough strength to help himself once the opportunity presented itself. When *Giffard*'s first lieutenant, John Patterson, dangled the fire hose from the fo'c'sle, Tate grabbed it, fastened a loose part of it around his waist and was hauled aboard bodily.

In a way, Irving Kaplan was just as lucky, but almost too close for comfort. Compared to others, the frigate's yeoman was in relatively good shape thanks to his heavy water-resistant "zoot suit." But by the time the Carley float he was clipped to edged against the ship, he was being dragged under the water by the weight of the overcrowded raft. When he tried to put out his arm to grab the clip to unfasten it, he couldn't reach it. In desperation he shouted for a knife: "Someone give me a dirk! Give me a dirk!"

One of *Giffard*'s seamen unsheathed the knife, reached out from the net and handed it to him. With a couple of quick slashes Kaplan severed the lanyard of his life jacket and freed himself. Then he clambered up the scramble net, hauled himself aboard and passed out from sheer relief.

What happened to Ed Munro when his corpse-laden Carley float eased up to the side of the ship was macabre to the extreme. The scantily clad coder was so unconscious that to the seamen from the corvette who secured the raft to the ship and climbed onto it Munro looked just like one more lifeless body to be picked up and taken aboard, laid alongside the rest of the corpses on deck and left for burial. There were more important duties for the crew to attend to.

The priority was to treat the living, provide warmth and comfort to the water-sodden, half frozen victims of the sinking, towel them off, wrap them in blankets, give them hot toddies to drink and bed them down on cushioned locker tops and any other available space to make them comfortable enough to allow them to rest. The sick-bay attendants assisted by the ship's coxswain and John Patterson, the first officer, played their part, working tirelessly to tend the wounded, who were suffering from shock, exposure and fever.

Someone must have been saying prayers for Ed Munro. The saints were on his side. He could thank his lucky stars that an alert engine-room artificer who happened to be passing the row of lifeless bodies laid out on deck noticed the leg of one of them twitching spasmodically. Hey! Startled, he let out a yell: "This one's alive! Give us a hand!" No longer just a corpse, *Valleyfield*'s coder was ceremoniously carried to the main deck for treatment. When he awoke from the stupor into which he had lapsed amid the dead in the Carley float, he could thank the Lord for the miracle that had brought him back among the living.

Giffard remained on the scene until the rescue had been completed, the last Carley float recovered, wreckage examined and no sign of anyone living or dying from the sinking left in the water, and those who had been taken aboard the sea boats were transferred to her. Then Petersen set course full speed ahead for St. John's, fully aware that the lives of many of those rescued from the sea depended on how quickly they could be taken to hospital.

Giffard's departure left the other three corvettes of the C-1 group, under the leadership of the most senior officer of all three, Lieutenant Commander Rafael Barrett, skipper of *Edmunston*, to continue the search for the German U-boat. Operation Observant went into full gear with a vengeance, Channel Fever temporarily on hold in the quest to search and destroy the enemy responsible for the death of so many of their comrades.

With the ships spread out in a line abreast, the hunt was thorough. They probed the depths for the faintest sign of the submarine they were sure was still within striking distance. No echo, no matter how faint, no radar contact, no matter how transitory, was ignored. Depth charges were dropped without hesitation at the slightest sign of their prey. But it was not until around one o'clock in the morning, about an hour and a half after *Valleyfield* had been torpedoed, that there was a firm indication that the U-boat had been found and *Edmunston* fired a Hedgehog pattern. But the sonar image must have been either a spurious echo or some other unidentifiable object.

Earlier, when Zimmermann heard the explosions of the first depth charges dropped, he had moved away from what he calculated to be the initial leg of the search and took *U-548* right down to the ocean bed. With engines stopped he nestled there.

An hour later he heard two ships directly overhead, their CAT gear shrieking through his hydrophones, and he decide not to press his luck any further. Time to move on. Just in time, too. At 4:00 a.m., he had no sooner got underway when an aircraft dropped depth charges almost on the spot he had just left behind. He steered south then turned west towards Halifax, leaving his trackers none the wiser. In fact, ironically, their efforts had been doubled.

When Petersen had signalled the other corvettes in his group that *Valleyfield* had been sunk, he had also notified St. John's of the disaster. The naval authorities wasted no time springing into action. They sent the frigate *New Glasgow* from port to team up with *Agassiz* and *Timmins*, which had already been searching for the U-boat and had passed *Valleyfield*'s group before she was torpedoed, sailing in the opposite direction. The objective for them now was to join *Edmunston*, *Halifax* and *Frontenac* and widen the search. Barrett was still in charge of what was now Operation Salmon.

It got off to what appeared to be a promising start. On one of the legs of the slow, intense, methodical sweep of the widening square, *Edmunston*'s sonar operator suddenly got a solid reflection from the ocean bed with no discernible indication of any movement. Optimism ran high that it might possibly be the U-boat lying doggo. Barrett moved carefully into the attack and dropped a stick of depth charges. The resulting explosions sent a fountain of spray cascading onto the surface. All eyes focused from the bridge as a pool of oil began to spread over the water, followed by a shapeless, grimy object about three feet square.

Hopes were quickly dashed, however, when it was unmistakably identified as a Canadian naval jacket and by its markings one belonging to *Valleyfield*. The depth charges had disturbed the once proud frigate's watery grave, where so many of her gallant crew lay entombed with her.

Morale sagged among the crews of the six ships, particularly the crew of the *Edmunston*, closest to the spot. But it soon became evident anyway that the search was futile, and after three hours the authorities called it off and ordered the group back to port. Far to the south, *U-548* was safely patrolling the Halifax area, Zimmermann highly pleased that the move on his own initiative would have the support of his superiors in Germany, who had come to the same conclusion, as he learned later—from a wireless message sent to him earlier—suggesting that he relocate as soon as conditions permitted.

Meanwhile *Giffard* steamed ahead at maximum knots to St. John's, her mess decks crowded with men rescued from the sea, her destination only hours away. Among the fittest of all was Yeoman Irving Kaplan, thanks to his waterproof thick "zoot suit" that kept him relatively dry and warm. He spent the time en route busying himself circulating among the others less fortunate, among them Ian Tate and Jake Warren. From Warren he learned of the fate of his captain, Dermot English. With the help of *Giffard*'s coxswain he compiled an estimate of those still alive and those missing. Out of *Valleyfield*'s ship's company of 160 officers and men, they calculated there were five dead and 38 living aboard. Only two of her 15 officers and 36 of the 148 crewmen had survived the sinking.

Ian Tate sensed that after the ship reached port and all immediate needs, such as sending the wounded to hospital, had been taken care of, the soulful *Valleyfield* saga and all the ramifications it entailed would not end there. Nor would they be passed over lightly. Naval history of such incidents, even lesser ones, dictated otherwise. Impressed by Kaplan's energy and interest in the outcome, Tate encouraged him to obtain instant depositions from the survivors, while their experiences were still fresh in their minds.

Kaplan, in typical high spirits and with his strong sense of duty, accordingly marshalled a team around him, including the ship's coxswain and, with pad and pencil in hand, began conducting a series of interviews. By the time *Giffard* pulled into the harbour an eerie metamorphosis began to take shape among the survivors. For the first time the significance of their salvation began to dawn on them. They were, as Charles Lamb put it, "a chosen few." They had survived while those less fortunate had perished.

All this was overshadowed by the excitement of going ashore shortly after midday on the afternoon of May 7, 1942, when *Giffard* docked at the pier on the city side of St. John's, which was closer to the hospital than the corvette berths. The long night of terror had ended. But for Charles Petersen, tired and bedraggled, the full agony and horror was only beginning.

The immediate concern was to take care of the wounded by transporting them to hospital as quickly as possible. Ian Tate and Jake Warren, the only two *Valleyfield* surviving officers, though classified as wounded (suffering from "shock"), refused to stand on ceremony. They commandeered a staff car to take them to hospital in style—as befitting their rank. On arrival they made a beeline for the showers to wash off the oil and grime while wallowing in the sheer joy of bathing themselves in steaming water—to the horror of a medical orderly and doctor who told them off in no uncertain terms. Standing under hot water after prolonged exposure to freezing temperatures for an extended period was asking for trouble; they ran the risk of permanent damage to their extremities, the severest being gangrene leading to possible amputation. The delinquent pair were promptly confined to bed for proper treatment for their condition. They could not have been in better hands. Surgeon Captain Charles Best, former partner of the developer of insulin, Sir Frederick Banting, and his assistant, Surgeon Lieutenant Andrew Johnson, had been flown into St. John's specifically to tend to the survivors. The cure for the seamen suffering from the effects of being severely chilled in the freezing sea was as effective as it was innovative.

The patients were propped up in bed, their extremities exposed to fans blowing air over pans of ice cubes to provide gradual warmth and avoid bringing on gangrene. The unique method proved so successful there was only a single casualty. One seaman had to have his little toe amputated.

The dead were not forgotten, either. The five dead seamen brought back aboard *Giffard* were given a burial in the city cemetery with full naval honours, a marching band and funeral procession of 1,000 officers and men and, finally, the three-gun salute.

After up to two weeks of cure and convalescence, the hospital released its charges, who were given an indefinite period of home leave. Behind them the final drama of the *Valleyfield* sinking was played out. Just as Ian Tate has surmised, the book could not be closed until a formal court of inquiry was held.

RefScs: FDS 227-29 TSIAOG 154 OTTR 139-213

St, John's, Newfoundland
May 19, 1944

BYRON James
DAVIS D.W.
GERITY F.O.
PETERSEN Charles
ROSS W.G.
ROWLAND James
TATE Ian
TAYLOR Cuthbert
WARREN Jake

"Court of Inquiry into the Loss of Valleyfield."

On May 10, 1944 at St. John's, the formal court of inquiry convened: "To inquire into the loss of HMCS *Valleyfield*, and the death and injuries of certain officers and ratings on board said ship at that time," Captain S.W. Davis, RCN presiding. The two other members of the board were Lieutenant-Commanders F.O. Gerity, RCNR, and W.G. Ross, RCNVR.

The inquiry boiled down to two fundamental aspects: the torpedoing of *Valleyfield* itself and the rescue operations conducted by Escort Group C-1, both of which directly entailed the tragic loss of so many lives. Because both the group's senior officer and the ship's captain were dead, it was impossible to establish cause and effect or affix responsibility at the command level.

Written reports from officers and from the five corvettes involved interviews, much of it vague and conflicting (and inevitably some of it second-hand), and revealed little beyond the fact that the frigate had been torpedoed by a submarine in the port bow and that the life-saving equipment was inadequate. Subsequently the board felt it prudent for the most part to refrain from an extensive statement. It was left to the two most senior officers at St. John's, Commander Cuthbert Taylor, RCN, Flag Officer, Newfoundland, and Captain James Rowland of the Royal Navy, Captain (D) [Destroyers], to provide the most relevant comments in the subsequent findings appended to the court's report.

They didn't pull any punches but at the same time their remarks were also fair and understanding. Special attention was paid to reports submitted by Charles Petersen, captain of *Giffard*, and to evidence of the two surviving *Valleyfield* officers on the bridge at the time of the sinking. Because Tate and Warren were still confined to hospital, in keeping with standard Navy protocol and to preserve service tradition, a white ensign was spread over Warren's bed, the hearing conducted with a secretary recording the proceedings by his bedside.

All this evidence, supported by other first-hand accounts at the time the torpedoing took place, led to a scathing condemnation of the actions—or lack of them—of the officer responsible for the conduct of Escort Group C-1, Commander James Byron.

He was found to be negligent on all counts. He had ignored the immediate threat of the U-boat even though he had been warned of its presence in the very area into which his group was entering and had failed to take precautions. On the contrary. He had cancelled the zigzagging, rendering the ships relatively easy targets to submarine attack. In spite of the recent losses attributed to the new acoustic torpedo, he had found it unnecessary to take countermeasures. In the detached confines of the boardroom, Byron, despite a distinguished wartime record, could well have been dismissed as a bumbling incompetent.

But Commander Taylor and Captain Rowlands, the key examiners, from their many years of ocean combat experience, clearly appreciated and understood the improbables of command at sea while in danger.

In fairness, the measures taken by Byron had to be judged against the circumstances surrounding them. His decision to cancel the zigzagging was understandable and acceptable, given that an erratic course multiplied the dangers of colliding with low-lying ice floes strong enough to pierce a ship's hull when weighed against the unseen and undetected threat of an enemy submarine. Likewise Byron's decision not to stream the CAT Gear as a deterrent to acoustic torpedo attack was acceptable because of the interference with asdic efficiency. Taylor's and Rowlands's defense of the group senior officer's actions in respect to these issues was duly noted—and appreciated—by the board.

The failure of the group to resume zigzagging once it had sailed through the floating-ice danger zone was not so easily explained away. But Byron could hardly be blamed for his failure to countermand his original order; he was asleep in his cabin after a prolonged period of two nights and days on watch under severe weather conditions, and his rest was well earned. Considering the circumstances, it was understandable that the junior officers he left in charge would be highly reluctant to disturb the exhausted group leader. The examiners had to take into consideration that blame had to be attached to the spirit of Channel Fever prevalent in every ship in the group and that all the crews were anxious to reach port as quickly as possible. Taking that into account, a direct route was preferable to an irregular anti-submarine one.

In any case the board was not about to besmirch the fine record of a distinguished commander who had given his life in the line of duty over something that, however the circumstances were interpreted—being asleep and not assigning responsibility before leaving his watch to resume zigzagging when conditions allowed—was understandable. (To stream or not to stream the CAT Gear was a toss-up.)

However, rescue operations in the wake of the sinking came in for much closer and more intense scrutiny than the events leading up to it. And responsibility on the part of *Giffard*'s commander, Charles Petersen, could not be so easily excused or dismissed. If there was a single factor for which he could be faulted it was procrastination. When his officer of the watch reported witnessing what amounted to an explosion in the spot 300 yards abeam to port where *Valleyfield* was positioned, coupled with the fact that his radar operator had suddenly lost contact under ideal conditions for a clear reception, Petersen hesitated to accept the fact that the frigate was actually sinking. Then, as *Giffard* reached the site of the survivors struggling in the water, which confirmed it, he couldn't make up his mind whether the sinking had been caused by an inner explosion, striking a mine, or a torpedoing, until the men freezing to death in the water, some seriously wounded, angrily responded that the latter had been the case. Even then he hesitated before signalling the other three corvettes in the group to close—without giving a reason—and by the time he realized that this needed clarification and that St. John's should likewise be informed, half an hour had been wasted since the officer on the bridge had witnessed what amounted to a sinking.

However, Captain Rowlands diagnosed the critical time lapse with a not ungenerous summation: "It is thought that the loss of the senior officer of the group will inevitably produce a certain degree of confusion. On this occasion much valuable time was lost before the situation was appreciated." In effect an understanding slap on the wrist—so far.

At the heart of the matter lay Petersen's indecisiveness in choosing which of the two actions left open to him to take: rescue the survivors or hunt down the U-boat. After notifying the other ships in the group he pursued the latter course. But going only half the distance—he certainly was no Solomon—amounted to a half-hearted gesture betwixt and between.

To avoid presenting the ship too clearly as a U-boat target, he had pointed it facing the moon and proceeded to the rescue of the survivors of the sinking at a reduced speed. But it was not slow enough to save the exhausted, half-drowned men who, without the strength to hold onto the scramble nets, fell back into the sea. Some were lost, including *Valleyfield*'s captain, while others were sucked under the propeller wash.

Senior court officer Commodore Taylor was less generous than his counterpart in his indictment of Petersen's conduct over this phase of the catastrophe. He put it this way: "The commanding officer HMCS *Giffard*, should have recognized the ships of the group were well placed to order 'Close and carry out Observant [search operation] anti-clock wise round *Valleyfield* (or my own position)' as soon as he knew something had happened to HMCS *Valleyfield*. It is considered that in this way there was a very good chance the U-boat would have been detected by HMCS *Halifax*. It is difficult to understand why, having realized that something had happened at 2343, as shown by his altering course towards *Valleyfield* at that time, the commanding officer HMCS *Giffard* made no signal to institute a search for the enemy until 0001, a matter of 18 minutes later."

About the ineffectiveness of the subsequent search at the cost of so many lives, Captain Rowlands was particularly scathing. "The lack of plot from *Giffard* gives reason to doubt the efficiency of her short radar search to detect the submarine. It is noted that even *Giffard* would not have reached the area before 0001 and that the other ships had not turned before this time."

To put it bluntly, Petersen's vacillation was directly responsible for the deaths of so many survivors. This the board could not abide. But by the same token it took into account that he had neither the training nor experience to cope with the unprecedented predicament thrust upon him; to take command of a group of ships in the absence of its senior officer. Normally such a responsibility would pass to the senior commander of that group. In this case the captain of *Edmunston*, a seasoned commander who, in fact, outranked Petersen in seniority—and experience. But this was not a normal situation. Far from it. Lieutenant-Commander Rafael Barrett, who doubtless would have handled the situation differently (notifying the rest of the group immediately, for one thing), was not at the scene. Petersen was. He simply did not possess the experience or initiative to cope with it. In sum: he was a victim of circumstances beyond his ken or control.

Taking into account all the various manifestations of the torpedoing, while Petersen was not exonerated for his part in the disaster, he wasn't censured either. The *Valleyfield* incident therefore passed into the naval record as another one of the tragic misfortunes of war.

Valleyfield's sinking was far from the worst sinking in World War II in terms of lives lost. Nor was it the last. For the record, however, it was the first and last RCN frigate to fall victim to a U-boat torpedoing. It was the timing that was significant. It was the second such Canadian defeat of such epic proportions to take place within "black week." Several days earlier HMCS *Athabaskan* had been sunk off the northern coast of France in a running battle with German destroyers, taking 125 of her ship's company to the bottom with her. These two major defeats were but a prelude to the torpedoing of six more RCN ships that summer at a cost of another 298 Canadian seamen lost at sea. All this came as an ominous shock to the escort groups, not to mention the merchant marine.

But before the final curtain came down on the *Valleyfield* affair there was one more act to be played out, perhaps the most painful of all. Although before retiring from the Navy Charles Petersen had been given various new naval assignments, including a command at sea, he never recovered from his part in the tragedy. It weighed too heavily for him to face life. In the end it was too much for him to bear and he drank himself to death.

RefScs: OTTR 206–219

TITANIC TEST FOR THE TRIBALS
JANUARY–APRIL 1944

In January 1944, the three RCN Tribal class destroyers
Athabaskan, Haida *and* Huron, *along with their Royal Navy
counterparts, were released from Russian convoy duty for an
even more challenging assignment. Two significant, though
seemingly unrelated, events brought this transfer about.*

*The first of these occurred over Christmas 1943, while the
destroyers sailed close escort to convoy JW-55, northbound to
Murmansk. Off the coast of Norway the powerful German battleship* Scharnhorst *suddenly appeared. A furious battle raged
between a flotilla of British cruisers, aided by the escort
destroyers, and the huge surface raider. A shell from one of the
Tribals temporarily forced* Scharnhorst *out of the fight. It
returned, only to become mincemeat when the RN battleship*
Duke of York *arrived on to the scene to send it to the bottom.*

Tirpitz, *the last German Dreadnought, still lurked undetected
within the Norwegian fjords, and the Murmansk run was still
threatened from the air and by U-boats. But a significant menace had been overcome, and this fact helped allow the
Admiralty to free up the Tribals for a second forthcoming event,
a job of vital importance—the Allied invasion of Europe.*

*The overall objective was to protect the western flank of the
assault force from German surface ships based in French ports.
To accomplish this, the RN assigned the heaviest destroyers it
could find to the 10th Destroyer Fleet at Plymouth. These were
backed up by two heavily armed* cruisers—Bellona *and* Black
Prince, *equipped with 5.25-inch guns.*

*The initial objective was to clear the English Channel of
German destroyers—but first they had to be found, or lured into
battle. A twin-pronged exercise was devised: Operation Tunnel,
aimed at disrupting enemy convoys from the northern French
coast into the Bay of Biscay, and Operation Hostile, protecting
RN minesweepers as they unclogged the approaches to enemy
harbours and other critical points. During each operation, Allied
ships stood a good chance of encountering German destroyers.*

The risks were high. Both exercises would be carried out at night, the only time the enemy ships would venture from port. They would be within range of German shore batteries, which were equipped with radar. And they would be wending their way through enemy minefields. As well, they were up against formidable opponents: Narvik and Elbing class German destroyers; the close escorts to German convoys, which included heavily armed flak ships, trawlers and minesweepers; and high-speed E-boats (comparable to the Allied MTBs—motor torpedo boats).

At first, the Canadians had little luck. In fact, between early January and late April, Haida *had completed 18 missions,* Huron *11, and* Athabaskan *nine, without once encountering a German destroyer or submarine. It was just as well—from the start they realized, and admitted, that they were poorly trained, and could use a good shaking down. But they adapted quickly, praised by Flotilla Captain Basil Jones as being "highly efficient and full of aggressive spirit."*

Before the month was out, they would show him they were as good as his word.

17 Miles Northeast of Ile de Bas
April 26, 1944

DeWOLF Harry George
RAYNER Herbert Sharples
STUBBS John Hamilton

"Scratch One Elbing"

British intelligence had revealed that three German Elbing class destroyers, known to be berthed at St. Mao on the north coast of Brittany, were expected to break out of port early on the morning of April 26. To intercept them, *Athabaskan, Haida, Huron* and a British destroyer, *Ashanti,* supported by the RN cruiser *Black Prince,* left Plymouth harbour at 9:00 on the evening of April 25; by 1:30 next morning they were in position, 17 miles east-northeast of Ile de Bas, 10 miles from shore. They began patrolling in an east-northeasterly direction.

The force was immediately picked up by German radar stations—their shore batteries opened up. Though the gun flashes were clearly visible in the dark, their range and aim were well off, and for the next half hour the patrol passed uneventfully. Then, at 2:00 a.m., *Black Prince* picked up a radar echo from 21,000 yards dead ahead, a contact confirmed moments later by both *Haida* and *Ashanti*.

At this point, the Allied flotilla's heading put them on a collision course with the German ships. But the Elbings abruptly reversed course and increased speed to 24 knots, heading back towards the French coast—neither soon enough, nor fast enough. The Tribal destroyers gave chase, all-out at 30 knots.

Nineteen minutes later, range closed to 13,000 yards, *Black Prince* lobbed several star shells over the enemy ships. Seeing them falling far to the right, Harry DeWolf, *Haida*'s skipper, signalled "More left." The next volley was right on target, their macabre light illuminating all three Elbings, at a range now reduced to five miles. *Athabaskan*, *Haida* and *Ashanti* opened fire simultaneously. The German destroyers laid down a smokescreen, but the Tribals continued to fire salvo after salvo.

At 1:31, *Ashanti* scored the first hit, followed five minutes later by a second strike; a hint of fire could be seen through the smoke. By 2:45, the range had narrowed to 7,300 yards, but the Tribals were still unable to clearly make out the enemy. Approaching 3:30, the Elbings were still in flight, staying within 12 miles of the jutting coastline, darting in and out of the smoke. Elbing *T-29* had even managed to fire off several torpedoes towards *Black Prince*, but they went wide of the mark.

The rocky inlets created a confused chaos on the radar screens. *Haida* nevertheless picked up *T-29*, which had broken away. DeWolf turned his ship sharply to starboard, at right angles to the enemy destroyer, crossing through a freshly laid British minefield as he did so. *Athabaskan*, skippered by John Stubbs, followed. *Haida*'s first shells smashed into the German ship's afterstructure; a second and third barrage struck the destroyer amidships. As fire erupted, *Athabaskan* fired off several more salvoes.

Huron, with Herbie Rayner at the helm, and *Ashanti* joined in, but their first torpedoes went astray. Now all four Tribals closed to within 400 yards for the kill. The Elbing, ablaze from stem to stern, mortally wounded and with its heavy guns out of commission, continued to fight fiercely. Its Oerlikons drummed along *Haida*'s side, struck *Athabaskan*'s superstructure and ripped into *Huron*'s bridge.

It was a simple matter of time, however, and time was fast running out for the Germans—shell after shell pounded the stricken ship. At 4:21 a.m., *Haida* reported to *Black Prince*, "Enemy has sunk." With battle ensigns snapping in the early morning breeze, the four triumphant Tribals formed up to set sail for Plymouth.

On the downside, *Ashanti* and *Huron* collided during the return voyage. Damage was slight, and there were no injuries, but it was enough to keep both destroyers out of action for five days of refitting.

RefScs: DHist f FDS 25 1–53 TSIAOG 161

East of Ile Vierge, off the Coast of Brittany
April 29, 1944

DeWOLF Harry
MacLURE William
HANNAN John
MURRAY Fraser
STUBBS John Hamilton

"Fiery End to Athabaskan"

On Friday, April 28, *Athabaskan* and sister ship *Haida* sailed from Plymouth on an Operation Hostile mission to cover a flotilla of British mine layers. The mines were being sown 10 miles to the east of Ile de Bas, where the destroyers had seen

Harry DeWolf aboard Haida. *(Herb Nott/DND/PA 141695)*

action two days earlier. The job took exactly one hour, beginning at 2:00 a.m. Saturday.

But, just before the mine layers headed back to England, Plymouth ordered the two Tribals to proceed southwest at full speed. Radar reception that night was exceptionally good. British stations had picked up contact with a German force steaming westerly towards the Morlaix River entrance. The enemy vessels were hugging the coast, and it was calculated that they would cross north of Ile de Bas by one mile.

Athabaskan and *Haida* figured they would intercept them after they had passed the island, while they were still west of Ile Vierge. Just before four o'clock, *Athabaskan* made radar contact—14 miles to port. The echoes indicated two destroyer-sized ships and a smaller vessel. In fact, they were *T-24* and *T-27*, the two Elbing destroyers that had escaped the Tribals just four days previous, and an E-boat.

Quickly closing range to 4,300 yards, "Hard Over Harry" DeWolf signalled "Ignite" from *Haida*'s bridge—*Athabaskan* fired a volley of 4-inch star shells. The German destroyers stood out clearly to port in the pinkish-orange glow. They discharged

John Stubbs, captain of Assiniboine *and* Haida. *(DND/PA 104250)*

smoke and started to veer away, but DeWolf had already given the order to engage, and both Canadian ships opened fire. At the same time, they turned their bows directly towards the German destroyers, to present as little silhouette as possible and to avoid the torpedoes the Elbings customarily fired when making a retreat.

But it was too late. A torpedo (whether fired from an Elbing or the E-boat was never determined) struck *Athabaskan*. An explosion, then fire erupted near her stern. "I'm hit and losing power," John Stubbs, her captain, reported tersely. DeWolf laid down smoke to protect his consort and continued the chase, now one against two.

Aboard *Athabaskan*, fires had broken out above and below decks. All the aft guns were out of action. The propeller and shaft were smashed. The main engines were finished. Then the forward guns failed, and the ship's stern began to mire. The situation was desperate. Stubbs had no choice: "Prepare to abandon ship."

Lifeboats were lowered and, in vain hope that the destroyer could be towed, cables were fastened. But now the flames were raging fiercely. A fire party managed to haul the ship's 70-ton fire pump to the stern, where the blaze was at its worst. They were connecting it to the hydrant when a second explosion—from the E-boat or shore batteries, in the confusion no one knew—heaved the ship to one side and then swung her back on keel.

She was finished. Listing to port, those still on board tossed Carley floats and jumped in after them. Slowly, *Athabaskan* upended and slid under the surface, steam and escaping air hissing her death knell. The survivors, some in boats, others clinging to floats and still others supported only by their life jackets, many of them barely alive, dolefully witnessed the demise of what had been one of the happiest ships in the Navy.

In the meantime, *Haida* had exacted revenge. Although the Elbings could barely be seen through their smokescreen, *Haida* trained her guns, guided mainly by radar, and she was able to inflict damage on *T-27*. Then, at the very moment *Athabaskan* was being struck a second time, *Haida*'s shells landed squarely on the wounded Elbing, setting her afire. Her captain decided that escape was futile, and deliberately ran his destroyer aground.

After delivering several more salvoes, and with dawn fast approaching, DeWolf decided to withdraw to render what rescue he could for *Athabaskan*'s survivors. He reached the position where life jacket lights were bobbing and blinking in the dark. Still within range of the shore batteries, he ordered engines stopped. He then lowered lifeboats and Carley floats, and dropped scramble nets over the side. At 5:15 a.m., with the tide pulling at the destroyer and dawn raising the probabilities for an imminent air attack, John Stubbs called to DeWolf from the water: "Get away. Get clear."

Haida lingered for several minutes longer—by then 42 crewmen had been plucked from the water. DeWolf gave the order: "Slow ahead."

During the rescue, *Haida* had also lowered her motor cutter (i.e., power launch) with Bill MacLure, a leading stoker, at the helm. MacLure had picked up two of his own shipmates, Jack Hannan and Fraser Murray, who had been swept into the water while manning the scramble nets. Together, they took another eight survivors aboard. But there was no time for *Haida* to hoist her cutter back aboard. MacLure and his party were left to fend for themselves and find their own way back to England. Heading north, they made off just in time. German minesweepers appeared, to take prisoner those survivors still in the water. One ship chased after the cutter—then, for some inexplicable reason, it broke off and turned back.

The cutter had fuel for three hours. It was equipped with emergency rations, and the weather was relatively calm and clear. But this was still not a completely happy arrangement—a voyage of some 150 miles lay ahead. And the engine was unreliable. Three times it stopped dead and, despite a band-aid patch-up job to fix a leaking fuel line, the best speed they could coax out of it was a paltry three knots.

Mid-afternoon, three German fighters—clearly identifiable by the black crosses on their wings—buzzed them from a height of 12 feet. But the tiny crew seemed blessed with luck—like the minesweeper earlier, the German pilots also broke away. That evening, two more aircraft suddenly appeared. The men held their breath and hoped for the best. Spitfires—the seamen began signalling wildly with semaphore flags. A short while later, a RAF air/sea rescue launch picked them up.

The number of those rescued from *Athabaskan* now totalled 50; 83 were prisoners of war; 128, including Captain John Stubbs, bearer of the DSO, were lost.

RefScs: DHist f FDS 254–58 TSIAOG 162–63

HIT-AND-RUN
MARCH–MAY 1944

*T*orpedo boats were the glamour ships of the Royal Canadian Navy. Quick—up to 40 knots or better—and lethal—four torpedoes, pom-pom, Oerlikon and machine guns— they could dart in among enemy convoys, mostly at night, strike hard, fast and often, and be gone, delivering maximum destruction in minimum time. Hit-and-run. Their speed and versatility allowed them to venture into places and situations the destroyers and their like could never dare. Thus they were an effective component for incorporation into the marine preparations for D-Day, and beyond it.

The success of Canadians assigned to RN motor torpedo boats (MTBs) and motor gunboats (MGBs) in the English Channel, the North Sea and Mediterranean had been such that the formation of all-Canadian motorboat flotillas had been conceived early in the war. A decision was not reached until November 1943, however, and the formation of two flotillas—the 29th and 65th—did not come about until March 1944. The 29th Flotilla comprised MTBS—70-feet long, known as "Shorts"; the 65th, of the longer (115 feet), but slower Fairmile D boats—known as "Dog Boats."

Their crews had, for the most part, served with RN coastal command. Compared with their counterparts on other classes of Canadian ships, their skippers were relatively young. Tom Fuller, for example—at 32, the oldest among them—was nicknamed "Gramps."

Working-up trials were held at Holyhead in Wales until late in April. The 29th Flotilla, under the command of Tony Law, was then assigned to Ramsgate, the coastal forces base of Dover Command. The 65th, commanded by James "The Brain" Kirkpatrick, under Plymouth Command, was based at Brixham in Devon.

The Canadian MTBs carried out their first mission on the night of May 16. Four ships from the 29th escorted two RN torpedo boats. They were to land engineers by dory on the French coast to steal German mines out from under the enemy's very nose—but heavy seas scrubbed the operation before it could get fully underway. The next night the wind had abated and the mission was carried out without incident.

The MTBs had been as conspicuous in the clear calm as silhouetted targets in a shooting gallery, yet there had been no enemy reaction whatsoever—not even from the shore batteries. The Canadians, brought to a fine fighting pitch, felt cheated in a sense. They had been trained for the attack! A week later, they would find exactly what they were looking for, and then some.

24 Miles off Boulogne
May 23, 1944

BISHOP Craig
CHAFFEY Charles Donald
LAW Anthony
MARSHALL Sherwood

"Night Action under Glare of Star Shells"

On the evening of May 22, Canadian MTBs *459*, *464*, *465* and *466* put out from Ramsgate, joined by four British torpedo boats to intercept a German convoy sailing between Dieppe and Boulogne. From intelligence reports, they knew the convoy would be heavily protected by the dreaded flak trawlers.

The sea was choppy and a stiff wind blew in a northwesterly direction. It was 2:24 in the dead of night before they found the enemy flotilla. Suddenly star shells erupted everywhere—the Canadians' red, the Germans' green—revealing the merchant ships, escorted by E-boats as well as the flak trawlers. Caught in the glare, and between the enemy ships and his own, Tony Law veered his MTB into the cover of darkness.

The British boats were forced to withdraw under a smoke-screen, drawing with them a barrage of shells from both the German ships and shore batteries. Now the Canadian 29th—Law, Charlie "Chuff Chuff" Chaffey, Craig Bishop and Sherwood "Barney" Marshall—pressed forward at full speed, flat out at 41 knots.

In the mix-up, Bishop found himself alone, one on one versus a German E-boat, an opponent faster by 10 knots. Closing to within 200 yards, the two ships blasted away, no quarter asked or given. Law ordered "Smoke," hoping a screen might help in reassembling his flotilla. Bishop was nowhere to be seen, and the convoy was by now lost to the darkness, although the Canadians were certain they had inflicted severe damage.

It was 7:00 in the morning before the three Canadian torpedo boats reached Ramsgate. There they found Bishop's 464, which

Tony Law (r.), who was awarded the DSC. (G.A. Milne/DND/PA 144588)

had joined the British MTBs on their way back to England. Though she was now safely berthed, she had sustained some battle scars; one shell had struck aft of the bridge, and her rigging had been shot away, along with the torpedo boat's white battle ensign.

Charles Chaffey joined the RCN in 1940 as an ordinary seaman. He was wounded in an air raid while serving aboard an RN destroyer off the coast of England. Subsequently earning his commission, he joined a mine-laying flotilla before being transferred to the MTBs.

Anthony Law had joined the Canadian army before transferring to the RCN in 1940. He subsequently served "on loan" to the RN, training in anti-submarine warfare. In 1941, he was posted to an RN MTB flotilla before taking command of the RCN 29th Flotilla in 1944.

RefScs: CN 139–45 FDS 247.49 VAS (L) 56–57 (C) 65–66

Off the Northern Tip of Brittany
May 23, 1944

COLLINS John
JONES Brian
KIRKPATRICK James
MABEE Oliver
McCLELLAND Jack
McLERNON Leslie
MORROW Albert

"Mistaken Identity Kills Gunners in Crossfire"

Farther to the west, on the same night as the action by the 29th, the 65th Flotilla set out from their base at Brixham, near Dartmouth. The flotilla consisted of torpedo boats *726*, *727*, *735* and *745*. James "Kirk" Kirkpatrick was in overall command, aboard John Collins's *735*.

They headed out at 22 knots, directly towards the northernmost tip of Brittany, where a convoy had been reported. Contrary to the weather conditions encountered by their sister flotilla, the 65th cruised through a calm sea, under a cloudless sky. At 3:27 a.m., Ollie Mabee, on the bridge of *745*, made radar contact. The blips indicated a convoy escorted by E-boats, north of Ile les Heux and Sept Iles.

The Canadians spotted the convoy 14 minutes later, from a range of 3,500 yards. But before they could launch a torpedo strike, the Germans had seen them and turned to intercept. Kirkpatrick split his forces in two. He ordered Mabee and Les McLernon (*727*) to attack the main convoy, while he and Bert "the Beard" Morrow's *726* tackled the E-boat escorts. The latter two torpedo boats closed to within 100 yards, all guns ablaze. They stopped two E-boats dead in the water—but before they were knocked out, the Germans managed to strike back. Two of *726*'s gunners were fatally hit.

Meanwhile, Mabee and McLernon closed in on the merchant ships—four torpedoes were fired. None of them found their target, and a smoke float was dropped to cover their withdrawal.

Jack McClelland, who served on MTB 726 as first officer, and carved a future in the Canadian publishing industry. (DND/PA 180071)

Now *726* was back in the thick of it. Brian Jones, the forward torpedo man on Morrow's MTB, spotted a boat looming out of the smoke, bearing directly down. It happened so suddenly, there was no time to properly identify the ship as either friend or foe. There was gunfire. Jack McClelland, on the bridge, was certain it had come from the approaching vessel—*726* returned fire—Mabee's *745* took the full brunt of the fusillade. One of her gunners was cut down by the rain of bullets. It had been a case of mistaken identity—the initial fire had come from an E-boat behind *745*.

The entire engagement had lasted only seven minutes. Hit-and-run. At 3:35, the shattered crews regrouped to return to

Brixham. Mabee's boat was so badly damaged she couldn't keep up. Her casualties were transferred to Morrow's MTB. Further en route, McLernon's *727* broke down from fuel contamination, and Collins's craft, *735*, had to be taken in tow. Nor was it the last of the 65th Flotilla's woes on her maiden mission. On reaching port, *735*'s crew learned that their MTB had lost all four of her engines—completely burned out.

After graduating from the Royal Military College in 1937, James Kirkpatrick studied law at Osgoode Hall in Toronto. He joined the Royal Canadian Naval Volunteer Reserve (RCNVR) in 1939, and his first sea duty was with an RN armed merchant cruiser, which was torpedoed in the Bay of Biscay. Kirkpatrick was later employed in air/sea rescue work; then, in 1942, he was transferred to an RN MTB flotilla.

Jack McClelland enlisted in the RCNVR in 1941. In 1942, he attended Royal Roads Naval College, and then was posted to a Fairmile flotilla at St. John's. He was later engaged in mine clearing, for which he was mentioned in dispatches. After the war, McClelland went on to become Canada's most famous book publisher.

RefScs: CN 139.45 FDS 247–49 VAS (K) 55–56 (W) 69–70 (Mc) 75–77

NEPTUNE
JUNE 1944

O *peration Neptune was just one aspect of Overlord, the Allied invasion of Normandy. It was the naval aspect—an assault armada of 10 columns, comprising 5,300 ships and landing craft—simply the largest naval invasion force ever assembled. For its part, Canada contributed 115 ships and some 9,000 Royal Canadian Navy seamen. And though there were several wounded, not a single RCN sailor was killed on D-Day, June 6.*

This notable fact could be attributed both to luck and good management, as well as meticulous planning—all three were

A view of the Allied invasion of France in which the 29th and 65th Flotillas played a vital role. (G.A. Milne/DND/PA 144576)

prerequisites to the success of the assault. The RCN's role was both various and onerous. And not without risk.

Probably the most exacting, not to mention nail-biting, role was that played by Canadian minesweepers. An operation known as the Oropesa Sweep was assigned to 16 Bangor class minesweepers. Six were distributed among three different RN flotillas. The other 10 made up the 31st Canadian Minesweeping Flotilla, commanded by Tony Storrs, aboard Caraquet.

Their job, along with 100 other Allied vessels in the same category, was to slice through the German minefields, clearing paths for the landing craft to follow. On the evening of June 5, five miles ahead of the invasion fleet, the minesweepers steamed into the Baie de la Seine and began cutting into the eight-mile-thick mine belt, which floated 40 miles north of the assault beaches; they carefully marked the alleyways then sliced through the defence barrier by dropping signal buoys along the routes. Their next task was to clear further channels to areas within seven miles of shore, where the troop transports and bombarding battlewagons would drop anchor. Finally, the minesweeping flotillas would clear the paths for the landing craft themselves, pushing as close as possible towards the beaches.

A task calling for the utmost accuracy and precision, the minesweepers were equipped with the latest electronic locating devices and radar-jamming sets. Fortunately, the enemy mines were moored by wires held down by weights—the sweepers simply cut the cables, releasing the mines to the surface. But, rather than the usual routine of exploding them with rifle fire and thereby alerting the Germans with their detonations, the mines were simply left free-floating. The danger was minimized due to the fact that, in most cases, the firing mechanism was neutralized when they surfaced.

To prevent interference from German destroyers, E-boats and, in particular, U-boats (considered the greatest menace by far), a 56,000-square-mile defensive rectangle had been defined—an area extending from the Atlantic approaches and the Bay of Biscay in the west, to the North Sea accesses in the east. Inside this area, Hurd Deep patrol, comprising of the Tribal destroyers, including Haida *and* Huron, *along with MTBS, were positioned to provide close protection to the assault fleet. Operation CA, made up of six escort groups, of which two groups were Canadian, guarded the outer phalanxes.*

Eleven Canadian frigates participated as part of the outer defenses in the west: Cape Breton, Grou, Outremont, Teme *and* Waskesiu *were assigned to RN Escort Group 6, while* Matane, Meon, Port Colborne, Saint John, Stormont *and* Swansea *formed part of Group 9. The inner defense was allotted to destroyers:* Chaudiere, Gatineau, Kootenay, Ottawa, *and* St. Laurent *made up Escort Group 11; Escort Group 12 consisted of* Qu'Appelle, Restigouche, Saskatchewan *and* Skeena.

The 29th MTB Flotilla had a job to do that night, as well—to protect the eastern flank of the British–Canadian assault force from E-boats, known to be berthed at Le Havre. Tony Law had split his boats into two divisions; however, once underway, the unit was reassigned to the western side of the assault formation.

After a thoroughly miserable night in the high, rolling sea and raging winds, the 29th headed back for Portsmouth at first light, just as the assault forces were approaching the Normandy beaches. On the north side of the Channel, their counterparts in the 65th MTB Flotilla had positioned themselves along the convoy routes heading out from Lyme Bay.

*As part of the attacking force itself, Canada provided 19 corvettes, 30 landing craft, two troop ships and two bombardment destroyers. The corvettes—*Alberni, Baddeck, Calgary, Camrose, Drumheller, Kitchener, Lindsay, Louisburg *(the 2nd),* Lunenburg, Mayflower, Mimico, Moose Jaw, Port Arthur, Prescott, Regina, Rimouski, Summerside, Trentonian *and* Woodstock—*were assigned a gamut of close escort duties, protecting landing craft, merchant ships, troop carriers, hospital ships and tugs towing sections of the Mulberry harbour (two prefabricated harbours capable of shifting 12,000 tons of cargo and 2,500 vehicles a day, as well as providing protection from inclement weather).*

The landing craft were divided into three flotillas. The 260th Canadian Flotilla consisted of seven craft, aboard which were 250 Canadian and 1,050 British troops (attached to the 3rd Canadian Division); 1,946 Canadians and 148 Brits (also from the 3rd) filled 12 craft of the 262nd Canadian Flotilla. Another seven LCTs, from the 264th Canadian Flotilla, carried 1,126 troops of the British Northumbrian Division.

Anchored seven miles offshore were the two Canadian troopships Prince David, *captained by Tom Kelly, and* Prince Henry, *by Stuart Godfrey. Formerly luxury liners, these 6,000 ton, 22-knot vessels were purchased from Canadian Steamship Lines in 1939; their metamorphosis to armed merchant cruisers required a year in the navy yards.* Prince David *was supported by* Algonquin, *skippered by Debby Piers.* Prince Henry *was escorted by* Sioux, *under the command of Eric Boak.*

The troop carriers began lowering their landing barges into the water at 6:17 a.m., June 6. As the tiny craft began their rough, hour-long run to the Juno beaches, destroyers Algonquin *and* Sioux *opened fire simultaneously—along with 76 other*

Allied warships. Sioux *targeted two buildings near St. Aubin, housing 75-mm guns—they were silenced within two minutes.*

Amphibious tanks—with collapsible canvas bulwarks—were to have gone in ahead, but they were delayed in the rough seas. Algonquin *and* Sioux *now undertook the task of clearing the beaches with their fire. Just before touchdown, their guns fell silent. By eight o'clock, the 800 first-wave troops of the Canadian Scottish Regiment and Le Régiment de la Chaudière began scrambling ashore.*

Later came a call for help—three German 88s two miles inland were holding up the Chaudières, who signalled Algonquin *to come to their aid. Debby Piers and his crew couldn't see the guns—their fire was directed by a forward observation officer ashore. It was right on. Several broadsides from* Algonquin *put the 88s out of business, and the Chaudières continued their advance. Perfect teamwork between army and navy was a theme that was repeated many times that day.*

Meanwhile, the minesweepers continued clearing the invasion area, a job that would go on for a week. By early afternoon, the follow-up convoys began to arrive, bringing in their landing-craft flotillas. Canadian units landed another 4,000 men before the day was through.

The first phase of Neptune had been carried out smoothly. In fact, it had succeeded beyond all hopes, and despite the anything-but-ideal sea conditions. A large share of the credit rested with the RCN Atlantic escort convoys and their ongoing battle against the U-boats over the years. On D-Day, only one German submarine was sighted—and it got nowhere near the invasion fleet.

Off Le Havre, at the Mouth of the Seine River
June 6–8, 1944

CHAFFEY Charles Donald

"MTBs Take on R-boats in Night Action"

A t mid-afternoon of D-Day, after a night spent in the rolling seas off Cherbourg, the thoroughly exhausted 29th Canadian flotilla put out from Portsmouth again. Their destination was Le Havre, which was known to be infested with German E-Boats and R-boats (*Raumboote*)—not as fast as the Es, but just as mightily armed. Hardly reassuring for the men manning the MTBs, their torpedo tubes were still damaged from a skirmish a few nights earlier—they were going out to do battle as gunboats against an enemy that would heavily outgun them.

And there was another new wrinkle, although it was in the form of a tactic that was ostensibly favourable. For the first time, British and Canadian ships would be directed to their targets by a central command vessel, in much the same way fighter aircraft were controlled by land-based command stations. On this night the controller was HMS *Scylla*, the flagship of Rear Admiral Sir Philip Vian (who, in 1942, had battled a cruiser squadron across the Mediterranean, from Alexandria to Malta, to relieve that besieged isle).

Another storm-tossed night. At 4:00 a.m. the four Canadian torpedo boats—*459, 460, 465* and *466*—were in position off the French port. Visibility was reduced to four miles. The crews kept their engines idling, constantly shifting to stay in position as they drifted to and fro. Suddenly, the hammering of cannon fire erupted to the south, and a kaleidoscope of star shells and flares lit the sky—a group of British MTBs clashed in a firefight with six German R-boats.

The Canadians raced in at full speed. They closed just as the RN torpedo boats withdrew to the north. At 4:30, the 29th was running 150 yards parallel to the enemy—firing pom-poms, Oerlikons and Vickers machine guns—raking the R-boats point-blank. The Germans returned as good as they got. In only three minutes, the MTBs expended 2,920 rounds of ammunition. The Canadians had suffered four wounded, and the attack had run them into a minefield. Now, withdrawing at top speed, mines exploded around them, star shells burst overhead, and tracers crisscrossed left and right, fore and aft of them.

With the help of a smokescreen, the MTBs finally made good their escape. For several hours, they searched for a hospital ship to which they could transfer their wounded—*Scylla*'s sick bay was full, as was a nearby hospital vessel. Eventually, they found a landing craft that had been converted to a hospital ship.

The four boats then tied up behind a battleship and stood down for the rest of the day, trying to get some sleep amid the constant booming of the guns from the Allied fleet. No rest for the weary—that night (June 8), they were back in action again.

The evening's activities got underway as the torpedo boats were bombed by mine-dropping enemy aircraft—no damage done. Then, while investigating a radar contact, they encountered two enemy destroyers. They opened fire at a range of 500 yards, but the German ships' barrage was too heavy. One shell landed so close to "Chuff Chuff" Chaffey's *465* that it deluged the boat. The MTBs dropped smoke floats and beat a hasty retreat.

RefScs: CN 15 1–155 WPA 82–83

Brittany Coast, between Brest and Ile de Bas
June 10, 1944

DeWOLF Harry George
RAYNER Herbert Sharples

"Western Flank Protected from Destroyer Menace"

Enemy naval action against the D-Day invasion had been uneventful. But at 5:00 that afternoon, the *Kriegsmarine* was readying a blow against the western phalanx of the Allied assault fleet. If it was too late to stop the landings—and it obviously was—the Germans were at least in hopes of seriously interfering with the flow of shipping to support them.

Three Narvik class destroyers left the Gironde River basin and steamed north through the Bay of Biscay. That evening they were twice attacked by Canadian rocket-carrying Beaufighter aircraft, but escaped unscathed. By June 9, the destroyers had reached Brest, on the northwestern tip of Brittany. There they were joined by a captured Dutch destroyer, *Tjerk Hiddes*, and an Elbing class destroyer. Under cover of darkness, the powerful five-destroyer flotilla ventured out of port. They headed due east to attack the western flank of the invasion forces.

Following an uneventful 10 hours in the Hurd Deep sector, Harry DeWolf and Herb Rayner, aboard their Tribal class destroyers, *Haida* and *Huron*, had returned to Plymouth by 4:00 D-Day afternoon. Next morning at eight bells, they received orders to rendezvous with and relieve two of six ships of the 10th Flotilla, currently patrolling along an east-west route 30 miles south of Lizard Point, off the southern tip of Cornwall. Objective: to intercept German naval craft reported sailing north from the Bay of Biscay into the western English Channel approaches.

At 10:45 the Canadians had taken their positions at the eastern end of the patrol line. For the rest of the day, and throughout that night, the watch continued without incident—not an enemy ship in sight.

Next morning at 10:55, the flotilla received orders from Plymouth to move their patrol farther west. The two relieved destroyers rejoined the squad; then another pair of ships—British destroyers *Ashanti* and *Tartar*, heading back to Plymouth to refuel—were ordered to about-face and reunite with the group posthaste. The 10th received instructions to concentrate its sweep in an area directly south of the ancient pirates' cove of Penzance. Clearly something important was brewing, but for the destroyer crews, their duty simply dragged on—one long, anxious, monotonous, sweat-it-out shift.

There were two groups of four. *Haida* and *Huron* teamed up with their RN counterparts *Ashanti* and *Tartar*, the latter being the senior ship in the group. Late that afternoon, the flotilla was ordered to make a horseshoe-shaped sweep: trace a wide arc across the southernmost entrance to the Channel, crisscross over Ile Vierge and Ile de Bas, then steer west until 4:00 a.m. of June 9.

The flotilla then began a zigzagging patrol, southwest at 20 knots, back and forth, north of Ile de Bas. Overcast weather, with intermittent rain squalls, low ceiling and poor visibility, made for poor radar readings. Nevertheless, that evening there were distinct echoes, albeit at distant range.

Then, at 1:07 of June 10, *Tartar* picked up a solid echo—range, 19,000 yards. The flotilla changed course and raced towards it, now estimating they'd be facing a force of four destroyers (there may or may not have been five). Star shells lit up two of the enemy, which immediately made smoke and veered away. *Tartar* ordered all ships to spread out. As they turned, the moon broke through the scudding clouds, illuminating the vessels of both sides in a pallid glow.

At 1:27, *Ashanti*, *Haida*, *Huron* and *Tartar* opened fire simultaneously from just 1,000 yards. While all ships were trying to maneuver to advantage, a German destroyer turned about and opened fire on *Tartar*. The result was devastating—shells ripped into her superstructure, killing three men and wounding 13 others. Reduced to a feeble six knots, she was compelled to retire. *Ashanti* had soon avenged her, however, in a fierce fight with *Tjerk Hiddes*. By 2:04, she had finished off the Dutch destroyer, which blew up in a cloud of smoke, flames and debris.

In the meantime, with one German target steaming off behind the smokescreen, *Haida* had joined in *Huron*'s chase. Each registered several hits on the enemy vessel, but they were also experiencing heavy return fire. A torpedo from *Huron* went wide of the mark. Then the German destroyer shifted to a course leading east, across a British minefield. The Canadian Tribals were under strict orders to avoid it at all costs—they had to skirt around it; in the process, they lost their prey. In frustration, they abandoned their chase at 2:15, returning to their original patrol position.

So far, the tally sheet read: one enemy destroyer destroyed; two escaped (one to the east, the other to the southwest); one entirely unaccounted for. Not for long—about half-past two, *Haida* reported radar contact, six miles off.

Initially, DeWolf thought it could well be the stricken *Tartar*, struggling home to Plymouth. As the Tribals closed in, they made out the silhouette of a destroyer, moving slowly to the northwest. They flashed identification signals, but the answer was gobbledegook. They tried again—the reply made even less sense. Though highly suspicious, DeWolf and Rayner wanted to take no chances—they considered it possible that *Tartar* might be under extraordinary distress.

They moved in closer yet, and the mystery ship dropped a smoke float, turned and made off south at 32 knots. Momentarily, they lost it to the dark. Then a star shell burst above the Canadians, and several salvoes crashed into the water around them.

The Narvik gradually altered her course to the east. It was clear she planned to take refuge in the Channel Islands. DeWolf and Rayner were determined to cut her off. At 3:11, the enemy ship turned even more sharply east—towards the same British minefield that had allowed the other Narvik to escape an hour earlier. Once more, *Haida* and *Huron* had to detour, fearful they might lose their target in a repeat performance.

By 4:00 they had circled the minefield and were steering northeast, with Ile Vierge 20 miles to the southeast. All they could do was stay the course and hope for the best, which arrived 11 minutes later in the form of a radar echo—the Narvik was due east, nine miles away and steaming northeast, evidently towards Cherbourg.

The Narvik had a good head start, and probably could have outrun the Tribals to Cherbourg, with room to spare. But, for some unexplained reason, the German ship suddenly swung round to southwest, in the general direction of Ile de Bas. It was too good to be true—the Canadians would be in perfect position to intercept. They steered across the Narvik's line of advance. At five o'clock, they were waiting as the German ship emerged from another British minefield.

The Tribals opened fire first. Flames erupted along the Narvik's decks. The enemy ship returned fire, but it was erratic and ineffective. She did hold her course and her speed, however, and at 5:17 the ship ran aground on the rocks of the island. *Haida* and *Huron* established a range of 6,500 yards, then kept up a steady barrage that left the destroyer ablaze from stem to stern. As dawn began to break, DeWolf signalled Plymouth: "One enemy destroyer beached off the Ile de Bas." Three hours later, the Tribals entered the British harbour, with battle ensigns flying.

Later that day, Allied aircraft reported the destroyer was still burning. She was listing at 35 degrees, with her bow on the rocks and her stern deep in the water, obviously long since abandoned. Canadian Beaufighters attacked with rockets; two days later, MTBs tried to finish her off with torpedoes. The ship remained on the rocks, derelict.

RefScs: DHist f FDS 286–93

Suppressing the U-Boats
June 1944

A *U-boat menace mounted against the Allied invasion fleet could only come from the west. Donitz deployed a dozen or more of his submarines out of Brest and St. Nazaire, with orders to penetrate the naval protective screens—none did. In fact, only two got anywhere close to the assault area. During a three-week period, six U-boats were sunk, seven damaged by planes of the RAF Coastal Command; naval ships accounted for four others, one sunk by two Tribals from the 10th Destroyer Flotilla.*

That victory represented retribution for the frustration experienced by four other RCN destroyers from Escort Group 12—Qu'Appelle, Saskatchewan, Skeena and Restigouche. During a 20-hour chase on June 7–8, a single U-boat had not only eluded its attackers; in addition to giving them a run for their money—both submerged and surfaced—it had managed to fire off eight torpedoes against them.

30 Miles South of Land's End
June 24, 1944

DeWOLF Harry George

"Sub Goes Doggo, Then Demolished"

On the night of June 23, *Haida* and the British destroyer *Eskimo* sailed from Plymouth, both vessels under the command of Harry DeWolf. The next afternoon they observed a Liberator bomber dropping depth charges in the distance. They raced full speed to the area where a marker had been dropped. The pilot advised that he had attacked a U-boat, but it had dived.

The two Tribals commenced firing depth-charge patterns, guided by an asdic contact from *Haida*, though they had strong reservations as to whether they were picking up a U-boat. The soundings were deep, very deep. The submarine had in fact dived straight down and was resting on the ocean floor. There, drifting with the tide and engine stopped, its captain hoped that confusing echoes would so addle his attackers they'd call off the hunt. He almost succeeded.

The destroyers continued their drops for two hours, with no results. The asdic echo was there—it couldn't be ignored, although it could have as likely been caused by a derelict, a shipwreck. But when *Eskimo* brought her own echo sounder into operation, the silhouette was clearly revealed—they indeed had a sub.

Now it was a test of wills, and the U-boat commander's broke first. At 7:20 p.m., tired of the constant pounding, he decided to surface and make a run for it. *U-179*'s periscope appeared 800 yards ahead of *Haida*, with *Eskimo* even closer. The British destroyer reversed engines to clear the range, and both Tribals brought all their guns to bear.

The U-boat didn't stand a chance. Her crew came scrambling out of the hatch and dove overboard. Most were in the water when the submarine, battered and riddled by the destroyers' fire, upended and sank. The victors pulled 52 German crewmen from the sea before returning to Plymouth.

RefScs: DHist f FDS 302–03 TSIAOG 172

Action on the East Flank
June 1944

*O*n the night of June 16, a new policy went into effect that
changed Escort Group 11's operations. Henceforth, the
destroyers, which included the Chaudiere, Gatineau, Kootenay,
Ottawa and St. Laurent, would continue by day to deal with any
U-boats that might penetrate the outer patrols, the third screen
on the west of the invasion fleet. But at night, the force would
split up—half the ships would cross over to patrol the eastern
flank.

The danger on the east was not from U-boats, but from the
hornet's nest of E-boats that swarmed from the harbour of Le
Havre. EG 11's new job was still defensive—protect the fleet.
And the task of the 29th Motor Boat Flotilla continued to be
offensive—harass the enemy torpedo boats.

17 Miles off the Hampshire Coast
June 27, 1944

GROOS Harold Victor
NIXON Charles Patrick

"Destroyers Tangle with E-Boats in the Dark"

*C*haudiere and *Gatineau* had been patrolling the eastern phalanx of the invasion fleet for several hours when, at 1:15
a.m., the sky lit up with star shells and gunfire 10 miles distant.
Destroyer skippers Harold Groos and Pat Nixon ordered: "Full
speed ahead!"

As they drew near, they fired their own star shells—four E-
boats appeared in the orange, luminous light, 2,000 yards
away—and let loose with their guns at the same time. The torpedo boats broke the formation they had assumed for harassing
the Allied convoy, dropped smoke flares and bolted north, with
the Canadian destroyers in pursuit.

The Germans steered a course that enabled the destroyers to cut across the lines of smoke and have an unobstructed look down the lanes between ships. The E-boats made the mistake of zigzagging back and forth between the smoke floats—each time they crossed through a lane the destroyers' Oerlikons were trained right on them. The E-boats fought back tenaciously, firing off their torpedoes, but none scored. In fact, neither *Chaudiere* nor *Gatineau* received a single hit.

In the long run, however, it was an uneven chase. The Germans could not continue northward for fear of being cut off from Le Havre. They had to break off—and with their superior speed, the E-boats easily outran the destroyers. The engagement had lasted 18 minutes before the enemy disappeared.

Groos was certain, however, that, at such close range, he and Nixon had inflicted damage. At the height of the encounter, he'd spotted a brilliant flash through the haze—sure sign of a strike.

This incident closed the first chapter of Neptune for Escort Group 11.

RefScs: DHist f FDS 301–02

North of Le Havre
July 2, 1944

CHAFFEY Charles Donald
DURNFORD Philip
HUNT Howard
KILLAM David
LAW Anthony
ROUSSEAU André

"Devastation at Dawn"

It was a hexed patrol. On the night of Dominion Day, MTBs *459*, *460* and *465* were speeding south towards Le Havre, 20 knots in a heavy, rolling sea, when Tony Law's boat struck some half-submerged debris. The vessel began to shake so violently he was forced to stop—examination revealed both propellers so badly damaged it was senseless to go on. Law turned his command over to Chuff Chuff Chaffey, then turned north and limped back to England for repairs.

Chaffey and Dave Killam, skipper of the other MTB, reached their assigned destination before midnight; they carried out their patrol without incident through the night. When it came time to withdraw, dawn was breaking and a sullen, low-lying mist was hanging over the choppy sea.

They were running single file, Chaffey behind Killam, when, to Chaffey's horror, the vessel ahead of him literally disintegrated before his eyes. A tremendous explosion lifted debris over 200 feet in the air. Pieces rained down on Chaffey's boat. MTB *460* had struck a mine.

A second explosion followed the first. Every one of the 17-man crew was blown into the sea. Chaffey maneuvered his ship into the midst of the carnage, but the heavy fog made rescue work difficult—*465* lowered scramble nets and launched Carley floats. Chaffey saw Dave Killam swimming among his men in the oily, flotsam-strewn water, giving encouragement.

Chaffey's crew had pulled two dead from the Channel and six survivors—all were wounded, most so critically it was vital to get them back to England as fast as possible. A British MTB arrived on the scene to assist in the rescue. Chaffey immediately made for Portsmouth; as *465* pulled away, he heard Killam shout, "Carry on! Don't worry about us." They were his last words. Killam, along with his first officer, Howie Hunt, were never seen again.

Of a full crew of 17, there were six survivors. Of the six, André Rousseau, an able seaman, considered himself the luckiest. The impact of the mine blast had knocked him cold. The second explosion had flung him into the sea, and the sudden shock of the chilly water had revived him in a hurry.

Philip Durnford was thanking his lucky stars as well; he seemed to lead a charmed life. This was the second time in three weeks he'd been plucked from the jaws of death. On D-Day plus two, he'd been wounded in a firefight against German R-boats off Le Havre.

RefScs: CN 156–57 WPA 102

Minesweeper Menace
June 1944

*G*erman minesweepers were a source of aggravation to Operation Neptune. They were a constant threat, not as warships themselves, but within the nature of the task they performed—minefields offered important protection from interference to both flanks of the invasion fleet. The work of the German minesweepers was always carried out under the cover of darkness. They were by no means easy targets—and they were escorted at all times by heavily armed trawlers, full of fight.

Off St. Malo
June 27–28, 1944

RAYNER Herbert Sharples

"Score Two for Huron"

In tandem with her RN Tribal companion *Eskimo, Huron* had sailed down into the waters of the Channel Islands, then made a sweep along the French coast 20 miles northwest of St. Malo. At 12:55 a.m., radar showed a German force in the vicinity, headed in their direction. Moments later, *Huron* commander Herb Rayner ordered a flare and star shell, revealing an enemy minesweeper and two trawlers.

The German ships immediately dropped smoke and headed south, the destroyers giving chase at full throttle. From 7,000 yards, both Tribals opened fire. *Huron*'s first salvo fell short—but of five subsequent shots, four were direct hits on the minesweeper, setting it afire.

Eskimo had meanwhile opened fire on the trawlers. These engagements had brought the ships uncomfortably close to the French shoreline, however, well within range of the coastal guns. When those batteries opened up, the destroyers observed their flashes and prudently altered course—north, then back east to attack the enemy again amid their swirling smoke.

Huron took aim on the minesweeper once more; this time, her guns sent it to the bottom. *Eskimo* had tracked down one trawler. She was pounding it with her heavy guns when the other trawler veered in, off the port bow at close range. A 3-inch shell stabbed the destroyer's hull and exploded in the engine room. The steering motor was knocked out as well as most of the electrical system—all the lights, and the power mountings for the guns and radar aerials, were out of action. *Eskimo* was blinded. *Huron* hurried to the rescue, circling the crippled vessel while she made repairs.

A trawler appeared once more, swerving out of the smoke-screen. *Huron* had a clear shot, from almost point-blank range. Rayner gave the order to commence firing—a sustained series that lasted four minutes, until the German ship blew up and sank. The second trawler, taking advantage of the smoke and confusion, was able to escape.

RefScs: DHist f FDS 339–40

CHALLENGE IN THE CHANNEL ISLANDS JUNE 1944

*U*ntil the night of June 11, the 65th MTB Flotilla's role in Neptune had been to patrol across the mouth of Lyme Bay, protecting that part of the convoy route leading from Devon and Dorset to the assembly area of the invasion fleet, south of Portsmouth. When it became obvious that there was no longer a danger to this sector, the 65th was switched from patrol duty to offensive missions.

Their new sphere of operation would be the Channel Islands, north of the Gulf of St. Malo, west of the Cherbourg Peninsula. Their objective was to prevent the evacuation of the islands' heavily armed German garrisons by small surface craft, and also to intercept any convoys that might be sneaking through the area. The MTBs were ideally suited for such work. Unlike even the smallest of warships, they could comfortably navigate the shallow waters around the islands. Their speed and low profile in the water also made them less conspicuous, harder-to-hit targets for the shore batteries.

In fact, their first outing into the area on June 11 was the only early outing during which the torpedo boats drew fire, and it proved totally ineffective. But, on subsequent forays, they had far more success finding significant action.

West of Cherbourg Peninsula
June 17–18, 1944

KIRKPATRICK James
MABEE Oliver
McLERNON Leslie
MORROW Albert

"Making Mayhem"

On the evening of June 17, a German convoy was reported to be leaving the port of Cherbourg to escape west to Brest. At 10:25, Kirk Kirkpatrick in command, Ollie Mabee, Bert "The Beard" Morrow and Les McLernon left their base at Brixham in Devon. They guided their MTBs across the Channel without incident, then passed the islands of Alderney and Guernsey to a point east of Sark. Four miles west of Cherbourg Peninsula, they changed course, steaming north again along the French coast. The convoy they were hunting was purportedly headed south from Cherbourg. The 65th Flotilla was in ideal position to cut it off.

By this time it was 2:00 a.m. On cue, radar indicated the enemy ships were 3,000 yards to the east. Perfect—the MTBs slowed to 10 knots and closed ranks, ready for an impending attack. Phantom shapes could barely be discerned in the darkness; creeping closer, they could make out two merchant ships, escorted by several trawlers and gunboats.

The German convoy now flashed a challenge by signal lamp. The Canadians ignored it. A second challenge was dismissed just as summarily. Kirkpatrick ordered "Open throttles," and the four boats bore down on the convoy. At 1,500 yards, Les McLernon fired two torpedoes. Kirkpatrick narrowed the range to 1,200 yards before letting go two of his own—but no results. Then a blinding star shell burst above the MTBs, followed by heavy fire from the enemy gunboats. But the Canadians persisted, bearing down on the west side of the convoy to within 400 yards, concentrating on a single merchantman and giving it all they had—two- and six-pound guns and Oerlikons. They completed their pass and headed north.

Kirkpatrick waited for the star shell to fizzle out, then turned his torpedo boats back around for an attack in the dark, circling around the convoy before breaking off. By now the enemy ships were in such a state of disarray they began firing at each other. Time to call it a night—the MTBs sped home to Brixham.

RefScs: FDS 304–05 CN 130

South of Jersey
June 22–23, 1944

JONES Tom
KIRKPATRICK James
KNOX Malcolm
MABEE Oliver
McLERNON Leslie

"Four Large Holes, but Nothing Serious"

MTBs *722, 743, 745* and *748* had arrived at a point south of St. Helier, the capital and main port of the island of Jersey, when they received orders to proceed to a location where British torpedo boats were attacking a German convoy. En route, they encountered an E-boat heading north, having broken off from the engagement. They chased it back to St. Helier, then swept back and forth across the rocky, treacherous harbour mouth for 30 minutes, hoping the enemy would venture out again. But it was to no avail, and they resumed their course south.

By the time the 65th was within 4,000 yards of the German convoy, the British MTBs had left. But they ran straight in for a torpedo attack, star shells bursting over them, followed by intense enemy gunfire, and they continued their course for three minutes, firing forward, broadside, and finally bringing their aft guns to bear.

Amid the smoke, fire, tracers, cannon shots and star shell bursts, Ollie Mabee's *745* took several hits, one shell exploding in the engine room, bringing the torpedo boat to a shuddering halt. All the MTBs were now within 500 yards of the convoy. Kirk Kirkpatrick circled Mabee's crippled craft and laid down a smokescreen.

Meanwhile, Les McLernon and Mac Knox continued the attack. Closing in further still, they could make out three enemy minesweepers and an E-boat. At point-blank range, Knox riddled one of the minesweepers. When the E-boat tried to come to its rescue, Knox turned his guns on that vessel—a direct hit knocked it out of action, its bow smoking.

James Kirkpatrick, commander of the 65th Flotilla. (DND/PA 180073)

Les McLernon ran alongside the minesweepers, raking them with fire, then spelled Kirkpatrick in *727*, standing by Mabee's damaged MTB. Kirkpatrick immediately turned his attention on a tanker he'd spotted in the convoy, opening fire and setting it ablaze. He ran in to finish it off, narrowly avoiding a collision with one of the sinking minesweepers. As McLernon joined him, the pair were suddenly confronted by two more E-boats—the Canadians fired quickly, and the E-boats were sent packing.

By this time, Mabee's engine crew had managed to get his ship running again, albeit at a very limited six knots. Even so, shepherded by the other three MTBs, *745* was able to head safely back to Brixham, the burning German tanker lighting the sky behind them.

Oliver Mabee, commander of MTB 745. (DND/PA 180068)

It had been a fitting finale to the first phase of Operation Neptune for the 65th Flotilla. In his diary, Tom Jones, Mabee's gunner on the forward 6-pounder, described this engagement as something less than epochal: "Four large holes in our ship and several other ships," he wrote laconically, "but nothing serious."

RefScs: FDS 305–07 CN 130 163–64

DREDGER
JULY 1944

In late June, air reconnaissance revealed a small but deadly squadron of German M-class minesweepers, escorting U-boats at night between Brest and a point 10 miles south of the island of Ushant (Ile d'Ouessant), presumably with the objective of attacking the west flank of the invasion fleet. Though slow, the trawlers were heavily armed with 5-inch guns, providing them with plenty of close-range firepower.

A plan was designed to wipe out the escort, leaving a clear shot at the submarines themselves. The operation was laid out in an order that read, in part:

Intention:
(A) To destroy the escort with a support group assisted by a striking force.
(B) The striking force will be routed outside radar cover to approach enemy's effected track from southward.
(C) The support group will keep clear westward until ordered by S.O. [senior officer] striking force to close in and assist in hunting U-boats.
Warning:
Attention is called to enemy mine fields.
Executive order:
The operation will be put into force by signal: Carry out operation "Dredger."

The directive was issued on the late afternoon of July 5, with instructions that it be carried out that night.

Off Brest
July 6, 1944

EASTON Alan
GROSS David
RUSSELL Patrick

"Le Nuit Chez les Pierres Noires"

Between Ushant (to Bretons, Ile d'Ouessant—The Isle of Terror) and the French mainland lies a treacherous archipelago of smaller islands, reefs and shoals. Outcroppings of rocks are numerous, and many are far out from the island. Added to those perils is an abundance of strong tidal streams. A navigator's nightmare.

Approaching 1:00 a.m., the four Canadian destroyers of the 12th Escort Group—*Qu'Appelle, Restigouche, Saskatchewan* and *Skeena*—had successfully steered through these hazardous waters, becoming the first Allied ships to enter the approaches to the famous Brest submarine base since the fall of France in 1940.

At 12:40, steering a course due west, they could make out the blinking red lights of *les pierres noires* (the Black Stones), the rocky, windswept Brittany coast just north of Brest. At 1:12 they picked up radar echoes—four vessels, some six miles ahead and to the north—the minesweeper escort the Canadians had been sent out to destroy. EG 12 sailed in as close to the coast as they dared (about half a mile), then turned north-northeast to cut the enemy off from any possible retreat to Brest. They increased their speed to over 30 knots and began to close the range.

At 1:30 the destroyers spotted the dim outlines of the enemy ships, three miles ahead. The Canadians were narrowing fast and in the next 16 minutes they had pulled up directly astern. They challenged by signal light. It went unanswered, whereupon *Qu'Appelle* called for illumination. Alan Easton, *Saskatchewan*'s skipper, ordered flares—six rockets soared over the German vessels, bursting with grandstand perfection and precision. The minesweepers were clearly visible, as were two submarines, which quickly made themselves scarce. The trawlers were assembled in a neat row, one behind the other.

Qu'Appelle, followed by *Saskatchewan*, then *Skeena*, captained by Pat Russell, and *Restigouche*, with David Gross at the helm, drew a parallel line alongside the German ships, 800 yards apart. Going full tilt, with the forbidding Black Stones' coastline less than a mile off their starboard, the enemy was trapped.

Both sides opened up, and the air filled with waves of gun smoke and concussions. Tracers whistled between ships. The din was ear-splitting—4.7-inch guns boomed away at 10 rounds a minute, the ships shuddering under each recoil, accompanied by the rattling, high-pitched, staccato fire from the Oerlikons and pom-poms.

Nine minutes later EG 12 had completed its initial run and left havoc in its wake. The leading German trawler was dead in the sea, wreathed in smoke. The second was turning away to the southwest, fire raging amidships. The third was also stopped and on fire. A fourth, like the submarines, had simply disappeared, probably escaping towards Brest.

The Canadian flotilla swept into a 180-degree turn, coming about to make a second run down the line, in the opposite direction. Up went the flares, and the destroyers opened fire once more. The remaining Germans were still full of fight. *Qu'Appelle*, *Skeena* and *Restigouche* concentrated on the lead ship, finally blowing it up. *Saskatchewan* drew within half a mile of the second minesweeper; she fired off a torpedo, but missed. Then, firing all guns, she blew the minesweeper's bridge away with a solid burst. Flames enveloped the ship and all return fire stopped.

The third German vessel was still immobile, but her guns were firing full out. The four Canadian destroyers now converged for the kill. Instead, 20-mm shells slammed into *Qu'Appelle*'s bridge, seriously wounding the senior officer and several others. A direct hit from a 5-inch shell severely damaged the steering gear. She was forced to break off.

Aboard *Skeena*, Pat Russell took over as S.O. Meanwhile, Easton's *Saskatchewan* had her radar blown out. One of her crew was killed and several others were injured.

Russell led *Skeena* on one more pass by the remaining vessel; by then, she was hopelessly afire and sinking. Russell then decided to initiate a search for the U-boats. But, with *Qu'Appelle* already turned north, and many wounded aboard the remaining three destroyers, some badly in need of attention (Russell himself had been wounded in the action), the search was soon abandoned. EG 12 called it a night and set sail for Plymouth, where they arrived at seven in the morning.

RefScs: DHist f FDS 341–42 TSIAOG 173

14 Miles South of Beachy Head, Sussex Coast
July 6, 1944

BERRY Peter
PRENTICE James Douglas
TIMBRELL Robert
WILLISON William

"U-Boat Doomed by Grapple"

About the time the 12th Escort Group was drawing within sight of Lizard Point from its successful "dredging" operation, two Canadian destroyers from Escort 11, Bill Willison's *Kootenay* and *Ottawa*, under Chummy Prentice, were ordered to a point south of Beachy Head. The British frigate *Statice* had made contact with a German submarine. They were in for a long haul, figuratively and literally.

The radar contact was firm and solid, but a strong tide allowed the U-boat to drift along the bottom of the Channel, varying its depth from 200 to 300 feet. And the seabed in that area was fraught with conditions that would give any asdic operator nightmares: changeable currents, schools of fish, wrecks of all kinds.

The destroyers' Hedgehog attacks were difficult, but they were not without tangible result. They concluded that the submarine was hurting when, at noon, flotsam began drifting to the surface—an assortment of books, clothing, pieces of wood, a cylindrical decoy. Then a diesel slick began spreading over the water.

Throughout the long afternoon the destroyers intensified their attacks, dropping one load of depth charges after another. By this time the U-boat was wallowing at a lesser depth of 150 feet. Aboard *Ottawa*, Bob Timbrell, Prentice's staff officer anti-submarine, was instrumental in devising a new technique.

A depth charge was armed with an electric detonator and lowered over the side by a wire, to the end of which was attached a grappling hook. The destroyer then pulled the rigging slowly over the U-boat, the Hedgehog bomb dragging along the bottom. The grapple caught the sub; the wire tightened; a ship's gunner triggered the charge—it split the U-boat wide open. Jetsam identified the victim as *U-678*.

The conquest was shared. It marked four submarine kills for Prentice, and two for Willison.

Kootenay's operations officer, Peter Berry, during this three-day period, spent the entire time in the operations room, with occasional periods of sleep at his post. Strictly against regulations, but with Willison's permission, he duplicated a chart of the action before sending the signal to the Admiralty.

RefScs: FDS 344 TSIAOG 173–74

Off Brest
July 20, 1944

BALFOUR St. Clair
BATES John

"Glider Bomb Attack"

Ships of Escort 9 had been ordered into the waters off the Brest peninsula to act as bait for some German ships reported in the vicinity, in the hopes of luring them into battle that afternoon.

St. Clair Balfour's Meon *taking* Commander Layard's Matane *in tow.*
(Courtesy St. Clair Balfour)

They were well underway when there was a loud explosion astern of the frigate *Meon.*

It was at first taken to be an acoustic mine, but then three Dornier bombers were spotted through a break in the clouds. Two hours earlier, a Junkers 188 reconnaissance plane had also been spotted shadowing the flotilla. RAF Mosquitoes had been ordered to investigate, but they'd found nothing.

The "Chase-Me-Charlie" glider bomb attack had flooded *Meon's* decks. Her skipper, St. Clair Balfour, called immediately for air support; meanwhile, all ships in the group rallied into formation, prepared to combat the enemy aircraft on their own.

A Dornier appeared directly above and to starboard of *Matane,* the senior ship in the flotilla. Its radio-directed missile shot ahead of the bomber in a sputter of white smoke. It wobbled for a moment, then zoomed down at a sheer angle, smashing through the Carley float on top of *Matane's* ammunition hoist. Shed of its wings and jet-propelled engine, the missile plowed through the quarterdeck bulkhead and exploded in the sea alongside the engine room.

John Bates was on the quarterdeck, setting the safeties on the ship's depth charges. He was blown over the side as the bomb struck. Then he was blown back on deck when it exploded—completely uninjured.

The "Charlie" had blown a large hole in *Matane*'s port side. The port engine had been knocked off its moorings—oil spurted from bursting tanks and the sea poured into the engine room. Steam and debris shot up in a great cloud, obscuring the entire aft end of the ship from the view of those on the bridge. Then a second bomb was seen diving down—it plunged into the sea astern, harmlessly.

Four of *Matane*'s crew had been killed; 11 were seriously injured. But things could have been worse. Had that first bomb struck six inches to starboard, it would have clipped the ammunition hoist in the magazine, and that would've been game over. And mercifully, the German shore batteries were well wide of their mark.

Balfour steered *Meon* through *Matane*'s raging clouds of escaping steam to take his sister ship in tow. The others in EG 9 fought off the Dorniers until Spitfires arrived in response to his SOS. When the attack ended, *Meon* got underway with the help of *Stormont*. All that stormy night and part of the next day the two frigates nursed the stricken *Meon* back to Plymouth.

RefScs: DHist f FDS 345–47 TSIAOG 174

MTB BATTLES
JULY 1944

*F*ollowing the debacle of the night of July 2 off Le Havre, when one MTB went down and 11 of her crew were lost, the 29th Flotilla struck back with a vengeance. Over a five-day period they kept up a series of attacks that marked the longest continuing action in the annals of the Allied coastal forces. Between July 4 and July 9 the flotilla took on 30 German E-boats and 10 R-boats, destroying one of the former and two of *the latter; they also severely damaged another three E-boats, and shot down a German Heinkel 111 bomber.*

Meanwhile, their comrades with the 65th Flotilla were engaged in search-and-pursuit. While poor weather along the Cornish coast kept them bottled up at Brixham through most of this period, on the night of July 3–4 they became embroiled in their most spirited and successful action.

Off St. Malo
July 3–4, 1944

COLLINS John
KIRKPATRICK James
KNOX Malcolm
MOORE George

"A One-Minute Victory"

Conditions were perfect. The sea was calm. Bright moonlight made for ideal visibility. Flotilla commander Jim Kirkpatrick was leading four MTBs of the 65th at 10 knots towards the coast of Brittany. They picked up radar soundings shortly after one in the morning. An actual sighting soon confirmed the echoes.

A convoy of three merchant ships, escorted by four gunboats, was hugging the French coastline in the vicinity of St. Malo, steering southwest. The torpedo boats fanned out in a line abreast, slowing to seven knots to ensure maximum firing accuracy, and crept to within 800 yards of the convoy without being detected.

They charged straight in. Kirkpatrick opened fire first. His torpedoes struck the lead merchantman. Swinging alongside with guns blazing, his vessel was hit by return fire. Five of his crew were badly injured. Shells slammed into the mess decks, and the bilges began to fill with water.

Mac Knox also fired two torpedoes at the lead ship. He observed the strikes, then let his other torpedoes go, aiming consecutively at the second and third ships in line. He scored hits in both cases. But neither did he escape unscathed. While he was veering away, return fire inflicted damage on the vessel and injured one crew member.

John Collins had also zeroed in, firing all four of his torpedoes. He scored hits on all three merchantmen. But again, turning away, a shell from one of the German escorts blew a hole in his MTB at the waterline. It began to sink. The hole was soon plugged; however, the emergency pumps were pressed into action.

George Moore's turn. His first torpedo missed the leader. His second hit the next merchantman in line. Then he sent another torpedo smashing into the third ship. It exploded with a roar and sank. Moore's was the only MTB to escape damage.

The entire attack had lasted just one minute. But in that short, deadly space of time the 65th had sunk two merchant ships and caused heavy damage to a third. Two of the escorting gunboats were significantly damaged as well. Kirkpatrick summed up the night's work succinctly: "It was the perfect setting for a torpedo attack and we took full advantage of it."

RefScs: FDS 337 CN 130 165–66

Off Le Havre
July 5, 1944

BISHOP Craig
LAW Anthony
MOYSE Robert

"Prolonged E-Boat Encounter"

Tony Law, commander of the 29th MTB Flotilla, Bob Moyse and Craig Bishop were holding a protective patrol line to the east of the Normandy assault anchorage when, just after midnight, radar blips indicated enemy ships approaching from Le Havre. They steered in the direction of the echoes; at a range of

2,000 yards, they fired a star shell that lit up a line of nine E-boats, sailing neatly in a row

The MTBs opened fire at once. The German craft turned tail and fled in the darkness, but one had been hit badly. It caught fire and, as the Canadian torpedo boats tore past it through the enemy smokescreen, it began to sink. During the half hour it took to track down the rest of the E-boat flotilla, the MTBs were subjected to a dive-bombing attack from a Heinkel 111. Not only did the aircraft fail to hamper their search—its bombs exploded harmlessly in the sea. The 29th gunners shot it down.

Nor was it of any help to the E-boats. The enemy torpedo ships proved incapable of getting themselves reorganized. As a result, the MTBs succeeded in damaging two more of them before they finally reached their haven at Le Havre.

RefScs: FDS 333 CN 129 158

Off Cap d'Antifer, North of Le Havre
July 9–10, 1944

BISHOP Craig
BURK Charles Arthur
CREBA Glen
LAW Anthony
MARSHALL Sherwood

"Shot in the Ass"

A new menace for Allied ships now loomed, in the form of a human torpedo. A German crew of one or two sat astride a missile to steer it. He or they then abandoned it at a safe distance from the target. On the night of July 6–7, MTBs from the 29th Flotilla were sent in close to shore, in the vicinity of the Ouistreham Canal on the east side of the British bridgehead, to search for the launching sites of these "manned" torpedoes.

The area lay just off the Allied anchorage and was heavily

mined via charges dropped nightly by the Luftwaffe. The torpedo boats would also have to navigate extremely shallow waters, along a shoreline still occupied by the Germans.

Miraculously, Glen Creba and Barney Marshall's boats survived the explosions of 25 mines as they whistled through the field at top speed. Next night their luck ran out. It was fortunate that only four crewmen were casualties. Creba's *463* struck a mine and immediately began to sink. Other MTBs rushed to her rescue. Although the torpedo boat was beyond salvage, all hands were safely taken off. It was the start of a mounting series of losses to befall the unit.

The following night saw a tempestuous clash with R-boats. The sea was calm and visibility clear as MTBs *459*, *461* and *464* patrolled off Cap d'Antifer, around the point to the north of Le Havre. At midnight star shells burst above them and shore batteries opened up with high explosive shells. The torpedo boats zigzagged frantically for nearly an hour before the shelling abated. At 1:00, they could see more star shells and gunfire to the north, and they promptly sped off in that direction.

They arrived on the scene to find three British MTBs, badly damaged after an attack on a line of 10 R-boats. Tony Law, Craig Bishop and Charles "Bones" Burk made a pass along the German line, taking on each R-boat in turn from as close as 100 yards. As they turned to make a second run, Burk circled the most severely stricken British ship, dropping smoke floats. In the process, his ship was hit by enemy fire.

Bishop had his own problems. Law was advised that Burk had no casualties, and then saw Bishop's *464* struck by several 37-mm shells. He called for a damage report. "Hello, Tony, Tony, Tony," came back the reply. "This is Bish. Have one killed and one wounded and damage to the boat. I've been shot in the ass."

All three torpedo boats now concentrated on rescuing the crew from the burning British MTB. Burk continued making smoke. Bishop and Law jumped back in among the R-boats, acting as decoys. Then they dropped their own smoke and returned to the rescue scene, by which time the enemy boats had stopped firing and were some 800 yards off.

The British boat was now an inferno. Its ammunition exploded. But the crew had managed to get off safely; they were clinging to two Carley floats when the Canadians picked them up.

RefScs: FDS 333–34 CN 129 158 WPA 106

Off Le Havre
July 16–17, 1944

ADAM Joseph
LAW Anthony
MARSHALL Sherwood

"Loss of MTB 459"

Around midnight, zigzagging to avoid fire from shore batteries, Tony Law's MTB *459*, Joe Adam in *464* (who had taken over for the incapacitated Craig Bishop) and Barney Marshall in *466* were vectored by their control frigate *Duff* onto some minesweepers, which were creeping close to shore, northward from Le Havre.

As the torpedo boats raced along the coast, flares suddenly burst above them, dropped by German aircraft. Then bombs rained down, falling in the sea around them. The shore batteries opened up again, shells shrieking down on the ships from a range of less than four miles. The MTBs resumed their zigzag pattern, narrowly eluding the first salvo. But the second barrage found the range—a shell smashed into *459*'s engine room.

Law and his coxswain were pinned to the bridge floor by a piece of deck that had burst from the engine room. The boat was already sinking at the stern. One of his crew managed to free Law and his coxswain; the skipper grabbed the RT (radio transmitter) and got on the blower to the other two ships. He ordered Marshall to pull alongside and for Adam to drop a smokescreen.

Marshall also dropped a smoke float—the screen covered the sinking MTB completely. Rescuers struggled to get to the engine room, but with two feet of water already covering the hatch their efforts were fruitless. From stern to midships the boat was totally mired, her bow jutting up at a 45-degree angle.

Three members of the crew were missing. One other was wounded and in a state of severe shock. Marshall had to wait for some of his smoke to clear before he dared pull alongside to take off the crew. Meanwhile, the shore batteries were lobbing star shells, and Joe Adam was chasing back and forth, keeping the smokescreen intact.

Once the crew were safely aboard his ship, Marshall took *459* in tow. Although shore batteries kept up a steady barrage of fire, the Canadians reached the assault anchorage without further incident, and the badly damaged torpedo boat was hoisted onto the beach. The action left the 29th Flotilla's commander without a boat. While this situation was being addressed, Law turned over the role of senior officer to Bones Burk, who soon demonstrated his skills as a leader and proved himself worthy of the responsibility entrusted to him.

RefScs: FDS 334–35 CN 129 158–59 WPA 116–18

Between Cap d'Antifer and Cap de la Hague
July 25–26, 1944

ADAM Joseph
BRAMPTON Joseph
BURK Charles Arthur
CHAFFEY Charles
MARSHALL Sherwood
MOYSE Robert

"In a Blaze of Glory"

The five ships of the 29th Flotilla still in commission were assembled for action. This was a calm night, with low clouds obscuring the moon—excellent conditions for torpedo boat operations. And Bones Burk, leading the pack—Joe Adam, Chuff Chuff Chaffey, Barney Marshall and Bob Moyse—was determined to take full advantage of those conditions. All but Moyse's boat were charged with torpedoes. His MTB was to act as a gunboat.

Burk pulled his team in as close to shore as he dared. He wanted a dark shelter from which to attack when the time came. While his ships rested undetected, the passing enemy craft would be silhouetted against the horizon—typical of Burk's tactical genius, with more to come. A little after midnight, radar reports from the control frigate indicated that an enemy convoy was moving north from Le Havre.

The MTBs continued lurking against the shore until they spotted the enemy ships: two minesweepers, two flak flotillas and several R-boats. The Germans weren't taking any chances. Against such firepower, the element of surprise was critical. The Canadian commander turned his ships in a line abreast to face the convoy. They roared out from the shadows at full throttle. As they closed they were met by withering fire from R-boats on the inside of the convoy. Yet within 15 seconds the MTBs had shot off six torpedoes. It would have been eight had not Barney Marshall been hit in the shoulder, slumping to the deck of the bridge. His first officer, Joe Brampton, took charge.

The MTBs now found themselves caught between the return fire from the convoy ahead of them and the shore batteries behind them. They chose to ignore them both, plunging into the line and raking the minesweepers as they sped on. The entire show was now behind them—one minesweeper blew apart in an immense blast, adding to the glare of star shells, red tracers and gun flashes along the coast.

It was time to retire, and the 29th went out in a blaze of glory, a credit to Burk's leadership and his propensity for sensing what needed to be done in any given situation. With Moyse's gunboat covering the retreat, the 11-minute escape through the pounding of the coastal guns and the relentless fire of R-boats and flak trawlers was nothing short of spectacular. Burk maneuvered his MTBs like hockey forwards rushing the defence—alternately slowing down, speeding up, changing course.

They made it—with only one torpedo boat slightly damaged and two men wounded—in one of the most dramatic shootouts ever experienced by the Coastal Command. And the bottom line was a plus—they had destroyed one enemy minesweeper and probably inflicted damage to several other ships.

Just as well that this was the last major action of the summer for the battle-weary 29th. The missions had begun to take their toll with the crews. They had suffered 37 per cent casualties—a disproportionately high ratio in killed and wounded, whether the fighting was on the ground, at sea or in the air. They had lost eight boats since D-Day. And those that were left were badly in need of refit and repair.

During the second week of August, the 29th, along with other flotillas, moved from Plymouth back to Ramsgate, where they once again came under Dover Command.

RefScs: FDS 335–36 CN 129 158–60

CORVETTES COURAGEOUS JUNE–AUGUST 1944

Compared with Atlantic anti-submarine duty, the part played by Canadian corvettes in Operation Neptune was, at least in the estimation of their crews, duller than bilge water. They spent most of their time acting as "cattle cowboys" or traffic cops or as signal posts, relaying messages between ships. It was duty that may have seemed routine and tedious, particularly to veterans of battle on the open seas—but not only was the work essential to the safety and success of the invasion, it did have its associated risks, and more than its share of casualties. Moreover, courage was called for, and never lacking.

Kitchener *and* Port Arthur *both survived near misses from Chase-Me-Charlie glider bombs. On the night of June 13,* Camrose, Baddeck *and* Louisburg *fought off a series of U-boat attacks. Early next morning* Trentonian *and a cable ship,* St. Margaret, *were erroneously and repeatedly shelled by an*

American destroyer that had mistaken them for enemy warships. St. Margaret's captain died of his wounds. The worst disasters of all were the losses of both Alberni *and* Regina *in August.*

Apart from these actions, the role of the corvettes in Neptune probably did seem pretty boring and routine; and there was precious little shore leave (as in none whatsoever for 40 days in one case).

But, in fact, the corvette crews suffered the highest losses of all Canadian naval forces during the operation—90 men killed and 30 wounded (out of a total of 120 Canadians killed, 159 wounded).

Off Trevose Head, Cornish Coast
August 8, 1944

FAULKNER Albert
GOULD Grant
HOGG Robert
MAIER Herman
MARSH Archibald
RACKER Lionel
RADFORD Jack
REUVERS John
THOMAS Roddick
WINN Jack
WOOD James

"Courage in Catastrophe"

For the past few weeks, *Regina* and her crew had settled into the regimen of shuttling convoys down the coast of Cornwall, "around the Lizard" and east to the assembly area south of the Solent. In contrast to some exciting moments on open sea duty, particularly in February 1943, when the corvette sank an Italian submarine off the coast of Algeria and took its crew prisoner, this work was pretty tame.

On this particular evening, however, the routine was rudely interrupted by a tremendous explosion. A merchant ship had been hit by a torpedo from German sub *U-667*. *Regina*'s captain, Jack Radford, took the precaution to order all depth charges set to "safe," then pulled alongside. Though badly damaged, the merchantman seemed salvageable, so Radford ordered an American TLC (Tank Landing Craft) to take aboard her crew and rig a tow line.

Regina pulled away to 100 yards to supervise the operation; as a safeguard, she cast off her own Carley floats—a fortuitous move indeed, as it turned out. At the moment the tow line tightened between the tank carrier and the freighter, *U-667* struck again.

This time the victim was the Canadian corvette. An enormous blast lifted the ship's bow—it pointed straight skyward and sent a pillar of smoke and debris another 100 feet into the air. For a brief moment it looked as if the ship would topple over backward—then it sank, stern first, straight down. It all happened in 28 seconds. Somehow, 64 of the crew managed to survive; 10 were seriously injured; all were coated with oil and in various stages of shock.

At the moment of impact, the ship's Number One, James Wood, and fellow officer Herman Maier were on the quarterdeck having a smoke. The explosion threw Maier on top of Wood. As the ship sank, Maier was pulled down by the suction. Luckily, and with superhuman effort, he was able to wrest himself free. He swam to a Carley float and hung on.

Wood found himself six feet under water after the detonation "blew the ship from under me." He struggled to the surface and was sucked under again. He managed to swim once more to the top. He was going down for the third time when he grabbed onto the barrel of a pom-pom long enough to save himself. Searching about, he found a floating plank to hang onto.

Another ship's officer, Roddick Thomas, was on the bridge. He was reaching for a sandwich when he heard a bang, saw a flash and was thrown against a bulkhead. As the vessel sank, his feet got tangled in some wire. Frantically, he broke away and swam for the surface for all he was worth, grabbing a piece of wood and working himself towards a Carley float.

Skipper Jack Radford was also standing on the bridge when his ship "just seemed to disintegrate." Torrents of oil and water swamped the deck. Radford climbed onto the rail, closed his eyes and jumped. He swam for nearly 20 minutes before he reached a Carley float, to which seven others were also hanging on.

Regina's coxswain Jack Winn was watching the merchant ship rescue getting underway when he was blown sky high. He landed on his back on the quarterdeck. Befuddled, he was tossed into the air again; this time he came down in the sea. The ship was standing on end. Winn found a plank and waited for the LTC to pick him up, along with the others floating around him in the water.

John Reuvers was blown 100 feet into the air. He landed on the ship's propeller and sank 20 feet before bobbing back to the surface. Archie Marsh, a leading seaman, was standing at the stern when he was thrown to the deck. Water swept over him, twisting and turning him in the turbulence. The suction dragged him down and he thought he was drowning. The next thing he knew he was on the surface, listening to the roar and hiss as the corvette plunged to the bottom.

Two able seamen, Albert Faulkner and Robert Hogg, were responsible for saving many lives that night. Faulkner got away from the sinking ship after being sucked under with one of his feet caught in a depth-charge rail. Hogg, like Jack Winn, had been blown into the air by the force of the explosion and landed on the stern. Once free, both he and Faulkner swam to recover two Carley floats. They brought them back to the small circle of survivors, many of whom were so exhausted they could no longer hang onto the pieces of wood to which they'd been clinging so desperately.

Aboard the LCT, Grant Gould, *Regina*'s ship's surgeon, half-choked with fuel oil and suffering so painfully from two broken ribs that he had to give himself a shot of morphine, nevertheless rendered yeoman service, tending to the injured under these most arduous circumstances and with supplies limited to first aid. Lionel Racker's left leg had been nearly severed below the knee.

It required amputation. Gould gave him a large shot of Pusser rum and, with several hands helping to hold the patient down, calmly performed the operation—on an open deck, on a rolling ship, by torchlight, with a butcher knife sterilized in the galley. His medical peers later judged the work an outstanding, unqualified success.

Though the number of crew to survive such a violent catastrophe was nothing short of amazing, the loss of 29 was no less horrendous.

RefScs: CCAN 261–62 DHist f FDS 329

Southeast of the Isle of Wight
August 21, 1944

BELL Ian
BREBNER John
BRYANT John
CRANDON Douglas
McVARISH Leo
O'MARA Zavier
WILLIAMS Frank
WOOD Donald
WORTHINGTON Donald

"Any Hesitation Was Fatal"

When a torpedo fired from *U-480* struck *Alberni* in broad daylight on this August morning, it brought to a close an illustrious three-and-a-half-year, action-packed career. The Yarrow-built corvette was credited with "probably" sinking one German submarine, had joined in on several other kills, had shot down a Junkers 88 bomber and had rescued countless numbers of men from the sea.

Commissioned at Esquimalt, B.C., on February 3, 1941, *Alberni* was the first western Canadian corvette assigned as a convoy escort, and she performed during the most bitter stretch of the Battle of the Atlantic. Before Operation Neptune, she had also put in her tour of duty in the Mediterranean with Operation Torch, surviving constant day-and-night bombing.

Late in the afternoon of July 26, 1944, while on an anti-submarine patrol off the Normandy beaches, a Junkers 88 had swooped in on the corvette, at deck level. *Alberni*'s starboard Oerlikon and pom-pom gunners opened fire. The bomber climbed and banked over the ship's forecastle at 200 feet. The port Oerlikon opened up, scoring several direct hits. The German plane burst into flames and exploded into the sea, 100 yards off *Alberni*'s port bow.

On the morning of August 21, the corvette was steaming south at 14 knots, ordered to relieve *Drumheller* from patrol duty on the eastern flank of the Channel. At precisely 11:46, some 25 miles southeast of St. Catherine's Point on the Isle of Wight, *U-480* attacked. The torpedo struck *Alberni* amidships just aft of the funnel. Only those of *Alberni*'s crew further forward survived, but even many of them never reached the upper deck. In moments the ship was awash. The stern sank first. The ship rolled to port, and then the bow went under. She was gone in 30 seconds.

Ian Bell had been *Alberni*'s captain for the past two years. He was in his cabin when the torpedo exploded. His immediate reaction was to dash to the bridge. He didn't make it past the wheelhouse door, where he found himself up to his ankles in water. The stern of the ship had already disappeared; the funnel was almost submerged. Bell was trying to reach a Carley float when he was pulled under the first time. As he came up for air, the bow was disappearing. The suction pulled him under again, but he resurfaced and was able to grab onto a wooden plank to keep himself afloat.

Donald Wood, the ship's writer, was in his office chatting with leading signalman Donald Worthington. As the pair rushed for the door, scalding steam from the funnel shot inside, and they slammed the door shut. It was a losing situation. Water began pouring in under and around the door. They had no choice but to get out. Worthington rushed to the port side and disappeared.

Wood was thrown in the opposite direction by a wave that engulfed him.

The boilers exploded—Wood was blown to the surface with such force it stripped away his clothing. The bow sank—he and others were being sucked down with the ship. But Wood managed to grab a life jacket floating by. It saved his life.

He was too weak to put it on. Frank Williams, a ship's officer, came to Wood's aid. A former football star and a powerful swimmer, Williams was indeed the star of the show that day. Many of those who survived the disaster could thank him for their lives and his efforts. When a British MTB finally arrived to pick up survivors, it was Williams who saved his captain's life, grabbing the semi-conscious Bell by the shirt and heaving him into the rescue craft.

Had it not been for the clear and quick thinking of John Bryant, the MTB might have never been of service in the first place. The able seaman was the only man with enough presence of mind to blow the whistle attached to his life jacket, attracting the ship's attention.

Telegrapher Zavier O'Mara had all his "luck o' the Irish" with him that day. He was in the radio shack when the explosion ripped his wireless equipment right off the bulkhead. With two other ratings, one ahead and the other behind him, he ran from the cabin—and never saw either of them again. O'Mara's life jacket snagged on something when he jumped into the water. He lost the jacket. But when he bobbed to the surface there it was, floating two feet in front of him.

It was a closer call for Doug Crandon. He was about to go on watch when he heard the explosion. He was making for the upper deck when his life jacket caught on something, so he abandoned it. A gush of water swept him into the sea. By the time he came to the surface, the ship was nowhere in sight. A strong swimmer, Crandon found the same log that O'Mara was hanging onto.

To John Brebner, a sick-berth attendant, the explosion felt like somebody had pulled a chair from under him: "The ship just seemed to drop." He started out from the forecastle, not taking time to grab his life jacket. He remembered how calm everyone seemed to be, no sign of panic. He got topside and began climbing the side of the wheelhouse. He could see the coxswain inside, trying to get out, but he didn't stand a chance—at that moment, the ship went down. Brebner was dragged under, and his head banged against something. He reached the surface and found O'Mara and Crandon hanging onto their log.

Leo McVarish was starting up the ladder towards the forecastle when everything went black. He was sucked down with the sinking vessel. His one fear was that the depth charges might go off. When he reached the surface, the forecastle was sliding away. In the confusion, he lost his life jacket. But there was no time for ruminations. "Any hesitation," he said later, "was fatal."

Alberni was the 18th Canadian warship lost in World War II, and the eighth corvette. In only 30 seconds, the disaster had claimed the lives of four officers and 55 ratings. Of a crew of 90, three officers and 28 other ranks were saved.

RefScs: DHist f FDS 330 CCAN 263

KINETIC
AUGUST 1944

*D*esigned to break up German coastal supply lines along the *Bay of Biscay, Operation Kinetic—literally, the science of force—was well named. The west coast enemy garrisons—Brest, La Rochelle, La Pallaice, St. Nazaire, Lorient and the mouth of the Gironde River—were holding out as long as they could. They could no longer operate as bases for U-boats, which were being withdrawn to Norway. But they were still a thorn in the side for Allied shipping, and they continued to cramp freedom of movement in the Bay. Though they were isolated, it would nevertheless require a sizeable force to capture the ports from the Germans. And, at this stage, men could not be spared.*

It had been reasoned, however, that, if the German bases were being fed from the sea, they could also be starved out from the sea. Heavily laden German minesweepers, trawlers and a

*few destroyers had been steadily moving up and down the coast
throughout July. The Allies had allowed the practice to continue—to the point where it had slipped into a typically Teutonic
routine, taking the lack of Allied interference for granted. Now
it was time to strike.*

*Kinetic got underway on the last day of July. For the first
sorties, a fairly sizeable force was assigned to cripple enemy
shipping—two cruisers, the heavies in the pack; an escort carrier, to provide fighter support; four escort destroyers; and a
strike force, made up of all the destroyers from the 10th Flotilla.*

*But, after three uneventful patrols, the force was reduced on
August 5 to one British cruiser,* Bellona; *two Canadians
destroyers,* Haida *and* Iroquois; *and the RN destroyers* Ashanti
and Tartar. *Fighter protection was considered unnecessary, so
the escort carrier was removed from the entourage. Three of the
RCN destroyers that had been part of the original strike* force—
Chaudiere, Kootenay *and* St. Laurent—*were assigned to an
independent patrol off Lorient.*

Off Ile d'Yeu and Belle Ile
August 5–6, 1944

DeWOLF Harry
HIBBARD James Calcutt

"Two Canadian Destroyers in on Kill of Two Convoys"

Sometime around 10:30 p.m., as *Bellona, Ashanti, Haida,
Iroquois* and *Tartar* drew abreast of Ile d'Yeu, 12 miles off
the coast of France and 40 miles south from the Loire River
mouth, they made radar contact at extreme range. As the echoes
strengthened, it was clear that an enemy convoy was steering
towards the seaward side of the island.

For two solid hours the cruiser and destroyers furtively stalked
the Germans, until the convoy was well beyond the range of
shore. At 10 minutes past midnight the destroyers increased

(l. to r): Harry DeWolf, Horatio Lay and James Hibbard. (DND/PA 115383)

speed to 25 knots, then cut in between the convoy and the land to the east. In its role as illuminator and controller, the British cruiser stayed astern and to seaward. At 12:33 *Bellona* lobbed the first shell, lighting up seven enemy ships.

All four destroyers opened fire. Jimmy Hibbard, at the helm of *Iroquois*, sank two vessels. *Haida*, skippered by Harry DeWolf, set a powerfully armed M-class minesweeper ablaze—in four minutes it was gone. Her gunners landed salvoes on another enemy ship. Then, as a shell was entering the gun breach, it exploded. *Haida* was badly wounded—her turret wrecked, the stern damaged, two gunners dead and eight others injured. But she stayed to fight on.

The encounter lasted only 12 minutes. In that time, six enemy ships, one of them evacuating more than 800 German troops, had been set on fire and sunk. Only one escaped, and the night was still young.

The force regrouped and sailed north along the coast for another two hours. They had just passed St. Nazaire when radio echoes indicated another enemy convoy, approaching Belle Ile, to the north on the inshore side. This was treacherous territory.

Quiberon Bay was heavily mined on both sides of the channel, which the Allied group was now entering. It was also shallow and extremely rocky, and the ships were well within range of radar-controlled shore batteries.

The destroyers and their controller were willing to gamble—they had gone this far undetected. Knowing the convoy would soon be moving into more open water, the Allies turned slightly seaward; they waited 15 minutes, then came about. Just ahead, clear of the shallows, were the enemy ships. Off went the star shells.

Closing to 6,000 yards, the destroyers opened fire, observing hits along the waterlines of several German vessels. They withdrew briefly when the shore batteries opened up, then returned again, a tactic they repeated three times. Two of the German merchantmen were so badly damaged they had to fall back. The destroyers were determined to finish them off. But 40 minutes had elapsed since the fight began and, with dawn approaching along with its imminent danger of air attack, the order came from Plymouth to withdraw.

RefScs: DHist f FDS 347–50

Between Brest and Lorient
August 7–8, 1944

DYER Kenneth
GROOS Harold Victor
WALLACE Dickson Carlile
WELLAND Robert Philip

"Action in Audierne Bay"

Shortly before eleven o'clock this night, a Kinetic flotilla made up of *Assiniboine*, *Qu'Appelle*, *Restigouche* and *Skeena*, commanded by Robert Welland, Debby Wallace, Harold Groos and Kenneth Dyer respectively, was moving south of Brest along with a British destroyer when they made radar contact with a

German convoy on the edge of Audierne Bay. An ideal venue for an attack, the Audierne was the only clear body of water between Brest and Lorient.

The destroyers moved on the enemy cautiously; it was nearly two hours before they decided to close in, just to seaward of the convoy. Then they charged forward at full tilt. At 2:24 they could make out three German trawlers, silhouetted by the moon at a range of 4,600 yards. The destroyers rocketed star shells over the enemy ships, which immediately dropped smoke floats. This worked to the destroyers' advantage, however. In the confusion created by their own smokescreen, the German vessels began firing on each other.

The destroyers made two passes, by which time one German trawler was on fire and listing, and the other two were headed towards shore to beach themselves. One made it; the destroyers came in for a third pass, sending the third ship onto the beach engulfed in flames. A cottage near the water's edge was hit by a stray shell. It too burst into flames, adding to the incendiary display the destroyers left behind.

RefScs: FDS 350–51

Off Les Sables-d'Olonne
August 14–15, 1944

HIBBARD James Calcutt

"A Night for Revenge"

In September 1941, Jimmy Hibbard had been senior escort officer to the ill-fated convoy SC-42, which, during a bitter 60-hour battle, lost 16 merchantmen to U-boats. Tonight, as skipper of the Tribal destroyer *Iroquois*, it was Hibbard's turn.

Along with a British cruiser and destroyer sailing south of Les Sables-d'Olonne, west of La Rochelle, *Iroquois* picked up such a strong radar echo that Hibbard immediately ordered a flare. The star shell lit up the area, uncovering an armed German merchant ship.

The enemy vessel made smoke and tried to squirm away from the light of the flare. Just as *Iroquois* opened fire, an Elbing was sighted. Hibbard shifted his attention to the German destroyer, following it towards the coast. He noted one solid hit, then was forced to weave out of the path of four torpedoes fired back at him. Hibbard ordered four of his own missiles fired, but failed to score. As the two ships approached shore the coastal batteries opened up. Hibbard was forced to break off. Meanwhile, the two British ships had set the merchantman ablaze and forced it ashore.

So much for such slim pickings in the southern patrol area. The Kinetic force now turned north. At 5:04 *Iroquois'* radar screen indicated movements to the north, 11,000 yards away. Thirty-five minutes later they came upon three minesweepers, inshore in water too shallow for the cruiser. *Iroquois* and her companion took over. Opening fire from 3,200 yards, within 20 minutes they had blown up one vessel and forced the two others to beach.

Hibbard was starting to avenge the debacle of three years before. Eight days later he exacted even greater satisfaction.

RefScs: FDS 351–52

Audierne Bay
August 22–23, 1944

HIBBARD James Calcutt

"Slaughter at Audierne—Climax to Kinetik"

With two British destroyers accompanying him, Jimmy Hibbard aboard *Iroquois* helped bring Operation Kinetic to a fitting culmination. Sweeping down from their base at Plymouth, they encountered their first prize when *Iroquois* registered a radar sounding at midnight—a German convoy in Audierne Bay, sailing southwest. The three destroyers waited

patiently for the enemy to appear. Then they raced in on the land-
ward side, and the convoy was trapped.

It was over in next to no time. Three enemy ships, ablaze from
end to end, beached themselves on the rocky Brittany coast. A
fourth simply blew up in a burst of flame and debris.

The Allied vessels were far from through for the night. Two
hours later, the other ships still burning, another German convoy
stole into the bay. *Iroquois'* long-range radar made it possible to
track it undetected until the moment came to strike. Up went the
flares again, and the three warships opened fire. Another quick
shootout. Two German ships were sunk almost immediately; two
others tried to run for the shore and collided, and both burst into
flames. One turned turtle and sank, the other rode up high on the
rocks, great plumes of flame illuminating the coastline.

As the Allied ships departed for home, the carnage they left
behind included three ships sunk, five others ablaze on the beach.
As far as Jimmy Hibbard was concerned, the losses he'd suffered
in the Battle of the Atlantic had at last been avenged.

Postscript: The action marked the beginning of the end for
German occupation of the ports along the Bay of Biscay. From
this point, Operation Kinetic would find few ships to attack—the
enemy vessels were hiding within their harbours, which could be
neither supplied nor evacuated.

Now the job of the Allied destroyers was to show the flag, to
encourage the Free French forces ashore and to land supplies for
the *Maquis* (French guerrilla) underground to assist in closing
down the ports.

Only four days later, on August 26, off Ile d'Yeu (Isle of God),
Iroquois was greeted by a party of Bretons that had put out from
the island in a fishing boat. The Germans had evacuated to the
mainland, and Free French Forces were now in control. A volunteer landing party from the Canadian destroyer was sent ashore to
set up a communications station and investigate the situation.
Nothing could have prepared them for the liberators' welcome
they received. They were embraced, lifted shoulder high, paraded
through the town, wined and dined.

By September 2, most of the German garrisons in the Bay had been evacuated, bringing Operation Neptune to a formal finish.

RefScs: DHist f FDS 352–53

COWBOY FLOTILLA
AUGUST 1944

*O*n *January 4, 1944, the all-Canadian 56th Motor Gun Boat/Motor Torpedo Boat Flotilla was formed at Malta, under the command of Doug Maitland. It comprised three gunboats (Dog Boats) and three torpedo boats. Most of the flotilla's officers had volunteered for Mediterranean duty as early as 1942. Four of its ships had set sail from Milford Haven in Wales at the end of April 1943. They had seen action in Sicily and had been instrumental in the seizure of the islands of Capri, Corsica, Carrera, Ischia, Prochida and La Maddelena. In September, they had acted in support of the landings on the Italian mainland.*

In July 1944, the three Dog Boats of the "Cowboy Flotilla" arrived at Komiza Harbour, on the island of Vis in the Adriatic Sea off Yugoslavia. There they were to harass enemy shipping, in support of Tito's partisans.

Canadian intrepidness had already preceded them in the person of Tommy Fuller, known among Yugoslavian partisans as the "black-bearded pirate of the Adriatic." Fuller's exploits had made him a legend. As commander of the 61st MGB Flotilla, he captured enemy ships and looted them for supplies, equipment and arms. On one occasion, he sank an enemy schooner by lobbing a star shell into an open fuel bucket—the ship exploded and took an E-boat down with it. Fuller had further pressed his pursuit that day, causing such confusion that his German targets began firing at each other. The episode was hailed by Coastal Command as "one of the most successful actions in the Adriatic."

The 56th had a lot to live up to. But they wasted no time proving their worth.

Between Mljet and the Yugoslav Mainland
August 17, 1944

BURKE Cornelius
LADNER Thomas Ellis
MAITLAND Douglas
REYNOLDS Rover

"Three Musketeers in the Battle of Mljet"

B efore they moved into the narrow patrol area that night, the "Three Musketeers" of the 56th Flotilla—senior officer Doug Maitland, Corny Burke and Tom Ladner—landed two Royal Marine commandoes on the northwest end of Mljet Island, to act as spotters for enemy shipping in the channel.

They had just started their patrol when Maitland called his fellow MGBs: "Hallo, Dogs, this is Wimp. I have a possible target. Four small ships moving fast up Mljet Channel. Am steering to intercept."

E-boats—much too fast for the MGBs to catch—and after a few frustrating minutes they gave up the chase. Their only consolation was that in the dull, moonless night they'd probably not been seen themselves. An hour went by, then Maitland was on the horn again: "Say, fellas. I think we're in luck! There are three targets at range three miles just entering the channel and running down towards us. Come to action stations and get into cruising line to port. I shall wait as long as I can before attacking."

After 20 minutes, Maitland announced: "Target now clearly eight or nine ships."

Burke, on the bridge of MGB *658*, peered through his binoculars. "Three in sight," he told his Number One, Rover Reynolds. "Right ahead."

Maitland waited until the enemy ships were almost on top of them before giving the order to attack, barking: "Here we go, Dogs! Speed eight knots. Attacking on port bow. Tommy—light please—range is 500 yards!"

Off went the star shells, and the four gunboats opened up with

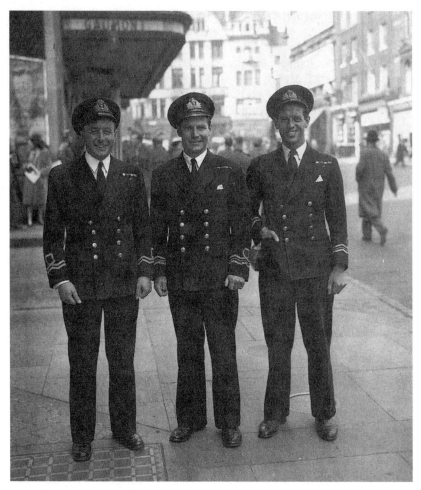

(l. to r.): Tom Ladner, Douglas Maitland and "Corny" Burke, known as "The Three Musketeers." (DND/PA 180065)

their pom-poms. Recovering from that hefty barrage, the German vessels fired right back. Burke's MGB was badly hit. He sent Reynolds below to inspect the damage. A 40-mm shell had torn a jagged hole in the port side, knocking out an engine. Burke steered away long enough to make hasty, band-aid repairs, then returned, with only starboard engines for power.

The MGBs now approached for a second attack, this time from astern, zeroing in on an E-boat and two landing craft. As they sailed by, they let fly from 200 yards with everything they had. Before the "Cease Fire" signal was given, all three enemy ships had been reduced to burning, lifeless hulks. They moved forward to attack three more ships at the head of the convoy. This time the range was 600 yards. The Three Musketeers each directed fire at a different target.

Burke's gunner hit the ammunition locker on their target, and the vessel exploded like a fireworks display. The other two convoy ships were soon out of action as well. But the night was still far from done.

Maitland's radar picked up more enemy ships approaching. As they came into sight, their leader challenged the MGBs by signal light. In response, all three gunboats—a total of 20 guns—opened up on the schooner, which promptly swung away out of the fight, irreparably damaged.

There were two other German ships holding course that still required attention. Maitland decided to lie in wait. Fifteen minutes went by before the MGBs could make out a schooner with a smaller vessel alongside. At 300 yards, the gunboats opened fire. Reynolds was amazed that the enemy ships could absorb so much punishment. Finally, however, they were completely silenced.

That cleaned out the channel for the night. Maitland now directed a mop-up operation. One of the schooners was still afloat. The MGBs finished it with the help of brush fires they set along shore with their tracers: silhouetted against the firelight, the German ship was a clear target.

The Battle of the Mljet Channel had lasted only five hours. But the havoc wreaked in that space of time had far-reaching ramifications. Coastal Command Forces lauded it as a "peak performance...In the light of reports from Intelligence," the statement on the engagement read, "it is thought that this action may be described as the shrewdest blow that the enemy has suffered on the Dalmatian Coast, and well may have speeded the evacuation of the islands."

The Three Musketeers had done themselves proud.

Cornelius Burke, son of the president of Boeing Aircraft of Canada, joined the Navy in 1939. After basic training he was sent on loan to the Royal Navy in the early part of 1940. His first taste of action came at the time of the evacuation of France as a member of a demolition force in the Le Havre area. There he acquitted himself and earned such praise and respect that his request to be transferred to MGBs was given hasty sanction.

Thomas Ladner left law school at Osgoode Hall in Toronto to join the RCNVR in 1939. He sailed to England in 1940. His first duty at sea was aboard an armed merchantman, which was torpedoed 100 miles off Iceland that December (his lifeboat was blown up, and he had clung to a Carley float in the frigid water until rescued). He was later accepted into Coastal Forces and, although he had never been to sea in one, he was given command of a motor gunboat thanks to his deportment as an officer and his high scholastic standing.

Douglas Maitland was already a sailor of some repute, having competed in sailing races in Vancouver, when he joined the navy at the outbreak of war in 1939. Like many others training as officers at the Naval Division there, he was sent to England on loan to the Royal Navy in March of 1940. Maitland first saw sea duty with an armed merchant ship, surviving an air attack and taking part in the capture of several enemy vessels. In 1941 he was posted as a First Lieutenant aboard a motor torpedo boat.

RefScs: CN 5 14 19–20 24 36 61–63 65–116 171–90 VAS 59–63

THE INEXORABLE TIDE OF WAR
AUGUST–DECEMBER 1944

*D*uring the late spring and summer of 1944, Canadian ships had supplied all the close escort duty for convoys sailing the North Atlantic. With Operation Neptune winding down, other navies began to contribute vessels. The overall challenge now was to maintain and strengthen the expanding Allied domination of the sea, and footholds on the continent itself.

Temporarily discontinued in March in anticipation of Neptune, Russian-bound convoys were renewed in August, and they required escort. Still more ships were required to enforce

Allied control of the English Channel, the North Sea and the coastal routes around Great Britain.

By August, Canadian ships were spread out from the Gulf of St. Lawrence to the United Kingdom; from the Mediterranean, where troop ships took part in the invasion of southern France, to mine-laying and air-support actions off the coast of Norway; and as part of the Murmansk run.

Driven from the Bay of Biscay, German U-boats now operated from bases in Denmark, Norway and northern Germany. Though they alone were no longer a great enough menace to threaten the outcome of the war, their very existence meant convoys and constant vigilance had still to be maintained, a process that tied down half a million Allied personnel. They may have been fewer in number, but they were progressively faster, and with steadily improved weapons and equipment, the subs were more dangerous than ever.

Hopes for an early victory had faded in mid-September with the failure of an airborne attack on Arnhem, the Netherlands, in a bid to occupy the Ruhr and cut off the Wehrmacht. The Normandy supply line had been overextended—after a bitter battle, the port of Antwerp had finally been freed, thus safeguarding the supply routes, but it took until December. It was apparent that the Germans intended to struggle desperately to an all-but-certain finish.

This war still had a long way to go. And if Hitler was prepared to fight to the last, so was Donitz. Though U-boat crews now lacked the training and experience of their predecessors (most of whom had by now gone the way of statistics—casualties of war), they were just as willing to sacrifice themselves for the Fatherland.

Allied—and Canadian—naval strength was at its zenith. But in the later months of 1944, Canadian ships took as big a beating as any they had suffered in the darkest stages of the early war.

Off Bergen and Tromso, Norway
August 10–24, 1944

BOAK Eric Eversley Garrat
LAY Horatio Nelson
PIERS Desmond William

"Tirpitz *and* Nabob *Reduced to Scrap"*

In August, naval operations off the coast of Norway were driven by two objectives. The first chore was to mine the waters in the Lepsoyren Channel and Harhamsfjord area north of Bergen—the "cursed corridor"—where German merchant ships were protected by the narrow channel, and sheltered by cliffs and a profusion of small outlying islands. The intention was to chase the enemy vessels out to sea and into the open, where Allied warships could take a proper crack at them.

The second aim was to mount carrier-launched air attacks to put away—for good—the last of the vaunted German battleships. *Tirpitz* had yet to initiate any action, though she had been badly damaged on several occasions. She was holed up at Altafjorden, far to the north in the vicinity of Tromso, and was still considered by the Admiralty to be a threat.

On August 9, a force composed of a fleet aircraft carrier, two escort carriers, two carriers and eight destroyers left Scapa Flow in Scotland, arriving at their destination off the Norwegian coast the following day. Included among the flotilla were two Canadian destroyers, *Algonquin*, captained by Debby Piers, and *Sioux*, captained by Eric Boak.

Sailing as well was the British escort carrier *Nabob*, manned by an RCN crew of 1,000 under the command of Horatio Nelson Lay. This was the largest ship at the disposal of the Canadian Navy at the time—492 feet long, with a displacement of 15,000 tons. Because Canada had no naval air designation at this point, the flying personnel consisted of the RN Fleet Air Arm, though there were Canadian pilots among them.

At 1:00 on that grey afternoon a squadron of 12 Avengers,

each carrying a mine, lifted off from *Nabob*, while a similar formation took to the air from the RN escort carrier. Flying cover were Seafire and Firefly fighters from the British aircraft carrier. The mission was a total success. Not only were all the mines laid; in addition, the fighters had taken the Germans completely by surprise, destroying six Messerschmitt 109s parked on Gossen airfield.

The enemy was better prepared next time. During a 6:00 p.m. sortie, flak was heavy and accurate, and two of the fighters failed to return. However, all the mine layers from Lay's *Nabob* and the RN escort carrier flew home safely.

Altafjorden lies north of Tromso, well within the Arctic Circle and far enough inland to make a surface attack on *Tirpitz* impossible. And *Tirpitz*'s concentration of flak guns, supported by those on the shore surrounding it, meant that an air raid, though possible, was certainly no piece of cake. Nevertheless, that was the objective of the next powerful strike force, which set out from Scapa Flow on August 16.

It consisted of the heavy British battleship *Duke of York*, three aircraft carriers, three escort carriers, of which *Nabob* was one, and a group of frigates and 13 destroyers, among them Piers's *Algonquin* and Boak's *Sioux*. *Nabob*'s role was to provide air cover for the flotilla with four of her Wildcats. The two Canadian destroyers acted as her guardians.

The force reached its flying-off position on August 20, but for the next two days the weather was so bad that flying was impossible. On the afternoon of August 22 two strikes were made on *Tirpitz*. The battleship took several hits. Escorting fighters shot down nine ME 109s, sunk several smaller vessels in the fjord and strafed enemy gun positions. But the pair of raids had been costly—11 British planes were lost.

Meanwhile, *Nabob*, along with British escort carrier *Trumpeter*, had moved westward, due to the rough weather, to refuel three destroyers; at four o'clock, they were 130 miles northwest of Tromso. An hour later, *Nabob*'s crew began laying out hose lines for refuelling. *Trumpeter*'s aircraft were patrolling the area for anti-submarine protection. At 5:16, *Nabob* took a torpedo that blew a hole 50 feet wide by 40 feet deep in her starboard side.

All electrical power was knocked out. Auxiliary machinery and ventilating fans came to an instant stop. Temperature in the engine room soared to an intolerable 150 degrees—the boilers and engines had to be shut down. Water flooded through the gaping hole, dragging the ship down. The stern sank 18 feet; the carrier began to list to starboard. Lifeboats were lowered, rafts and Carley floats cast over the side, as the crew prepared to abandon ship. One of the RN destroyers pulled alongside, taking off 214 men, 10 of whom were injured.

In the meantime, damage control parties in the engine room had closed off flooded compartments and shored up the bulkheads. By 7:00 p.m. the situation had improved dramatically—internal structures not damaged by the explosion were holding; and the engines, shaft and propeller had escaped damage. A diesel generator had been hooked up to the main switchboard, putting the ventilators and auxiliary machines back in business. Now the engines could be restarted. By 9:30 *Nabob* was underway once more, albeit at a sharply reduced speed.

Now she faced a 1,100-mile return voyage. Because it had been impossible to recover the rafts and Carley floats so hastily thrown overboard, she had very little left on board by way of lifesaving or rescue equipment. The real question was how well the engine-room bulkheads would hold—they were the ship's only hope as water battered against the metal walls through the gash in her side. Constant vigilance on the part of crewmen was called for; the crew worked waist-deep in water in the stifling corridors for the next three days and nights.

At 2:30 a.m., August 23, *Nabob*'s radar detected a U-boat 4,000 yards to starboard. The submarine had surfaced and was preparing to attack. The crippled carrier, with 800 aboard, was struggling along at a bare 10 knots, a very large and extremely slow-moving target. Lay immediately ordered his aircraft aloft, severely testing the skill and daring of the carrier's airmen.

Two Avengers were catapulted away. They made straight for the submarine. The U-boat commander wanted no truck with dive bombers—he quickly submerged his craft. The Avengers patrolled for two and a half hours, to no avail. The submarine had disappeared. Now came the trickiest maneuver—landing on *Nabob*'s sloping, buckled deck. Being 6:00 a.m., it was at least light, though the weather was far from fair. The first plane touched down gingerly, but safely. The second dropped out of low cloud, bounced onto the deck, overshot and crashed into the barrier at the far end—but the pilot climbed out unscathed. That night *Algonquin* took off another 200 of *Nabob*'s company.

For three more days the weather steadily deteriorated, and the escort carrier continued to plow through rough seas. Her condition also gradually worsened: her stern had settled to the point that her quarterdeck rode only four feet above the surface. But finally, on the morning of August 27, she sailed through the gate at Scapa Flow. Her toll was 31 dead, 10 injured. As a warship, *Nabob* was through. She never again saw action.

In the meantime, the air strikes against *Tirpitz* had continued. By the time the force set sail for the return to Scapa Flow on August 24, *Tirpitz* had been severely battered—in fact, mortally wounded. That didn't satisfy the Admiralty. On November 12, three Lancasters from RAF Bomber Command, carrying 12,000-pound blockbusters, finally sent her to the bottom of Tromso fjord.

RefScs: DHist f FDS 37 1–76

800 Miles West of the British Isles
October 4–12, 1944

OLIVER Maurice Franklin

"The Plight of HMCS Chebogue*"*

While on close escort duty, *Chebogue*'s master lookout spotted a surfaced U-boat, 13,000 yards distant. Maurice Oliver, the frigate's skipper, ordered full speed ahead. At 10,000 yards the submarine submerged. Oliver continued the search well

Maurice Oliver aboard Chebogue *inspecting damage inflicted by U-1227 on October 4, 1944. (F.R. Kemp/DND/PA 141532)*

into the evening, but without result. Then, a few minutes past ten, a Gnat acoustic torpedo exploded into the ship's stern. *Chebogue* was left rudderless, a cripple. Other vessels in the group rallied and began a search, but the culprit was nowhere to be found.

By 1:00 next afternoon the frigate was in bad shape. She had to be taken in tow. She was towed in relays, ship after ship, for the next week, the full 850 miles back to Wales.

On October 9 she was in sight of shore, and a rescue tug arrived to guide her along the last lap of her torturous journey. But on October 11, at the very mouth of Swansea Bay, she took the full force of a blizzard, the worst storm to hit the area in 20 years. Around midnight the tow lines broke and *Chebogue* floundered in the rough sea, blown broadside into the wind. Her stern settled at the bottom of the bay in 20 feet of water as the gale began to abate and it was finally possible to get the crew off-loaded.

By morning at high tide, the frigate's stern had lifted off the bottom just enough that she could be eased into the jetty at Port Talbot. *Chebogue* had been rescued, but her days as a fighting ship were over.

RefScs: DHist f FDS 380–81 TSIAOG 177

Pointe des Monts, the Mouth of the St. Lawrence River
October 14–15, 1944

HILL Henry Knox
QUICK Lewis Dennis

"Magog Sunk Close to Home"

Only five months after the frigate was commissioned, HMCS Magog gained the dubious distinction of being the Canadian vessel sunk by enemy action closest to the community after which she was named—Magog, Quebec, some 600 miles west of Pointe des Monts, at the mouth of the St. Lawrence River.

Part of Escort Group 16, along with the Canadian frigate *Toronto*, *Magog*, under the command of Henry Hill, was on her way to join a Sydney-to-Quebec City convoy. At 1:25 on the afternoon of October 14, five miles off Pointe des Monts Light, they came under the watchful eyes of *Kapitanleutnant* Kneip, captain of *U-1223*. Though ground visibility was clear, with low, overcast skies, even the Catalina flying boat acting as air escort had no inkling of an impending attack.

Magog was zigzagging on the starboard side of the convoy at an incredibly low speed of seven knots when Kneip locked her in his sights and fired two acoustic torpedoes from 6,000 yards. The first Gnat ripped into the stern of the frigate, sheering off 65 feet of afterstructure; the second exploded in the stern as well. Three of *Magog*'s crew were killed instantly. Damage-control parties went to work immediately; they had only recently undergone intensive training at the Navy's base in Bermuda.

Meanwhile, *Toronto*'s skipper, Lewis Quick, sighted what he thought to be a periscope. The frigate's gunners let fly with their 4-inch and Oerlikon guns. Below, Kneip's U-boat crew could hear the explosions and the scream of the Cat Gear being deployed by the Canadian ships. Kneip decided to call it quits, for the moment.

Half an hour after the attack, *Toronto* was maneuvering to take the stricken frigate in tow. Lifeboats were being lowered to rescue three of *Magog*'s crew, blown overboard. But *U-1223* had returned to the scene. *Toronto* made contact, and just in time—a torpedo was heading for her starboard bow. She broke off the tow and began a series of Hedgehog attacks. Aircraft dropped sonobuoys (whose signals could be picked up by asdic), while ships from EG 16 carried on a series of searches into the following evening. But Kneip had again escaped to safety.

The most seriously wounded were taken from *Magog* and transferred to a waiting Catalina, in wind and a running sea that made the task almost impossible. The frigate was eventually towed into Quebec City—but she was nothing more than a hulk. In December, she was paid off. *Magog* was sold for scrap the following year.

RefScs: FDS 380 TSIAOG 177 UBAC 237–39

Near the Faeroe Islands
October 16, 1944

BALFRY C.P.

"Annan Claims 'Unauthorized' Submarine Kill"

C.P. Balfry's frigate *Annan* had been built by the Royal Navy and commissioned into the RCN in 1944. Fresh from a work-up at Tobermory in the New Hebrides, Balfry had taken command of her in May. In October she was part of Escort Group 6, released from Neptune duty the previous month.

On the afternoon of October 16, *Annan* dropped a depth-charge pattern on what appeared to be a very promising target. A lengthy follow-up search continued until dark, when Balfry called off the hunt to rejoin EG 6. *Annan* was almost in sight of the group when her radar operator reported a fix astern. Balfry swung his ship about and bore down as the echoes strengthened. It became apparent that the submarine was on the surface, following a sharp zigzag pattern. In fact, *U-1006* had been so badly damaged by the earlier depth charges that she was unable to submerge.

As the frigate closed range to 2,700 yards, Balfry ordered star shells fired, and he turned towards the U-boat beam on. *Annan's* gunners opened fire, and the frigate was met with a return barrage that wounded four of her own crew and knocked her radar out of action. But Balfry continued to bear down, 4-inch guns and Oerlikons blazing at point-blank range. He brought his ship in so close that gunners dropped depth charges on top of the U-boat. They bounced off its deck and exploded in the water.

The engagement had lasted 18 minutes, and the submarine had begun to sink. Men were pouring from the hatches and jumping overboard. Two minutes later the submarine disappeared, still on an even keel; 46 Germans were rescued and taken prisoner.

Balfry's attack had actually contravened Navy tactical instructions, which suggested that, due to the menace of the Gnat acoustic bomb, solo assaults on enemy submarines were to be avoided at all costs. In effect, Balfry's victory was an "unauthorized kill"—it succeeded, official instructions to the contrary notwithstanding.

RefScs: DHist f FDS 381–82 TSIAOG 177–78

Off Hoek Van Holland
November 1, 1944

BEVAN Alan
BISHOP Craig
BROADLY Harold
BURK Charles Arthur
CREBA Glen
LAW Anthony
WELDEN Frederick

"Fierce MTB Battle off Dutch Coast"

Operating out of Felixstowe on the coast of Suffolk, four motor torpedo boats from the 29th Flotilla led by Tony Law went in search of a German convoy, reported off the Hook of

Holland (Hoek van Holland), just south of The Hague. It was a clear, moonlit night with visibility eight to nine miles; it was also bitterly cold, with winds blowing at near gale force.

The MTBs picked up the enemy on radar at seven miles. Drawing near, they could make out several flak trawlers, a gunboat, a tug towing a barge and a 3,000-ton merchant ship. Closing in further, and still undetected, they spotted seven German E-boats. Law and Glen Creba turned about to charge the E-boats, giving Craig Bishop and "Bones" Burk a chance to take on the convoy.

Selecting the merchant ship as their target of choice, the latter closed the range to 800 yards for a torpedo attack, despite heavy fire. A hit below the waterline stopped Bishop from launching his "fish." He nevertheless persisted with his attack, sweeping the convoy with gunfire. The action became fierce. Burk's 6-pounder ran out of ammunition; Bishop's main gun was knocked out; Burk's torpedoes found their mark. A blinding white flash and ugly, black cloud of smoke shot from the merchantman.

Bishop's *464* had casualties. Harry Broadly had been killed outright; Alan Bevan was badly wounded. Fred Welden, damage-control officer, organized a bucket brigade while he worked to block the hole first with clothing, then with "instant" planking fashioned by smashing the mess deck table with a fire axe and using the handle to wedge the works in place. The bucket brigade had to keep slogging until the volume of water was reduced sufficiently for the MTB to pick up enough speed to get the ship's suction pump working.

Law and Creba had meanwhile been in a savage fight, managing to set fire to one E-boat. With Bishop on his way back to England, the remaining three MTBs engaged four flak trawlers, armed with powerful 88-mm guns, known as the Four Horsemen of the Apocalypse. In a game of hide-and-seek, each side batted shells back and forth. It was a draw, neither side scoring. The MTBs headed home only after spending their ammunition.

CN 202–03 WPA 144–46

Near Halifax
December 24, 1944

BATT Alex
CAMPBELL Craig
CLARK Norman Vincent
FINLAY Paul
MUNRO William

"Year Closes in Fateful Finale"

Craig Campbell had been given command of the Bangor minesweeper *Clayoquot* only days earlier. On December 20, he'd been in Chester, Nova Scotia, celebrating over a glass of rum when he was recalled from Christmas leave. An American liberty ship (each was manufactured in one day by Henry Kaiser) had been torpedoed 40 miles east of Halifax, and an anti-submarine sweep was needed immediately to protect two convoys moving south in the vicinity.

Three ships were assigned the mission—*Clayoquot, Transcona* and *Kirkland Lake*, skipper Norman Clark in charge. Two-thirds of Campbell's crew remained on shore leave—most of the personnel he sailed with were temporary, the majority inexperienced in submarine hunting.

Two miles off Cape Sambro, *U-806 Kapitanleutnant* Klaus Hornbostel, having torpedoed the US freighter, was biding his time. On Christmas Eve, around 10:30 a.m., the order was given for the Canadian ships to take up assigned positions around the convoy, reduce speed to 12 knots and begin zigzagging. Campbell was reacting faster than the other ships because *Clayoquot* was to move to the far side of the convoy. Hornbostel, watching from periscope depth, was under the impression the minesweeper had spotted him; in fact, *Clayoquot* was totally unaware of the U-boat's presence.

Hornbostel fired off a Gnat to protect himself. It struck the ship astern, followed by two detonations—one from the torpedo itself, the other from a magazine of small charges belowdecks.

Clayoquot's entire stern section launched into a vertical position, plastered against the hatch of the after-officers' cabin.

The blasts peeled back the quarterdeck. They threw the minesweeping winch over the mast and onto the forecastle. Parts of depth charges landed on the bridge. Other bits of explosives shot through the galley skylight, under which the off-watch hands were mustering for their daily grog. That they were there—forward rather than aft—when the torpedo hit saved their lives.

Belching clouds of smoke and steam, *Clayoquot* listed sharply to starboard, and the order was given immediately to abandon ship. Paul Finlay and William Munro, two of the ship's officers, were trapped in the after-cabin. They yelled for axes to chop their way out. Such tools had already sunk to the bottom, and the officers went down with their ship.

Craig Campbell was the last to leave. He swam to a rescue raft, from which he watched *Clayoquot* go down. A letter from his parents, congratulating him on taking over his command, was still in his pocket.

Nine minutes had elapsed since the torpedo struck. The evacuation had been orderly and disciplined. Only eight of the crew were lost, most of them trapped on the ship. Alex Batt, a coder with an irrepressible (if sardonic) sense of humour, wrote the epitaph to the episode, bellowing from a Carley float: "Flash! Canadian minesweeper destroys German torpedo!"

RefScs: FDS 384 TSIAOG 177–78 UBAC 257–63

ROUND-UP—THE FINAL CHAPTER 1945

*T*o all intents, the Germans were already beaten by the beginning of 1945. Their brief Ardennes counteroffensive (at the Battle of the Bulge) had failed. The Russians were closing in from the east. In the west, the Americans, British and Canadians stood poised to cross the Rhine. Germany as a nation was doomed, caught in a giant vise. But she was far from defeated at sea.

Kriegsmarine *surface ships—what remained of them—had been withdrawn to the Baltic in support of the troops retreating from the Red Armies. But U-boat warfare continued relentlessly. Assisted by E-boats, the submarines harassed the Thames-Antwerp supply line. Coupled with Luftwaffe air attacks, they preyed on the ships along the Murmansk Run. And they were still a major factor in the North Atlantic.*

Nearly 150 U-boats were still in action. In the last five months of the war, they sent half a million tons of Allied shipping to the depths. That figure represented just over 10 per cent of the total tonnage conveyed to Europe—production for the same period amounted to four-and-a-half million tons. The submarine menace could never be ignored.

The main role for the Royal Canadian Navy reverted to convoy escort duty, though some ships worked with the Royal Navy on the Murmansk route, and the two MTB flotillas continued their work in support of the Thames-Antwerp shipping lanes. The Atlantic convoy escort vessels saw the most action off their own home shores. Heralding the new year on January 4, two merchantmen were sunk by Kapitanleutnant Dobritz's U-1232 off Egg Island, only 20 miles from Halifax.

And so the situation remained status quo until May 8, when the U-boats in Canadian waters finally hoisted their flags in surrender.

Off Falmouth, the Cornish Coast
February 22, 1945

ABBOTT Patrick
GLASSCO Colin
KINSMAN Burnley

"10th and Last Canadian Corvette Lost"

At 5:30 on the evening of February 21, the Canadian corvette *Trentonian* joined coastal convoy BTC-76 off Bull Point,

Colin Glassco who, along with Burnley Kinsman, was the last to leave the torpedoed Trentonian. *(F.R. Kemp/DND/PA 163150)*

bound from Bristol to the Thames. Only a few days earlier, her captain, Colin Glassco, had given the ship's company a pep talk on the importance of wearing life jackets—timely advice that was to save many lives.

By noon next day, having safely rounded Land's End and Lizard Point the night before, the convoy was proceeding east at seven knots, *Trentonian* leading two columns of seven ships each. The fog had cleared, the sea was calm, the wind light, and visibility was about 10 miles.

At 1:20 p.m., the second of the inshore column of ships took a direct hit from a torpedo. *Trentonian* sounded action stations and swung back towards the stricken merchantman. Glassco ordered the

Cat Gear streamed out, while cutting through the convoy towards the area from which the submarine had most likely attacked. He had just ordered depth charges dropped when, at precisely 1:30, *Trentonian* was herself struck by a torpedo. As the corvette started to slew to the right, Glassco ordered: "Stop engines."

Fortunately, most of the crew had already reported to action stations. They were on the upper deck, and all hands had heeded the skipper's earlier warning. They were wearing life jackets, or casualties would have been much higher.

Burnley Kinsman, first lieutenant, went aft to investigate the extent of the damage. He reported that the engine room was flooded and the ship was rapidly sinking by the stern. It was impossible to save her. Glassco gave orders to abandon ship, lower the lifeboats and drop Carley floats. The time was 1:34. The abandonment of *Trentonian* was efficient, orderly and systematic. The crew's discipline and training stood it in good stead.

Pat Abbott, the navigating officer, destroyed all the ship's charts; then he helped toss a Carley float into the water before jumping in after it. After three-quarters of an hour in the icy water, he was so stiff he was "just barely able to climb out."

Colin Glassco and Burnley Kinsman were last to leave the ship, and then only after they were certain all living personnel were clear of it. Kinsman climbed aboard a lifeboat and directed rescue operations. Glassco jumped over the port side of the ship. He hung on to an oil drum, finally making his way to a Carley float, where he "felt much safer."

Trentonian sank at 1:40 p.m., exactly 10 minutes after she had been torpedoed. Before she went under, her bow stood straight up—so vertical that those in the water feared she might topple over on them. Much to their relief, she went straight down and disappeared. The survivors numbered 95. One officer and four ratings lost their lives, and 11 were injured.

A search force continued to sweep the area for the U-boat all afternoon and throughout the night. It yielded no results. The following morning the hunt was called off.

RefScs: CCAN 265–66 DHist f FDS 390 TSIAOG 180

St. George's Channel between Ireland and Wales
March 7, 1945

ALLEN John
BROCK John
McLEESE Willis
MISENER John
QUINN Harold
WALLER Dalton

"Relentless Sub Kill"

For John Misener, HMCS *La Hulloise*'s asdic officer, it had been a particularly busy afternoon—and a frustrating one. All the pings he had been picking up turned out to be nothing more than shipwrecks on the ocean bed. The gunners were just as disconcerted; they'd spent all the ship's ammunition in vain. In itself that might have been misleading. Though the war on the continent was drawing to a close, in the sea there was still a lot of bite left in the enemy. The three frigates of Escort Group 25, *Strathadam*, *Thedford Mines* and *La Hulloise*, were skippered by Howard "Hank" Quinn, John "Smash" Allen and John "Panner" Brock. The three skippers insisted on keeping their crews on a high state of alert, false pings or no false pings. And with good reason. With the introduction of the "*schnorkel*," which had been added to the German submarines' equipment two years earlier, the U-boat menace to all Allied ships at sea—men-of-war and merchant shipping—remained as big a threat as ever.

The *schnorkel* had solved one of the chief problems facing submarine operations. It did away with the need for the submarine to surface while recharging batteries and running on diesel engines. Consisting of an air intake and exhaust the height of a periscope, it allowed the submarine to run on its diesels and recharge its batteries, at the same time discharging the noxious engine fumes. As a result the U-boats could remain submerged for indefinite periods of time. And the odds of the *schnorkel* tube being detected were slim indeed, even at close range.

In fact, at 5:30 p.m. late on this mild late March afternoon, sitting down to supper with rest of his officers in the ward room, "Panner" Brock might well have laid bets on it. Ironically, in the light of subsequent events, he could have easily been persuaded to change his mind. Suddenly his evening meal was interrupted by word from the watch on the bridge that a two-masted fishing ketch had been sighted approaching from ahead, range about 2,000 yards.

By the time Brock reached the bridge the "fishing" vessel was almost within shouting distance and closing fast, now unmistakably identifiable as a *schnorkel* U-boat, its air and exhaust tube and periscope "masquerading" as the twin masts of a ketch. In no time at all it was abreast of the frigate, no farther than 100 yards away

"Action stations!"

Willis McLeese, the frigate's engineering officer, rushed to his post in the engine room. Others took to their stations as Brock alerted the other two frigates in the group. With *La Hulloise*'s ammunition gone, it was up to *Strathadam* and *Thedford Mines* to take over the firing duties, something the latter's gunnery officer, Dalton Waller, looked forward to with relish. All three frigates made a 180-degree about-face and gave chase, Brock directing the operation, the other ships dropping depth charges and lobbing Hedgehog bombs.

Thanks to John Misener's ingenuity, *La Hulloise*'s crew belowdecks had a running commentary of the action by remote control. The ship's asdic operator had rigged up a series of loudspeakers by cable from his office in the chart room off the bridge belowdecks so that McLeese and the others could listen in on the proceedings.

By now it was beginning to get dark. When Dalton Waller's gunners aboard *Thedford Mines* scored a direct hit with their first depth-charge volley, the flash from the explosion was so vivid it seemed to confirm a kill. Nevertheless other firings followed, bringing *U-1302* close to the surface, its lights clearly visible just under the water. Then suddenly it disappeared. Shortly afterwards oil and miscellaneous rubbish bubbled to the surface. Was this for real? Or was it the old U-boat ruse of releasing ersatz evidence indicating it had been sunk when all the while it was making its escape?

"Panner" Brock wanted to make sure. He promptly ordered John Misener and Willis McLeese to man the ship's motor launch and verify the debris—true or false. By the time they reached the spot where the submarine had allegedly met its demise—exact position 52.19 N, 05.23 W—there was no longer any question that the *schnorkel* had been sunk. Oil was quickly spreading over the surface of the sea. Amid the debris vomited up from the deep were pieces of engine room equipment, clothing, shoes, log books, paybooks and ration kits, as well as personal items of all sorts such as letters, diaries, snapshots and other assorted paraphernalia—including a harmonica. It was revealing. Confidential naval publications identified the wrecked submarine as *U-3102*, which had a full complement of 52, most of the crew young, some in their teens. McLeese and Misener concluded that this must have been the cause of their inexperience in so wantonly sailing into the midst of an escort group of anti-submarine frigates. Wrong. Captured German documents showed that the submarine had a fine record. Indeed, only a few hours earlier, it had sunk two merchantmen.

La Hulloise engineering and asdic officers became so engrossed in pursuing their findings, which they signalled by flag to all ships in the group, that they lost all track of time. It was getting late, and "Panner" Brock, concerned that they might become easy prey to a submarine attack, ordered them back to the ship post haste.

EG 25's destruction of its first U-boat, which in fact was the second-to-last RCN enemy submarine kill of the war, was hailed by the British Admiralty's Anti-U-Boat Division as "outstanding." *Strathadam*'s captain, "Hank" Quinn, held his cohort Brock in the highest esteem for his conduct in coordinating the subsequent attack once he had identified the "fishing" vessel as a *schnorkel* submarine. It was, he said, the most notable feature of the entire episode.

RefScs: FDS 159 FDS 392 IWM MMM 9 TUBH 238–24

North of the Azores
March 17, 1945

LAMB James
McCORMICK Frank
POTTER Harry
RUSSELL Benjamin
SLOPE Stan
WALKER Dennis

"22nd Warship Lost—55 Perish Awaiting Rescue"

When two torpedoes struck RC Bangor minesweeper *Guysborough*, 88 of her 90-man crew were able to reach the Carley floats that had been flung overboard. But by the time a rescue ship reached them the next afternoon, 55 had died from injuries and exposure to the cruel, wintry waters of the North Atlantic.

Lieutenant Frank McCormick, the ship's communications officer, was not among the fatalities. He credited the luck of the Irish for his survival; after all, it was Saint Patrick's Day. Having finished supper, he left the wardroom and, because he was not scheduled to take his turn at watch for the next two hours, he retired to his cabin to do some sketching, his pastime while not on duty. At 7:00 p.m. he was comfortably seated on his bunk, sketch pad on his lap, when the first torpedo struck. The sudden blast threw him into the air against the deck head and temporarily knocked him out. He flopped down on his stomach against the back of his chair, hanging there head first, his feet dangling obscenely inches from the floor.

That initial explosion had badly battered *Guysborough*'s stern. The ship staggered, then began listing to port. Litter cluttered the deck but there were no casualties. Benjamin Russell, the ship's captain, gave orders to muster the crew and put on winter clothing and to remain on deck until further notice.

McCormick regained consciousness. Although he was only wearing socks, underwear, grey slacks and shirt, he dashed out to make his way up to the main deck without bothering to retrieve anything else, not even his belt. Then he hit a snag. Blocking his path, ascending the gangway was Stan Slope, the ship's asdic operator. Clad in his sheepskin coat, Slope had been standing watch and was so obviously dazed by the explosion he had lost his bearings. It took some persuasion on McCormick's part to convince him to turn around and go up instead of down, but he finally succeeded "I had a hell of time," McCormick recalled.

By the time the pair reached the top, Slope still in a state of shock, McCormick hardly conforming to the captain's "winter clothing" dress code directive, most of the crew was assembled on deck. At first, although the explosion was treated as an emergency—the ship's whaler and motor boat had been secured alongside the ship for one thing, a misjudgment as it turned out—no one, including Russell, was quite certain of the cause. A pile of twisted metal, bits and pieces strewn all over the bow, indicated she had probably struck a mine. Closer inspection, however, revealed that a torpedo had smashed into the propellers and practically demolished the quarterdeck, scattering debris and blowing it over the mast onto the bow. Russell took all necessary precautions, ordering the guns manned, the watertight doors closed, the bulkheads shored; he then set damage-control parties to work. Then he consulted with the ship's engineer and coxswain, and they agreed that by shoring up aft they might save the minesweeper. They decided to continue on course. At this point the ship's gunnery officer, sub-lieutenant Harry Potter, tried to inject some levity into the grim situation. Taking an armful of bottles of wine from his locker, grinning from ear to ear, he began distributing them on deck. Irish to the core, he joked to the captain, "Bloody jerries have a nerve pickin' this day of all days to put a fish in us." Russell was not amused; this was no time for pranks. Angrily he grabbed the bottles one by one and pitched them over the railing into the sea.

Russell instructed McCormick to fix the ship's position and send off a wireless message to all ships in the area. McCormick made a quick calculation (which turned out to be remarkably accurate) then he and Russell drafted out an SOS message, which he gave to his two telegraphers to tap out. Although they repeated the signal countless times, McCormick never learned until later whether or not they were received because there was no acknowledgement. Then at 7:45 the second torpedo struck.

Several of the crew were injured, including McCormick, who was standing a mere 10 feet from the explosion, and, on the upper deck, gunnery officer Harry Potter. McCormick was knocked unconscious for a second time. He felt a tremendous pressure, as if he was tumbling through outer space. When he came to he climbed up the steps to the companionway leading to the upper deck. The only other people there were the skipper, two ratings and Potter, lying on his back, so badly injured he couldn't move.

The damage to *Guysborough* was so severe this time that there was no longer any question of saving her. Russell had no choice but to give the order to abandon ship. An ominous prospect what with the limited rescue craft available. The ill-advised command (from a source never determined) to tie the motor launch and whaler to the side of the ship instead of lifting them back onto the deck resulted in the total destruction of the former; the latter capsized from the blast when the second torpedo hit. That left five Carley floats, four of them lashed together. With about a dozen men on each, they began to drift away from the sinking ship. Together with a single float, they were split up among the crew of 90 men overboard. The remaining 42 men in the water, many of them badly injured, struggled to climb aboard the fifth float. Before jumping into the water himself, McCormick had picked Potter up and gently dropped him over the side close to the hull. Then he jumped into the water, closely followed by Russell, the captain and the last man to leave his sinking ship.

By this time Potter had begun to drift dangerously close to the gaping hole in the side of the ship caused by the torpedo's explosion. Assisted by a Royal Air Force officer who had joined the ship in Halifax as a passenger, McCormick swam over and pulled the gunnery officer away just in time to save him from being sucked under.

HMCS *Guysborough* had been commissioned in Vancouver in 1942 and first saw service on the Canadian Pacific Coast. She took part in Operation Neptune and was twice cited by the United States government for rescue work, all under the leadership of Benjamin Russell. In early 1945, she put in to Lunenburg, Nova Scotia for a refit. Then, with a full complement of 90 officers and men, most of whom had never been to sea before, she set sail for Halifax to stock up on supplies. From there she crossed the Atlantic to Plymouth Harbour in England, where she rejoined the minesweeping fleet to which she had been assigned a year earlier. She was returning to England after mine-clearing duty, having stopped in the Azores to replenish her supplies, when she was torpedoed.

Miraculously, the critically wounded minesweeper remained stubbornly afloat for an hour and 10 minutes after the initial torpedo explosion. At 10:10, the veteran of the Battle of the Atlantic finally succumbed to the depths. Just as amazing was the fact that not a single member of the crew went down with her.

During the interminably long, uncomfortable night, the two parties of survivors began drifting apart. A bitterly cold breeze sprang up, chilling the men to the bone. Waves sloshed across the floats so that no one could stay dry. Many of those in the water hanging onto the sides of the float kept drifting off to sleep, periodically lifting their heads up to keep from drowning. Men died from injuries, exposure and shock. But they did so bravely, stoically. "Both the air and the water were cold," reported stoker petty officer Denny Walker. "Most of the men died smiling. If they suffered any, you never would have known it." Some simply gave up. According to McCormick, "They swam off a distance and put their heads under."

On the crowded single float, coats were removed from the dead to cover the living. They took turns slipping into the water, slipping over the side to make room, many of them never seen again. Twice a float was turned over completely by the buffeting swell. Each time 10 men were lost.

At 8:00 the following morning an aircraft was sighted. But it failed to spot the floats. It wasn't until 2.30 p.m. that day, March 18, 1941, that HMS *Inglis* arrived to pick up the survivors. There were only six of the original 42 from the once-overcrowded single float. On the other floats only 31 were still alive. All of the survivors were too weak to climb up the scramble nets. They were hauled above by lines, all of them thankful that McCormick's wireless messages had got through after all and proud of having the distinction of having been afloat for 19 hours as castaways—a wartime record for the Battle of the Atlantic. Author James Lamb aptly christened the incident "Canada's Finest Hour."

RefScs: DHist FDS 393–94 PW11S 84–87

Lough Foyle, Northern Ireland
March 20, 1945

CHENOWETH Ian
HANBURY Ross

"Accidental Collision—Victory over U-boat"

It was a moonlit night, but hazy. As part of Escort Group 26, *New Glasgow*, commanded by Ross Hanbury, was just clearing Lough Point, moving into North Channel at 16 knots, when an object was sighted off her port bow. One lookout took the vague outline to be a low-flying aircraft. By the time it was identified as a U-boat, it was too late.

There was a resounding crash as the Canadian frigate collided with *U-1003*. The snorkel and periscope scraped the ship's side just below the wing of the bridge. As the ship lurched to starboard, action stations were rung. By the time an emergency depth-charge pattern was set, the U-boat had escaped 200 yards astern. Moving in the opposite direction, it disappeared.

Ian Chenoweth, *New Glasgow*'s first lieutenant, organized a damage-control party, to make repairs in case the submarine surfaced to engage the frigate in battle. These were accomplished in record time. Meanwhile, 50 rounds of star shells were fired, but they revealed nothing.

Hanbury ordered a series of Hedgehog attacks, but these too failed to yield results. Joined by others in the group and four more Canadian vessels from Londonderry, a two-day search for the submarine began. *New Glasgow* was then forced to return to port; the collision damage was found to be more serious than had first been believed.

The search had proved fruitless and was about to be called off when, on March 23, *Thedford Mines* came upon a group of German sailors on rescue rafts 16 miles off Ballygorma—the survivors of *U-1003*.

The ramming had been far more serious than the Canadians had reckoned. The U-boat had gone right to the sea floor to wait it out. The crew heard the depth charges exploding around them, but they inflicted no further damage. The U-boat's snorkel and periscope were out of action, however, and the sub was flooding so badly the pumps were unable to stem the tide. At midnight on March 22, the crew gave up and abandoned ship.

RefScs: DHist f FDS 394–95 TSIAOG 180

Near Falmouth
March 29, 1945

HARVEY Denis

"Teme's *Last Voyage*"

At dawn the RCN frigate *Teme*, Denis Harvey at the helm, was sweeping astern of a convoy when she made asdic contact. Investigation showed it to be another of the false echoes so common in that area of the English Channel. She picked up another contact as she started back to the convoy. This time it was the real thing, and a torpedo had already been fired; it was too late to take evasive action. The missile struck the port side under the quarterdeck.

The explosion knocked 60 feet off her stern. Depth charges

blew debris into the air. One man was blown from the quarter-deck onto the gun deck. He died moments later. Three others on the quarterdeck were never seen again.

Harvey ordered his crew to "stand by boats and floats." The engineering officer reported that the propellers were gone and the main engines and number two boiler were shut down. Damage control went to work, shoring up the aft section of the ship. Harvey and his officers decided that, for the time being at least, the vessel could be kept afloat.

Teme passed a tow line to the corvette *Moose Jaw*, another Canadian ship in the escort group. The forepeak was flooded, so two fuel oil tanks were pumped overboard, and the ammunition and deck stores were moved to keep the ship on an even keel. But the weather refused to cooperate. The swell was steadily rising and a high wind was blowing. Inevitably, the tow line broke.

At that point Harvey opted to play it safe. He had 57 members of his crew transferred to a lifeboat that had come alongside. *Moose Jaw* made another attempt to take the frigate in tow, but the line gave way again. Finally, a tug took *Teme* in tow, and after a hectic, 12-hour struggle through atrocious weather, she finally reached Falmouth.

This was the second time *Teme* had been towed back to port since being commissioned in February 1944. In June that same year, under the command of Douglas Jeffrey, she was rammed by an aircraft carrier while on anti-submarine duty in the Bay of Biscay. Though badly damaged with a hole in her port, there were no casualties. She was towed by the RCN frigate *Outremont*, a trip that lasted 48 hours, then repaired and returned to action. But with the March 29 incident, *Teme* was through for the duration.

RefScs: DHist f FDS 395

Halifax Approaches
April 16, 1945

CAMPBELL Albert
KAZAKOFF Michael
KIDD Thomas
KNIGHT Herbert
MacMILLAN Robert
MANUEL Terrence
McDONALD Duncan
McINTYRE Thomas James
RICHARD Frank
SMITH Frank
WARE Jack
WHITE Don

"Last Canadian Warship to Be Lost"

The end of the war with Germany was only weeks away, and everybody knew it. That might explain the casual, relaxed manner in which the Bangor minesweeper *Esquimalt* was carrying out her anti-submarine duties off the coast of Nova Scotia. She had left Halifax in the early hours of the morning and was about to break off to rendezvous with the minesweeper *Sarnia* at 7:00 a.m. There was a sense of euphoria aboard. It was a beautiful morning. The sun was shining. A light wind blew from the west, accompanied by a long, low and easy swell to the sea. And the barometer kept rising.

Contrary to patrol regulations, *Esquimalt* was neither streaming her two Cat Gear nor following a zigzag course. After the loss of *Clayoquot* in the same area in December, a board of inquiry had reported that areas "in the vicinity of the swept channels offer excellent opportunities for the use of Gnat torpedoes," and recommended strongly that "greater use be made of Cat Gear in those areas." Zigzagging on such an assignment was standard procedure.

The old-fashioned radar had been turned off; it was so ineffectual that it couldn't detect a periscope or snorkel anyway.

Robert MacMillan, skipper of Esquimalt. *(R.G. Arless/DND/PA 157026)*

Besides, the weather was clear, with visibility ranging from 10 to 15 miles. The minesweeper was relying on her asdic. The operator routinely made a constant search, sweeping ahead from one side of the ship to the other. But, though they were getting a variety of echoes, both the asdic operator and the officer of the watch failed to recognize that they had picked up a submarine.

U-190 was lurking five miles off the Nova Scotia coast. *Oberleutnant* Hans-Edwin Reith, listening to the asdic pings and crackling emissions bouncing off the hull of his submarine, was certain the minesweeper had discovered him. He was preparing to attack. Meanwhile *Esquimalt*'s skipper, Bob MacMillan, steering straight ahead at 10 knots, had no idea that he was practically on top of the U-boat. MacMillan unwittingly turned his ship towards *U-190*, steering directly into the submarine's periscope.

Reith was certain that *Esquimalt* was about to drop depth charges. He turned his stern towards the minesweeper; in desperation and self-defence he snapped off a Gnat torpedo, aimed at her bow.

Esquimalt sank by the stern like a ton of bricks. In less than four minutes, the sea swallowed her up. Miraculously, when the torpedo smashed into the starboard side at 6:27 a.m. with shattering force, not a single member of the crew was killed. Many were injured, however, some severely. All 70 managed to abandon ship.

There'd been no time to radio a distress signal or fire off flares to alert the lighthouse vessel, only five miles away. The minesweeper went under with the lifeboat still locked in its davits. Only four of six Carley floats were released.

Michael Kazakoff, an officer, was asleep in his cabin when the torpedo struck. He felt himself falling to the deck, grabbed his life jacket and put it on. When he stepped into the hallway all he could see was a maze of twisted metal. A few feet away, water poured in through several jagged holes. Pulling off his life jacket, Kazakoff squeezed through one of the openings, tearing his clothes and gashing himself on the edges of the metal.

Stoker Jack Ware was on duty in the engine room. Because it was so hot and stuffy, he had opened the escape hatch of the dummy funnel about 20 minutes before the blast. That action saved his life. With the explosion, the engine room filled with black smoke and powder; except for emergency bulbs, all the lights went out. Ware climbed through the escape hatch and onto the deck.

Terrence Manuel, a writer, credited his life jacket with saving him. Starting down the starboard side of the ship, he suddenly remembered that he couldn't swim; he went back to get it. He struggled out through an escape hatch only a moment before the ship sank.

Skipper Bob MacMillan, true to Navy tradition, was the last to leave his ship. He almost left too late. One of his crew in the water, watching the minesweeper's bow about to disappear, yelled: "Jump in, you silly old bastard." MacMillan happily complied, and he chose to do so with a graceful headfirst dive.

Now began a terrible, torturous ordeal. The blazing sun scorched the survivors; the freezing water chilled them. It was a fight, a test of will, to simply stay alive. It was a story of tragedy, but it was also a saga of bravery, of concern for comrades and, at times, good humour.

Leading seaman Herbert Knight found himself crowded onto a Carley float with 16 others. A strong swimmer, he plunged into the sea and swam to another raft. He remained in the icy water and pushed the float back to the one he had just left, so that the two could be lashed together. That accomplished, he was pulled aboard, but the cold and exertion had proved too much—he died an hour later.

Frank Smith, an able seaman, had lost his shorts and pants when he jumped over the side. He was naked and chilled to the core by the time he reached a Carley float. Frank Richard was wearing a windproof Navy "zoot suit." He gave Smith his flannel shorts and underwear.

Duncan McDonald, a leading seaman, along with a ship's telegrapher, kept stoker Thomas Kidd alive by repeatedly slapping him back to consciousness each time he passed out from the cold. Realizing he was in the hands of fate, McDonald owned up to his captain that he was the one who had been dipping into MacMillan's bottle of rum.

Albert Campbell had lashed two Carley floats together with a woollen sock. He later braced them with an oar to prevent them from drifting apart. With the help of the ship's signalman, Campbell held onto a comrade in the water whose leg had been broken; it was a losing battle. The man finally succumbed to the cold.

Don White's arms as well as his legs had been broken when the torpedo exploded. Incredibly, he had managed to reach a Carley float despite his injuries, then died moments later.

Some men simply accepted the inevitable. Thomas McIntyre, the ship's leading cook, tried to cheer up his near-naked, oil-drenched, shivering mates by promising them T-bone steaks as he helped to haul them aboard a float. He later slipped off, and was forced to hang onto the side. The ordeal was too much for him; after half an hour, he knew he'd had it—he waved goodbye with a smile and wink, and disappeared.

Twice the survivors thought they were on the verge of rescue. Aircraft flew over them, but their crews mistook the yellowcoloured rafts for fishing boats. Then two minesweepers were spotted on the horizon. The survivors waved and shouted themselves hoarse.

It was fully six hours before help arrived. Ironically, the rescue was provided by *Sarnia*, the minesweeper that was to have rendezvoused with *Esquimalt*. By this point, however, there were only 26 survivors—the ship's full complement was 70. Sixteen bodies were taken aboard. Those lucky enough to be among the living were suffering from extreme sunburn and frozen feet; they were so exhausted from exposure they were unable to lift themselves. Only one man among them, Jack Ware, was able to walk on his own. The rest were helped aboard by *Sarnia*'s crew.

Postscript: A frantic search for *U-190* began. It lasted a week, every ship available in the area—RCN and RN alike—taking part. The war might be ending, but the enemy was still very much at large in Canadian waters. Hans-Edwin Reith, however, managed to keep his submarine lying doggo on the ocean floor while depth charges burst above him, none to effect.

On April 30, he slipped away to make a run for home. He didn't make it far. On May 11, three days after the war against Hitler's Third Reich had ended, Reith received a signal from German high command, notifying him to surrender his ship. He reported his position to Boston, New York and Cape Race, Newfoundland. That night a boarding party from the corvette *Victoriaville* took charge—marking the first U-boat surrender to the Royal Canadian Navy.

On July 24, in accordance with the terms of the Potsdam Conference, the submarine was scuttled—in the same waters off the coast of Nova Scotia that held the remains of *Esquimalt* and the 44 of her crew who had died.

U-190's periscope was saved as a souvenir, placed on display in the Crow's Nest Club in St. John's, Newfoundland.

RefScs: DHist f FDS 397 TSIAOG 180–81 UBAC 287–92 298–99

IN THE PACIFIC
1945

*A*s the war against Germany came to a close, plans already *underway for two years for RCN participation in the Pacific theatre were being put into effect. The plans composed were of an entirely different nature than they had been in Europe; they proposed to fight an entirely different war. For one thing, anti-submarine operations would play a very minor part. For another, distances in the Pacific were beyond the range of corvettes, the mainstays of the Battle of the Atlantic.*

The Canadian contribution was to consist of 60 ships in all. Two would be aircraft carriers, still under construction in Belfast. The fleet was to be manned by 13,500 men. In actual fact, only one Canadian cruiser took part in the war against Japan, and the role it played was far from a major one.

However, a singular naval action in the Pacific theatre was one of this country's most spectacular achievements in any war. It was performed by a pilot serving with the Royal Naval Fleet Air Arm, and it won him a posthumous Victoria Cross—the only member of the RCN to be so decorated, and the last Canadian to earn the British Commonwealth's highest award for valour.

Okinawa, Truk and Honshu
May–July, 1945

MAINGUY Edmond Rollo

"Uganda *in Pacific Operations*"

O n April 6, *Uganda*, under the command of Rob Mainguy, set sail from Leyte in the Philippines to join Royal Navy Task Force 57, taking part in the naval portion of the struggle to capture Okinawa. Operation Iceberg saw the first sustained use of *kamikazes* by the Japanese. On May 9, the suicide planes concentrated their attacks on the British aircraft carriers *Victorious* and *Formidable*. *Uganda*, which escaped damage, had a ringside seat from 3,500 yards away.

On June 12, after the conclusion of Iceberg, the force commander transferred his flag to *Uganda* and led his cruisers on a naval bombardment against Truk, shelling landing fields, shore installations and a seaplane base on Dublin Island.

At the beginning of July, the British Pacific Fleet joined the United States Third Fleet. The combined force sailed into the waters of the Japanese homeland to attack Honshu by air via the aircraft carriers. Moving within sight of land, their planes bombarded Kure, Kobe and Nagoya. It was the beginning of the end.

On July 26, the British Fleet withdrew to refuel; next day, *Uganda* was recalled. She reached Esquimalt, B.C., on August 10, the day after the Americans had dropped the second atomic bomb, on Nagasaki.

RefScs: FDS 409–13

Onagawa Bay, Northern Honshu
August 9, 1945

GRAY Robert Hampton

"Canada's Last Victoria Cross Winner"

It happened the same morning the United States Air Force dropped the second atomic bomb. Three hours earlier, at 8:00 a.m., some 800 miles northeast of Nagasaki, Robert "Hammy" Gray was in the cockpit of his Vought Corsair fighter-bomber, his engine running. He sat on the deck of the aircraft carrier *Formidable*, waiting to take off. One section of Corsairs from 1841 Squadron of the Royal Naval Fleet Air Arm was already airborne. Gray, the senior pilot in the unit, was to follow with his two sections of eight aircraft as soon as the carrier turned into the wind.

Their target was to be a Japanese airfield at Matsushima. At the last minute, however, with radio silence being observed, he

Robert Hampton Gray, who won Canada's last Victoria Cross. (PA 133296)

was given fresh orders verbally. Now his flight was instead to attack Japanese warships in Onagawa Bay.

His pilots were well equipped to tackle such an assignment. The Corsair was one of the most maneuverable fighter-bombers built—designed to outclass the Japanese Zero. Its cranked wings gave it a lethal, inverted gull-like appearance. It had a top straight-and-level speed of over 300 miles per hour, and carried two 500-pound bombs.

Gray climbed his sections to 10,000 feet westerly, and after flying 150 miles over the sea, they crossed the Honshu coast north of Kinkasan. As they proceeded inland they could see the town of Matsushima and the airfield, their original target, on their left. To the right was their new objective, Onagawa Way—the bay. Several major ships were stationed there, including the sloop *Amakusa*, two minesweepers, a training ship and several smaller submarine chasers and shipping vessels.

The Corsairs reached a point northeast of the bay, then turned 180 degrees. They began losing height and picking up speed, racing down the valley towards the harbour mouth. They crossed the shoreline around 9:45, at low altitude and in sight of their targets. This was a skip-bombing attack—assured of maximum accuracy, the bombers were also highly vulnerable to anti-aircraft fire. The ships in the harbour, combined with the shore batteries that surrounded the bay, put up a curtain of intense fire, enveloping the eight Corsairs.

Gray took aim on *Amakusa*, anchored in the middle of the harbour. As he swept in, a cone of fire—from everywhere it seemed—zeroed in on him. Ack-ack struck his aircraft, knocking one of his bombs away and setting the Corsair on fire. But Gray persisted in his attack, holding a steady course. Flames streaming behind, he closed to within 50 yards before releasing his remaining bomb. It was a perfect strike amidships. Gray's plane turned slowly to starboard, then rolled onto its back and dived into the water.

Neither the pilot nor the Corsair was ever found. For his heroic attack in the face of withering fire, Gray received the Victoria Cross. He was also honoured by his enemies. In 1989, the Japanese erected a cairn and memorial plaque in Saklyama Peace Park, overlooking the site of Gray's action. It is the only memorial to an Allied officer or serviceman on Japanese soil.

Robert Gray was born in Trail, B.C., in 1917. Before joining the RCNVR in July 1940, he had attended the Universities of Alberta and British Columbia. In December that year he transferred to the Fleet Air Arm. After graduating as a pilot and completing his training, he served with several squadrons in Africa.

In August of 1944 he joined 1841 Squadron, aboard *Formidable*. For his part in the raid on the German battleship *Tirpitz*, Gray was mentioned in dispatches. In March 1945, the aircraft carrier joined the British Pacific Fleet where, in May, she teamed up with the USN Third Fleet as part of Task Force 37 for the final assault on Japan. On July 28, Gray led a low-level strike against the Japanese naval base at Maisuru north of Kyoto, where he sank a destroyer, which action earned him the DSC.

Lt VC DSC MID Born November 2, 1917 KIA August 9, 1945
RefScs: CNAG DHist f FDS 415–17 TTS

THE RCN MUTINIES 1949

*B*y William Bligh–Fletcher Christian standards, insurrections *aboard His Majesty's Canadian Ships were tame as sit-ins. But they were mutinies all the same, involving collective insubordination, even though they were more in the nature of peaceful protests than rebellions. Only one of the five incidents could be construed as serious by strict military measures, and only because it took place in wartime. Even so, the stern disciplinary action taken over a trivial offense that gave rise to the insurgency was entirely unwarranted, not to mention irresponsible. Fortunately, in the case of the other four, which occurred in peacetime during the years immediately following World War II, cooler heads prevailed. The protests were reasonable without any display of rancour—dissatisfaction with outdated rules of conduct, regulations and dress, unsettling routines, unfair and indifferent treatment, and lack of rapport between officers and other ranks. Conducted in an orderly manner with discretion and proper respect for authority, they received a sympathetic hearing that showed the concern and understanding they deserved.*

About time. Long overdue. Unrest belowdecks in the RCN had been simmering since the early days of the war. This could be directly traceable to British naval autocratic class distinction between officers and other ranks dating back to the days of Admiral Nelson and certainly Captain Bligh. Such discrimination stuck in the craw of the average Canadian reared and educated in a classless society. Nevertheless an undertow of that form of militant snobbery seeped into the commissioned ranks of the RCN as well as the RCNVR. Many Canadian officers on temporary loan to the RN were impressed with British standards and enthusiastically passed them along. In addition, British officers serving with the RCN provided their input. Following the outbreak of hostilities, the germ of this groundswell proliferated in popularity among the more militaristic-minded ship's commanders and remained a cross to bear after peace was signed. Though fractional, like a burr under the saddle, they were effectual. And it was just such a pinprick that led directly to the RCN mutinies to begin with.

The first incident served as a prime example. On July 20, 1943, in Plymouth, HMCS Iroquois' *ship's company refused to report for duty after being subjected to what they considered to be unnecessarily harsh discipline over a trifling infraction. When the clothes of three U-boat survivors rescued from the Atlantic by the Canadian warship were being cleaned and washed someone stole the German submarine commander's badge, which he angrily demanded be returned to him. Because such an offense contravened the Geneva Convention,* Iroquois' *Captain, Bill "Scarface" Holms, took it as a personal reflection on his ability to command and promptly cancelled all shore leave on the night before the ship was scheduled to return to active duty.*

Next morning the crew shut themselves in belowdecks and adamantly refused to fall in. That was too much for the arrogant, autocratic Holms. Such deliberate defiance fortuitously brought on a heart attack that ended the crisis. His Number One took over and calmed the waters.

An isolated instance? Perhaps. But a mutiny is a mutiny is a mutiny and, no matter how passive, particularly in wartime aboard ship, not something that can be taken lightly or simply washed away by emptying it overboard like so much bilge. The Iroquois *insurgency went into the record—and stayed there.*

Holms had it coming to him—and that was the point. Unbending and harsh from the moment Iroquois *was commissioned in November 1942, his strict treatment of the ship's company proved unpopular with everyone, not only among the ratings but his officers, CPOs and petty officers as well. Resentment had been brewing from day one. Something had to give, and his impulsive reaction to the stolen badges incident piped it aboard. His command was taken over by Jimmy Hibbard who, in contrast, inspired such confidence that* Iroquois *went on to acquit herself with distinction, although the stain of Holms's irrational behaviour and lack of judgment left an indelible mark in the RCN log.*

The salient fact was that the mutiny itself per se had set a dangerous precedent for future such incidents to materialize as a medium for expressing dissatisfaction and discontent over a growing unrest belowdecks that had been steadily surfacing since the end of the war.

In 1947 a case in point. Ironically, the veteran Jimmy Hibbard, as captain of HMCS Ontario, *was once again called upon to smooth troubled waters. The problem rested with the ship's executive officer, Commander Jeffry Vanstone Brock, a particularly crusty character who had inherited his aloof manner and lack of rapport with those under him from his wartime service, most of which was spent with the RN. On April 22,* Ontario *was on a shakedown cruise off Nanoose Bay on Vancouver Island when Brock's failure to provide assurance and understanding for his officers and hands came to a head—an incident that might have been avoided had the insensitive XO shown the slightest interest in the welfare of the ship's company. As it turned out, right after dinner some 50 disgruntled able-bodied seamen locked themselves in one of the mess decks to express their dissatisfaction over the manner in which they were being treated, with an ultimatum that they would not answer the evening pipe to "fall in" until they had been given a chance to air their grievances.*

Jimmy Hibbard once more to the rescue. Overriding Brock, who had urged disciplinary measures even though there was nothing disorderly about the way the men had conducted themselves, the ship's captain prudently cancelled the pipe, cleared the decks, assembled all hands and encouraged them to voice their complaints. For the most part they were pretty routine—dissatisfaction about having to wear night uniforms, resentment over unfair assignment of duties and the like—nothing too onerous that couldn't be quickly redressed and to which Hibbard promised his immediate attention.

The Iroquois *and* Ontario *scenarios shared a common denominator: the cause of their discontent was aimed at the command level of the ship. In both cases the crews had the satisfaction of knowing that neither Holms nor Brock ever held another sea command. Similarly, the other three Canadian mutinies, which occurred in rapid succession during February and March of 1949, were levelled at ships' XOs also. This was significant. It pinpointed exactly where the trouble lay: right on the bridge.*

HMCS Athabaska, *successor to her wartime namesake sunk off the coast of Brittany in April 1944, was refuelling at Manzillo, Mexico, when the junior hands went out on strike, refusing to fall in until their demands were met.* Crescent *went through somewhat the same experience in mid-February in Nanking while guarding the interests of Canadian citizens caught in the communist advance on the Chinese Nationalist capital. Then, early in March, when* Athabaskan *joined* Magnificent *in the Caribbean, after sailing through the Panama Canal, the ships' crews met ashore at Colon, where talk naturally centred around the destroyer's recent mutiny. Not surprisingly, the carrier's crew decided to take similar steps. After breakfast at sea several days later, 32 of the aircraft handlers remained in the mess deck when the order came to fall in.*

In each case the post-war mutinies had been handled with propriety on both sides, the aggravation momentarily mollified. But far from cured; the underlying cause for the unrest was not about to be simply blown away. It had too much substance to be quelled so quickly and easily. The malaise was spreading—and with good reason. The once-proud Royal Canadian Navy, universally respected as the third most powerful naval force afloat, was no longer a happy ship—far from it. Life at sea for the seaman was barely tolerable. Working conditions, still labouring under rigid Royal Navy, British-oriented standards, were deplorable, discipline unnecessarily harsh, at times down-right unreasonable. Time at sea was invariably for extended periods. Skilled tradesmen were frequently overworked for lack of personnel being trained to supplement their depleted ranks. Food by any measurement was substandard, a disgrace. And pay and allowances were shamefully low compared to civilian remunerations.

The average leading rating struggling to support a family on $120 a month was forced to moonlight. While he was at sea, his wife—and children—were frequently forced to move in with parents or in-laws, inevitably creating domestic problems. In fact in Halifax and Victoria, where most RCN personnel were based, housing for families was inadequate. There were no married quarters save for senior officers. Quarters for the single man lacked privacy, and were often cramped and uncomfortable and bleak in winter. What recreational facilities existed were inadequate. To the young man with a family considering a future Navy career, these were hardly incentives auguring a positive decision. Inevitably, recruiting suffered as well. Nor did it encourage re-enlistments, particularly among the old salts who were certain conditions elsewhere could hardly be worse. Alternately there was a rash of requests for transfer to more comfortable, less inhibited postings, such as an air force station.

These were the real roots that generated the demonstrations of discontent aboard ship. They should have been recognized deep down for what they really were: bellwether warnings of

*the heavy seas into which the Navy was sailing. They weren't.
Now distress signals were flying that could no longer be
avoided or ignored. A state of emergency was rapidly approaching—the crisis of an outright rebellion calling for immediate
"Action Stations!"*

Ottawa
1949

AUDETTE Louis de la Chesnaye
BROCKINGTON Leonard
CLAXTON Brooke
MAINGUY Edmond Rollo

"Tour de Force—The Mainguy Report"

The prospect of a full-scale mutiny was frightening enough,
the menace of communism tied to it terrifying. Three insur-
gencies in as many weeks. The possibility of subversion at a time
when the Russians had just exploded the atomic bomb. Enough to
create panic as far afield as Washington.

On April 4, 1949, Canada was among six nations that signed
the North Atlantic Treaty Organization (NATO) pact pledging
their armed forces. So it was not out of the realm of possibility
that mutinies could be part of a plot to undermine those forces.
Nor, that being the case, to assume that the RCN, because of its
size and proximity to the United States, could be a logical target.
A distinct possibility.

But realistically the more logical probability was that the reason underlying the insurrections was a provincial problem that
lay right at the foot of the Navy's gangway—getting down to
basics, one that called for a thorough housecleaning.

This did not call for disciplinary measures or recriminatory
steps. Sober judgment was needed to place matters in proper perspective. Fortunately it prevailed where it was needed most—in
the offices of the Canadian Minister of National Defence. Brooke

Claxton wasted no time appointing a commission "to improve conditions of service, the relations between officers and men, the machinery for the ventilation of grievances and...the training of personnel."

His choice of a panel to make a study of events surrounding the mutinies and come up with recommendations was equally judicious and sound—an impressive trio headed by Rear Admiral Edward Rollo Mainguy, ably assisted by lawyers Leonard Brockington and Louis de la Chesnaye Audette.

Mainguy was ideally suited for the job of chairman of the commission. Rugged and athletic-looking (Maritime squash champion), six foot tall and weighing over 200 pounds, he had a reputation for putting the concern, comfort and welfare of those serving under him above all other considerations. As Captain (D) [Destroyers] in St John's, he started the recreation camp for men as well as the Crow's Nest Seagoing Club, a Newfoundland Navy hallmark. While on duty in the Pacific with the Royal Naval Fleet as captain of HMS *Uganda*, he inaugurated "Town Hall," open forums with the ship's company where he established himself as an accomplished speaker. He became known and respected as a leader for his open-minded fairness. In fact he admitted that his procedure in relieving Jeffry Brock of his duties over the *Ontario* kafuffle was, without a prior investigation, "neither completely wise nor completely fair." His impressive war record earned him three decorations for, among other commendations, "never failing to set an outstanding example of wholehearted devotion to duty."

The awesome responsibility of chairing Claxton's commission could best be summed in three words—Save Our Navy—and no one was better qualified for the task. Leonard Brockington brought unparalleled wisdom, experience, knowledge, insight of and understanding of both national and foreign affairs to the commission. The first chairman of the Canadian Broadcasting Corporation, during World War II he acted as special adviser to Prime Minister Mackenzie King. His radio broadcasts on major affairs were a national institution. "Uncle Louis" Audette, a veteran of the Atlantic convoy battles, after retiring from the RCN with the rank of Commander, pursued his career as a lawyer and served as chairman of the Canadian Maritime Commission. An aggressive, knowledgeable and highly respected individual with a keen perception of Navy affairs, he was, in the words of his wartime naval contemporary former Captain St. Clair Balfour, "a real cracker-jack."

Entrusted to such qualified commissioners, a thorough investigation was assured. Full steam ahead, casting off with a series of 28 interviews conducted in camera—immunity guaranteed— they ran the gamut from the chief of the Naval Staff down through every rank and station to the lowest rating including currently enlisted recruits. In addition, newspaper and radio notices asking for volunteers to come forward to testify attracted 50 witnesses, among them chaplains, medical officers, civil servants and two journalists. As part of their probe, the panel went aboard three of the ships involved in the mutinies, *Athabaskan*, *Crescent* and *Magnificent*, for hands-on testimonies. To compare the modern American methods and facilities with the outdated Canadian ones, the commission visited the U.S. naval establishment in Seattle, Washington.

Out of these exhaustive studies over a year emerged the watershed of Canadian naval history, which became widely celebrated as the Mainguy Report, a remarkable manifesto, a true tour de force.

High on the list of conclusions was the fact there was "no evidence of subversive or political activities," a major concern. Investigation into the *Iroquois* and *Ontario* mutinies revealed that among members of their crews who were later transferred and turned up on the other three ships involved in the protests, there appeared to be no collusion or subversion, although the possibility of successful incidents rubbing off on other ships could not be ruled out. Ironically, the all-too-frequent transfers were a serious bête noire. Nothing new about that. As early as 1783 Horatio Nelson wrote: "The disgust of Seaman to the Navy is all owing to the infernal plan of turning them over from ship to ship so that men cannot be attached to their officers or the officers care two pence about them."

If there was a focal point to the report, it was the lack of communication and grievance procedures in the RCN all down the line. The commission called it "the most useful and proper safeguard against insubordination resulting from mass grievances." Some effort had been made to redress this shortcoming, but it never got off the deck. A month before the *Ontario* mutiny a bulletin had been dispatched from Headquarters to all ships to set up welfare committees to be chaired by the XOs for "free discussion between officers and men."

Reaction: you don't run ships by committee. *Athabaskan*'s captain and his XO chose to ignore the dictum. *Crescent*'s, ditto. *Magnificent* followed suit. A little salesmanship, perhaps some friendly persuasion, might have helped. But too late; all three were already mutiny bound, but for reasons that had nothing to do with welfare committees. The commission's findings indicated otherwise. Its report read: "We do not believe that sufficient care was exercised in the selection of Executive Officers. A great deal of the trouble arose from [their] unpopularity." The report added: "As a subject of criticism, he [the XO] seems to be the equivalent of the proverbial Sergeant-Major...he is the pivot of the ship's routine and general discipline. If he fails to handle the ship's crew with tact, humanity and firmness and common sense, there is always the danger of trouble..."

The commission alleged that throughout all three ships— indeed throughout the Navy—changes in officers and men were made much too frequently to allow sufficiently close relationships between them, and relationships are needed to inspire mutual respect. In fact there was found to be an absence of confidence even between officers and petty officers, nominally the strongest link in naval discipline. As one high-ranking officer put it: "I have heard several complaints—and that's the only thing I have heard—told to me by Chief and Petty Officers that apparently they just don't matter, they are ignored, so there you have the middle of the string sagging; you have a void in your connection with the men. The backbone, you well know, is the Petty Officer. That is the only way you find out what is going on—those fellows are useful, but not unless they get the support of the Officer."

All this had a bearing on what the commission termed an "artificial distance between the officers and men." The men didn't deny the officers their privilege, but when the officers failed to live up to their responsibilities, resentment replaced respect. As the report pointed out: "The only discipline which in the final analysis is worthwhile, is one based upon the pride in a great service, a belief in essential justice, and the willing obedience that is given to superior character, skill, education and knowledge. Any other form of discipline is bound to break down under stress."

The report continued: "In Canada, many officers and men come from the same kind of home, and spend their boyhoods in playing basketball in the same lot, swimming hole and in playing 'hooky' from the same school. With such a national background, it is more important that discipline should be based on the realities we have mentioned rather than on artificial distinctions."

Another factor was the quality of officers. In 1776, Admiral John Paul Jones applied this criterion: "The naval officer should be the soul of tact, patience, justice, firmness, charity and understanding. No meritorious act of a surbordinate should escape his attention or be left to pass without reward, even if the reward be only one word of approval.... He should not be blind to a single fault in any subordination; at the same time he should be quick to distinguished error from malice, thoughtlessness for incompetence and well-meant shortcoming from heedless and stupid blunder. As he should be universal and impartial in his rewards and approval of merit, so he should be judicially unbending in his punishment or reproof of misconduct."

In summary: leadership, that centurion's age-old mantra upon which all military structures depend. The Mainguy Report revealed that while RCN officers in the early stages of their commissioning were given more than adequate hands-on junior training, fundamentally they were poorly educated to begin with compared to their United States Navy counterparts. A parallel even close to home: to qualify for a pre-war career commission in the RCAF, the basic requirement was a university degree.

To a great extent Canadian naval shortcomings in this regard could be attributed to the influence of the RN dogma that there was no need to teach leadership, it was something that the young gentleman learned for himself and developed as his career progressed. The RCN, to its regret, applied the same principle. The USN, where discipline was, in fact, much stiffer, took a modern, far more realistic approach—it taught leadership to the extent it produced a manual on the subject. It would have been auspicious had the RCN dusted off the RN's musty anachronism and done the same.

Another complaint from the lower deck—and to some extent from officers as well—was the lack of Canadian identity. Too much emphasis on RN tradition—Drake, Nelson, Jellicoe, "Britannia Rules the Waves" et al. But the RCN had created its own proud legend—Hendy, Hennessy, Hose, Pierce, Prentice, Stubbs, deWolf to name a few, and "Victors of the Atlantic."

The Mainguy Report put the problem in this perspective: "The absence of identification on the uniforms of the Canadian ratings gave rise to many unpleasant incidents in which American sailors were present. While the incidents often resulted from ignorance, ill manners, and unfortunate national prejudices, there is no doubt that the relations between Canadian, American, and British sailors were greatly impaired by the continual mistaking Canadian ratings for British sailors...the men were vehement in the demands that they be identified as Canadians." The addition of Tony German's comment: "How easy it would have been to give Canadian names to *Warrior* and *Magnificent*" seems an appropriate postscript.

Recruiting methods also came under fire, with harsh criticism from almost every witness interviewed. It was charged that promotion had been left in the hands of advertising agencies that hadn't the faintest notion of what the Navy was all about. Furthermore, they were guilty of false promises, misleading claims: "The Navy's the Life—Travel and Adventure in Fast New Ships. Financial Security Now and a Pension for the Future," was a typical message. This, both men and officers agreed, was the wrong approach. The hardships of the sea, the manliness of the service and the practical patriotism were rarely, if ever, mentioned.

In the same breath, Navy public relations was judged seriously unsatisfactory. The commission had this to say: "There is the occasional suppression of stories of public in the Press. The Navy is traditionally the 'Silent Service.' The result of this tradition is that many senior officers, not aware of the change in conditions which have brought about the war, are not sufficiently conscious of the necessity of good relations with the press and public. In peacetime at least, a prompt statement of the plain truth is in the public's interest and right."

The Mainguy Report concluded its findings with 30 recommendations. As a start it emphasized training. "It is our opinion," the commission asserted, "that the navy should be given breathing space for essential training and strengthening of its men and ships." It suggested the establishment of one or more training ships and that these be commanded and staffed by officers specially selected "both for teaching and learning." The report recommended that the "bed and roses" or "beer and skittles" approach to advertising be eliminated, and that naval officers be encouraged to take part in recruiting campaigns. It also stressed that neither design nor content of the publicity should be left to commercial and advertising houses.

The Commission also dealt with the education of recruits. "They should be taught the traditions and customs of the Naval Service, and efforts should be made to make them understand their own importance in the navy, no matter how humble their tasks may be, and to realize what patriotism and service to one's country means. To this end it is recommended that a booklet be published on the history of the Canadian Navy and issued with the Seamanship Manual."

The report went to great pains to recommend vast improvements in living conditions for both single and married men. These had been found inadequate to the extreme, lagging behind the other Canadian services and, compared with USN facilities and services on their bases, filled the RCN with envy. This extended to overhauling and broadening recreational facilities ashore and afloat.

One item that came in for attention was the showing of films at sea. There had been complaints that poor-calibre movies were the usual fare. That put it mildly. A glaring example was a film on venereal disease that was shown "over and over again!" The commission recommended that negotiations be made at the highest level with film distributors. The report tabled the commission's conclusions by summarizing that while the incidents were indeed mutinies, apart from barring the doors aboard *Athabaskan* and *Crescent*, no force was used, nor was there any defiance of higher officers' orders. However there was no justification, and could be none, for any form of mass insubordination, and in future, insubordination should be most severely punished. The report also pointed out that had the various captains and executive officers been fully informed and had there been proper welfare committees in place, the incidents might have been prevented. The report ended by urging that "legitimate grievances which have been outlined in our report should be promptly and sympathetically investigated and remedied."

The Mainguy Report was indeed a masterpiece, a classic example and a lesson of how an inquiry into military misdoings should be properly conducted. The fine hand, mind and wisdom of the learned Leonard Brockington were reflected in the calibre of the manifesto. The sympathy and understanding his words project are worth remembering:

"The times in which we live, like all post-war times, are full of restlessness, uncertainty and change. Wise men throughout the ages have observed that just as the sea after a great storm is troubled for many days, it is a long time before the winds are lulled and the calm settles upon the waters, so after every great conflict, there are turmoil and ferment in the affairs of mankind. The social and economic uncertainties and changes, which affect Canada as they do the world, and the general deterioration in the discipline of family life, which is one of the misfortunes of our times, press with particular intensity on the lives of young men. It would be a miracle if the comparative isolation of men within the walls of a ship at sea should protect them from the disturbing influences which harass their companions and contemporaries ashore."

RefScs: TMR TSIAOG 207–211

War is the province of uncertainty.
—Clausewitz

The RCN in Korea 1950–1953

On July 5, 1950, 11 days after the outbreak of the Korean War, three RCN destroyers sailed from Esquimalt, B.C. They arrived at Sasebo harbour in Japan 25 days later. Before the end of the conflict, in 1953, five other destroyers had joined them. At all times, there were at least three Canadian ships present in Korean waters.

Along with other warships of the United Nations forces, the Canadians performed multifarious tasks, mostly off the west coast of the peninsula. They maintained a continuous blockade, prevented amphibious landings by the enemy, screened carriers from the threat of submarines and aerial attack and supported UN land forces with strategic bombardments. They also protected the "friendly" islands, and brought comfort to the sick and needy living in South Korean fishing villages.

It was tough slogging, at times monotonous, but there was the constant danger of enemy mines and gunfire from coastal batteries. And the waters offshore were often hazardous.

The eight Canadian destroyers carried out 21 tours of duty, in which 3,621 officers and men served. The ships spent 65 per cent of their time under sail, with patrols lasting up to 50 days unrelieved. Three men were killed in these operations; two were severely wounded.

The last Canadian vessel left Korean waters in September 1955.

Chinnamp'o
December 4, 1950

BROCK Jeffry Vanstone
COLLINS Andy
TAYLOR Paul
WELLAND Robert

"Sea Evacuation from the West Coast"

The invasion by the Chinese into North Korea at the end of October shattered the US 8th Army in the west, forcing a retreat to the capital of P'yongyang. The evacuation had to be made from its port of Chinnamp'o, roughly 100 miles south of the Chinese border. Jeffry Brock, in *Cayuga*, was to lead a flotilla of six destroyers—three Canadian, including his own, two Australian and one American.

The evacuation was not a particularly pleasant prospect. To reach the harbour, the ships had to navigate up the Daido-ko estuary, rife with small islets and mud flats, as well as having been heavily mined by the North Koreans in their flight north two months earlier. Two of the destroyers, an Australian ship and *Sioux*, commanded by Paul Taylor, got stuck in the mud, eventually having to withdraw.

The consummate skill of *Cayuga*'s navigator, Andy Collins, working with the new Sperry radar, led the other four ships safely through the channel during a four-hour ordeal. The next morning, the docks of Chinnamp'o were swarming with refugees crowding into junks, sampans—any kind of vessel that would take them south.

Amid all the confusion there was work to do. War equipment had to be loaded onto landing craft and transports. Brock laid down the order that all the ancillary vessels were to be clear of the estuary by dusk; after night fell, any ship running aground could block the withdrawal of the rest.

Landing parties went ashore. Meanwhile, the destroyers fired on rail lines, boxcars, workshops, warehouses, factories—any target they could identify. *Athabaskan*, commanded by Bob

THE RCN IN KOREA 301

Welland, moved back down the delta towards the sea, acting as a rescue ship if needed. She sailed past the ragged native fleet of junks and sampans, while sailors aboard her lifeboat searched them for mines. Ship's gunners opened up on concrete boxes along the shore, demolishing them with their 4-inch guns.

With all troops and equipment back aboard the ships as darkness fell, the shore parties set fire to the docks, lighting them up for the gunners, who laid down a barrage. One shell struck an oil tank, creating a tremendous blaze. As the destroyers pulled out in the morning, escorting the landing craft downstream, the entire harbour was wreathed in flames and smoke.

Refscs: TSIAOG 220–22 VR(3) 22

Yalu River, and the Vicinity of Songjin
May 1951

FRASER-HARRIS Fraser
SLATER Anthony

"Bombarding the Bridges"

L ate in the spring, *Nootka*, under the command of Fraser Fraser-Harris, an ex-Fleet Air Arm pilot, had captured an entire Chinese fishing fleet. The action was part of the naval blockade between Inchon to the south and the mouth of the Yalu River to the north, which separates North Korea and China.

Later in May, her target was a railway bridge near Songjin, spanning a gully between two tunnels. Fraser-Harris decided that this assignment called for a landing party to plant explosives, rather than trying a sea bombardment. He dispatched an armed demolition crew under Tony Slater. Fog moved in just as they started—there would be no cover from *Nootka*; she couldn't see the target area.

The sea was calm and the cutter was easily beached on the rocky shore. But the party was suddenly confronted with a band of North Korean soldiers. They emerged from the tunnels, laying down a furious fusillade. Slater's crew at first returned fire—then, observing the axiom that discretion is the better part of valour, they quickly withdrew.

Some days later in the same vicinity, *Nootka* drew another railway bridge as a target. Because any damage was always repaired overnight, no matter how much it was shelled, it had been dubbed the "Rubber Bridge." Fraser-Harris decided the trestle needed to be attacked at almost point-blank range to ensure proper results. A substantial problem—the inshore area was heavily mined, and he had no sweeper at his disposal. He assigned the task to the ship's two motor cutters—towing a length of wire between them.

As an additional precaution, Fraser-Harris lobbed "squid" bombs ahead to explode the mines—none were encountered, and *Nootka* was able to draw within 1,300 yards of the coast. As she did so, North Korean soldiers poured from tunnels bordering the bridge. Fraser-Harris had his gunners lower the ship's 4-inch and 44-mm guns to fire over the cutters.

The enemy scurried for cover. Now *Nootka* concentrated all her armour on the bridge. A US destroyer followed suit with her own 5-inch guns. In no time, the Rubber Bridge was reduced to fragments of metal.

Nootka's crew celebrated with a load of fresh fish caught by the cutters. The North Koreans spent weeks filling in the gully so they could rebuild their rail line on top of it.

RefScs: TSIAOG 227–28

North of Inchon
April 1953

BOVEY John
COPAS Frederick

"The Train-Busters Club"

Late in the war, one of the main naval objectives became the destruction of trains running the length of North Korea. The rail lines had already taken a fearful hammering over the past two years, but the trains continued to roll. Now the trains themselves became the targets. Attacking them became the grounds of competition for membership in the "Train-Busters Club." To qualify as a kill, the engine had to be destroyed—no easy goal. Tunnels along the railway offered a good deal of protection—if a train was halted by shell fire, the engine was often uncoupled and shunted to safety.

Crusader, commanded by John Bovey, became the UN's leading train buster. She had already destroyed several locomotives when, on a dark night (trains were too vulnerable travelling by day) in April, her gunnery officer, Fred Copas, spied a southbound train—he had spotted the sparks flying from its firebox. Pressing all his guns into action, Copas knocked the vehicle off its tracks. Next morning, *Crusader*'s gunners further reduced the wreckage to smithereens, shot by shot.

That afternoon lookouts spotted another train. Bovey brought his destroyer to the very edge of the coast. Copas levelled his sights on the target from 14,000 yards. Dead on—the locomotive was stopped in its tracks. Minutes later, another train appeared. *Crusader*'s gunners finished it off with the same finely tuned precision. *Crusader* now officially led the train-buster parade.

RefScs: TSIAOG 230–31

Abbreviations

GENERAL DESIGNATIONS

asdic anti-submarine detection equipment (later known as SONAR)
CNAG Canadian Naval Air Group
HF/DF High Frequency/Direction Finding
HMCS His Majesty's Canadian Ship
HMS His Majesty's Ship
KIA Killed in Action
LCT Landing Craft—Troops
MGB Motor Gun Boat
ML Motor Launch
MOMP Mid-Ocean Meeting Point
MTB Motor Torpedo Boat
NATO North Atlantic Treaty Organization
NEF Newfoundland Escort Force
RCN Royal Canadian Navy
RCNVR Royal Canadian Naval Volunteer Reserve
RN Royal Navy
RT Radio Transmitter
SC Slow Convoy
TLC Tank Landing Craft
UN United Nations
USN United States Navy
WW1 World War 1
WW2 World War 2
XO Executive Officer

RANKS

ADM Admiral
CAPT Captain
Captain (D) Captain (Destroyers)
CGS Chief of the General Staff
CMDRE Commodore

CNS Chief of the Naval Staff
COMNDR Commander
E/O Engineering Officer
Lt Lieutenant
LTCOMM Lieutenant Commander
M/O Medical Officer
NOIC Naval Officer in Charge
P/O Petty Officer
QC Queen's Council
RADM Rear Admiral
SEO Senior Executive Officer
SO Senior Officer
VADM Vice-Admiral

DECORATIONS

BCRM British Crimean Medal
BSM Bronze Star Medal (United States)
CB Commander of the Order of the Bath
CBE Commander of the Order of the British Empire
CD Canadian Decoration
CdeG (Fr) Croix de Guerre (France)
CdGaP (Fr) Croix de Guerre avec Palms (France)
ChM China Medal
CLM (US) Commander of the Legion of Merit (United States)
CM Canadian Medal
COL (Nor) Cross of Liberation (Norway)
COV (Pol) Cross of Valour (Poland)
DFC Distinguished Flying Cross

DSC Distinguished Service Cross
DSO Distinguished Service Order
IMM Indian Military Medal
KHCOL (Nor) King Haakon
  Cross of Liberation (Norway)
KStLJ Knight of the Order of
  Lazarus of Jerusalem
Ld'H (Fr) Legion d'Honneur
  (France)
LoM (US) Legion of Merit
  (United States)

MID Mentioned in Dispatches
OBE Officer of the Order of
  British Empire
OLH (Fr) Officer of the Legion of
  Honour (France)
OLM (US) Officer of the Legion
  of Merit (United States)
TM Turkish Medal
VC Victoria Cross

REFSCS: Reference Sources

50N   *50 North*. Alan Easton. Markham, Ont.: PaperJacks, 1980.

ABW   *A Bloody War*. Hal Lawrence. Toronto: Macmillan, 1979.

AIHOTCN   *An Illustrated History of the Canadian Navy*. Jack MacBeth. Toronto: Key Porter, 1989.

BW   *Bloody Winter*. John M. Waters. Annapolis, MD: Naval Institute Press, 1984.

CAAC   *Canada's Admirals and Commodores*. John M. MacFarlane. Maritime Museum of British Columbia, 1994.

CCAN   *Corvettes Canada*. Mac Johnson. Whitby, Ont.: McGraw-Hill Ryerson, 1994.

CCC   *Corvette Cobourg*. Tom Blakely. Cobourg Branch: Royal Canadian Legion, 1985.

CE   *Canadian Encyclopedia*. Edmonton: Hurtig Publishers, 1988.

CN   *Champagne Navy*. Brian Nolan. Toronto: Random House, 1991.

CNOIK   *Canadian Naval Operations in Korean Waters*. T. Thorgimsonn and E.C. Russell. Ottawa: Department of National Defence, Historical Section, 1965.

CS   *Canada's Submarines*. Dave Perkins. Erin, Ont.: Boston Mills Press, 1989.

C&TOTCN   *Customs & Traditions of the Canadian Navy*. Graeme Armbuckle. Nimbus Publishing, 1984.

CVC   *Canada's VC's*. Lt-Col George Machum. Toronto: McClelland & Stewart Ltd., 1956.

CWMC&F   Canadian War Museum, Correspondence & Files.

DHIST   Directorate of History.

DND   Department of National Defence.

FDS   *Far Distant Ships*. Joseph Schull. Toronto: Stoddart, 1987.

HA   *Haida*. William Sclater. Markham, Ont.: PaperJacks, 1980.

H&ACNFWWII   *Honours & Awards: Canadian Naval Forces in World War II*. Lt Cdr Edward R. Paquette and Lt Charles D. Bainbridge. Vancouver Island: E.W. Bickle Ltd., 1986.

HOTSWW   *History of the Second World War*. B.H. Liddel Hart. London: Cassell, 1970.

IWM   Interview with Willis McLeese, ex-RCN.

LAET   *Lusitania: An Epic Tragedy*. Diana Preston. New York: Walker Publishing Company Inc., 2002

MM   *Maclean's* Magazine.

MMN   *Maritime Museum Notes*. Maritime Museum of British Columbia Society.

NAC   National Archives of Canada.

NAR *North Atlantic Run.* Marc Milner. Toronto: University of Toronto Press, 1985.

NSO Naval Service of Canada.

OTTR *On the Triangle Run.* James B. Lamb. Toronto: Macmillan, 1986.

PD Pamela Dunn, private files

PWIIS *50 Personnel World War II Stories.* Joan Donaldson-Yarmey. Edmonton: Jomet, 1995.

RAR *Ready, Aye, Ready.* Jack McBeth. Toronto: Key Porter, 1989.

RCNIR *The RCN in Retrospect: 1910–1968.* James A. Boutilier. University of British Columbia Press, 1982.

SD (1)(2)(3) *Salty Dips.* Vols. 1,2 & 3. Ottawa Branch, Naval Officers' Association of Canada, 1983.

STS Starshell Naval Officers' Association of Canada.

TCAW *The Canadians at War.* The Reader's Digest Association of Canada.

TCN *The Corvette Navy.* James B. Lamb. Toronto: Macmillan, 1977.

TDBS *Dark Broad Sea.* Vol. IV, "With Many Voices." Jeffry V. Brock. Toronto: McClelland & Stewart Ltd., 1981, 1983.

TGM *The Globe & Mail.*

TL *The Legionary.*

TLS *The Lusitania.* Colin Simpson. Boston: Little Brown and Company, 1872.

TLUTM *The Lusitania: Unraveling the Mystery.* Patrick O'Sullivan. New York: Sheridan House, 2000.

TM&ME *The Mediterranean and Middle East.* Vol VI. Maj-Gen S.O. Playfair, Brig C.J.C. Molony, Capt. F.C. Flynn and Gr Capt T.P. Gleave. London: Her Majesty's Stationary Office, 1954–1988.

TOTNA *Tales of the North Atlantic.* Hal Lawrence. Toronto: McClelland & Stewart Ltd., 1985.

TPAPS *Tin Pots & Pirate Ships.* Michael Hadley & Roger Sartt. Kingston: McGill-Queen's University Press, 1991.

TSIAOG *The Sea Is at Our Gates.* Tony German. Toronto: McClelland & Stewart Ltd., 1990.

TSOCNF *The Ships of Canada's Naval Forces 1918–1981.* Ken Macpherson and John Burgess. Toronto: Collins, 1981.

TSOTVC *The Story of the Victoria Cross.* Rt. Hon. Sir John Smyth. London: Frederick Muller Ltd., 1965.

TTCOH *Through the Corridors of Hell.* George H. Evans. Antigonish, N.S.: Forman Publishing Ltd., 1980.

TTS *The Toronto Star.*

TUB *The U-Boats.* Douglas Bottling. Alexandria, VA: Time-Life Books, 1979.

TU-BH *The U-Boat Hunters.* Marc Milner. Toronto: University of Toronto Press, 1994.

TWABOWWII *The World Almanac Book of World War II.* Peter Young. New York: World Almanac Publications, 1981.

TW *Total War.* Peter Calvacoressi and Guy Wint. New York: Pantheon Books, 1972.

Name Index

KOREAN WAR